THE TEN POUND POM

BY

Andrew Robert Baker

Dedicated to.

To my Mother Cecilia Josephine O Malley and Father Robert Henry Baker

A shining example of a thrifty, committed, loving couple, determined to do their very best for their children Susan and Andrew.

Thanks Dad for opening my eyes to the benefits of travel, without doubt in my opinion it is the best education in the world.

Both my Mother, Father and sister are now deceased. they are finally achieving the tranquillity of peace they fought so hard to enjoy on earth.

I wish to thank Bernadette Challener and other ladies who over the last few years have helped me turn my collation of words into my story.

This is as recalled when I was a ten year old boy.

It never hurts to say thank you.

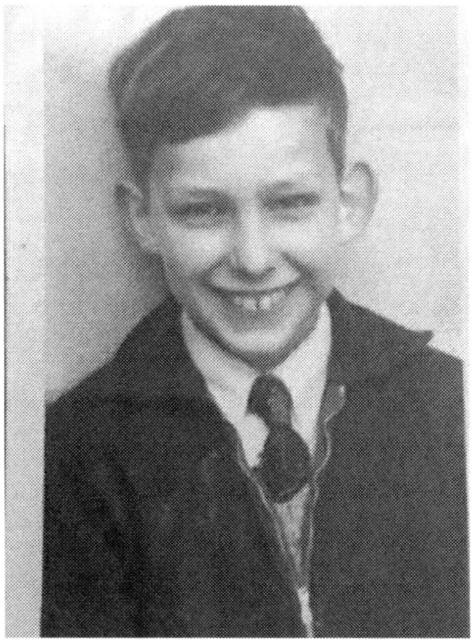

CONTENTS

CHAPTER 1   **EARLY DAYS**

The fishing rod

Broughton Park

Heaton Park

The Canal

Going to the Cinema

The Attic

The Anniversary

Visit from the Postman

The Frogs

The Model Boat

Nanny

The Football Boots

Nanny Comes Home

The Summer Holidays

Malcolm's Snake

A Trip to the Swimming Pool

Watching Television

A surprise for Andrew

Nanny; A Sad Momentum

Delamere Forest

Heaton Park Boating Lake

Blackpool

Chapter 2   AUTUMN

Preparing for Bonfire Night

A Day Trip to the Countryside

The Robbery

The Fire

The Fireworks

Bonfire Night

Dad's Birthday

The Shambles

Farewell to the Toys

Benediction

Snow

Malcolm's Snake Goes Missing Again

Mum Gets a Job

Saturday Morning

The Shoplifter

Saturday Night Entertainment

Sunday Outing

Exam Week

Preparing for Australia

Christmas 1958

CHAPTER 3

Friday 2 January 1959	**Leaving Bradshaw Street.**
Monday 5 January 1959	London

CHAPTER 4   THE VOYAGE

Tuesday 6 January 1959	**The Voyage**
Wednesday 7 January 1959	The Bay of Biscay
Saturday 10 January 1959	Gibraltar
Sunday 11 January 1959	Naples
	Cruising Through the Mediterranean
Thursday 15 January 1959	Approaching the Suez Canal
	Port Said
	The Suez Canal
Monday 19 January 1959	Djibouti
Sunday 25 January 1959	Colombo
	Kandy
	Mount Lavinia
Monday 26 January 1959	The Merit Badge
Tuesday 27 January 1959	Crossing the Equator
Thursday 29 January 1959	The Cocos and Keeling Isles
	The swimming Lesson
	A visit to the Bridge

CHAPTER 5

Sunday 1 February 1959   Freemantle
                               The Ball
Wednesday 4 February 1959   The Southern Ocean
Thursday 5 January 1959   The Australian Bight
Friday 6 February 1959   The Final Destination.

                               The End

Foreword

This is the story of how I, as a ten-year-old boy, witnessed and experienced the events which unfolded a few years after my father returned to Salford at the end of the Second World War.

Both Mum and Dad were in the forces; Dad was a Royal Marine and Mum a WAAF based at Squires Gate, Blackpool. She was born of Irish heritage in higher Broughton, and consequently spent her childhood and adolescent years around Manchester and Salford. It was a natural progression for Dad to come to Salford after the war, although he was a countryman from the Lincolnshire fenland's. Mum had been married at the start of the conflict but unfortunately her first husband was killed after only four days of wedlock. For five years she was a widow but eventually married Dad towards the end of World War II.

Job opportunities were scarce or at best very limited. Dad unsuccessfully tried to become a greengrocer but alas wasn't cut out to become a businessman. Eventually he got a job driving lorries for Wimpey; he was happy driving and stayed with it, but he always wanted to get away from the city and back to the country.

My sister Susan was born in 1947 and I came along in 1948. We lived in a typical three-storey terraced house in Higher Broughton, Salford.

At this time, several of Dad's workmates were migrating to Australia or South Africa and sow the seed of a better life elsewhere was planted in his mind. Australia was harvesting groups of people from many social combinations and walks of life; various miscellaneous trades and professions were being cobbled together by the Australian Government.

The process of selection for the new adopted countries was based on trades and professional qualifications rather than social demographics; background and previous economic standing was fairly judged and providing you didn't have a prison record most people were welcomed. The consequences of this assessment meant that everyone had a similar goal; this was to provide for their families a better way of life in a warmer climate. The Australian government offered plenty of work with good salaries and a quality system of education. The majority of migrants came from the more densely populated parts of Britain, and not the villages or from the more gentrified or well-educated folk of England

Chapter 1   Early Days

The Fishing Rod

In a backstreet of one of the great cities of England lived a young schoolboy.

'Andrew!'

A yell came from behind just as he was about to scramble over the back yard gate. 'Watcha mate!' It was Eddy, Andrew's best mate. 'Are you coming out?'

Andrew replied, 'Hang on a minute; I've not got home yet. Let me change out of my uniform and I'll meet you on the Croft in five minutes. Shall we go up to the park for an hour?'

'Yes, why not,' came the reply, 'but I'll have to be home before its dark. My Mum nearly skinned me alive the other night for being late.'

'Okay, see you in five minutes.'

Andrew was full of mischief, fairly typical of the boys in his area; plenty of determination but with very limited pocket money, therefore most of the things they wanted, they made themselves.

The boys sauntered up to Broughton Park about two miles away, wandered around and chatted to the anglers. They always ended up climbing the fence and sitting at their own favourite spot.

'I'm going to make a rod Eddy; I'm fed up with coming up here and never been able to fish.'

Andrew had asked his dad for a rod, but money was scarce and there was always something more important to spend it on. His father drove a lorry for a construction company. One day he brought home a long bamboo cane, 'There you are son, see if you can make a rod out of this cane.'

'Wow, thanks Dad!' Andrew said to his father, 'I can make a beautiful rod from this bamboo.'

Andrew immediately asked his mum for an old wash-leather which he bound round the end to make a handle, tying it tightly with string to make sure it didn't come loose. Next he asked his father if he could have his pocket money early, but Dad, who always gave Andrew his pocket money on Friday said, 'No son, you will have to wait, just as I have to wait for my wages.' Andrew felt a little downhearted, but did understand and started planning how he was going to fabricate his rod.

The next day, Thursday, he woke bright and early, washed, dressed, had breakfast and then cleaned his teeth. On his way to school Andrew stopped at the fishing shop to gaze at the many different rods in the window. Alongside these, were all the accessories; the reels, the fishing hooks, the spinners and the eyes to thread the line up the rod, and many other items of equipment. Andrew decided that first thing on Saturday morning he would buy the eyes and the brightly coloured nylon to bind them onto his new bamboo rod. But first, he had to get through a day at school and that meant a bit of concentration.

At school he tried hard not to allow his mind to wander, but somehow it kept on drifting back to his new rod and all the fun he was going to have with it. The day passed quickly and on his way home, once again, Andrew, drawn to the shop window, examined the articles he intended to purchase.

The next evening, before he went to bed, his father gave him his pocket money. Andrew carefully put the money away; this week he wouldn't be able to buy any sweets for himself. His mother had a habit of giving him a bar of chocolate on Sunday afternoon, after their big dinner, so Andrew didn't mind waiting. He kissed his Mother and Father goodnight and climbed the stairs to bed. Slowly he drifted asleep, thinking about his fishing rod.

He woke early the next morning with great excitement. His big sister Susan was asleep and he didn't want to wake her. It was traditional within their family that on Saturday morning they lay in bed for an extra half hour, but that morning Andrew just couldn't contain himself, he just had to get up.

Unfortunately, his father heard him. 'Is that you Andrew? Get back to bed! The shops aren't open yet; don't forget I've been working all week.'

'Sorry Dad,' sighed Andrew and scurried back to bed.

Susan, Andrew's sister, had woken up by this time, 'What is wrong with you getting up so early this morning? Normally you like to stay in bed.'

'I know,' replied Andrew, 'but this morning is special. This morning I'm going to buy the guides twines for my fishing rod.'

'Oh,' said Susan 'so that's what this is all about.'

Both children lay in bed talking quietly for almost an hour. Eventually they rose, washed and dressed and went downstairs.

'Can I have boiled eggs for breakfast, Mum?' asked Andrew.

'Al right,' said Andrew's mum and she went to the kitchen to prepare them, while the children had their cereal and Dad made the tea.

Knock! Knock!

'Someone's at the door,' shouted Mum from the kitchen.

'I'll get it,' said Dad and went to open the front door.

'Is Andrew coming out to play, mister?' said a small voice. It was Eddy.

'You'd better come in,' said Mr Baker, 'He's just finishing his breakfast.'

Eddy came in and sat down by the fire and the two boys chatted for a while, Andrew telling Eddy all about the bamboo and the handle he'd made and the accessories he was going to buy that morning.

A short while later, the two boys said 'Goodbye' and ran up the street to the fishing shop. The man in the shop was very helpful and advised them on how to fix the eyes and then wrap the nylon tightly round to secure them in position, and finally to apply a little fibreglass resin to secure it all.

The boys thanked the man and rushed back to Andrew's bedroom to turn the advice and the shopkeeper's demonstration into reality. Finally, after about two hours, the rod was finished with all the eyes on and the nylon carefully fixed; the boys left it to dry. They told Andrew's mum so she would not touch it and went for a walk to their favourite place, Broughton Park.

At one time a well-to-do gentleman resided in the park, and more recently the local community used it. Within these grounds was a large lake which contained roach, rudd and perch, and on its water swam many varieties of duck and moor hens, occasionally a few graceful swans also dropped in for a swim.

BROUGHTON PARK

The main attraction was the fishing. Men and boys alike all loved fishing the water of Broughton Park. Andrew and Eddy stood beside the green railings watching the men casting their lines into the water; each line had a float, lead shot weights and a hook baited with maggots or bread paste. These were the favourite baits, at that time of year, for these waters.

Andrew's eyes gleamed when he saw all the brightly coloured floats; some were cork with bright red markings on, some were oblong with bright orange tops. Besides this, there were many types of quill floats; all the fishermen had quill floats, they were very popular.

'Have you caught anything, mister?' asked Andrew.

'Got a couple of perch,' the man replied, 'want to see them?' He bent down and proudly pulled the long green keepnet out of the water to display his prize.

'They're beautiful,' said Eddy, 'look at the stripes on them.'

'Look at the marks on their sides,' said the fisherman. 'You should always be careful when handling perch—you see the spines on their backs? Well, they can give you a nasty cut if you're not careful. It's a good idea to wrap a piece of cloth lightly round when you're taking the hook out of their mouths.'

'We'll remember that,' said the boys and watched as the fisherman returned the fish from the keep net back into the water. The boys told the fisherman about the rod they were in the process of making, and agreed this was a really good idea.

'Time I was heading home for tea,' said the angler and started to pack everything away. As he was putting his reel into his bag he pulled out a half used spool of nylon line. His hand dived back into the bag and he brought out two quill floats. 'Here you are boys, take these to start you off, the old quills have always been lucky for me.'

'Gee, thanks mister!' The boys said their goodbyes and promptly made their way home.

Time has a habit of vanishing, especially when you're enjoying yourself. So with the nylon and two floats to start them off, the boys ran until they were exhausted, but full of excitement. They quickly put the two miles behind them and arrived safely home. Eddy went off and Andrew went in for tea.

He told his Dad about the perch, the floats and the nylon and what the fisherman had said about handling the perch. Andrew's Dad saw how excited his son was about the day's activities and was well aware of what Andrew had done with the bamboo cane he had given him.

'Why don't you hand me up your Mum's sewing box,' he said to Andrew. Andrew looked puzzled but he obeyed. His Dad looked through the bobbins and then selected a really large one that was nearly empty. He transferred the cotton onto another reel and then turned to his son, 'Go and fetch that fishing rod, son.'

Andrew brought the rod to his father. They went downstairs into the cellar where Mr Baker put the big reel into his vice on the work bench, then selected a piece of dowelling suitable for a handle and cut it to length with his panel saw. Andrew got the glue off the shelf, and Mr Baker drilled a hole in the reel to fit the dowelling as a handle. Next he put the fishing rod into the vice and very carefully drilled a hole into a solid part of the thick bamboo. Then he took a piece of threaded bolt and placing them either side of two light washers he had shaped, he threaded the long bolt through the bamboo and locked on a nut with a little solder. He handed over the fishing rod, complete with reel to his son.

That night when Andrew went to bed, he could think of nothing but his fishing rod and where he was going to go fishing. With that he drifted off to sleep.

Sunday morning dawned and the sun peeped through the bedroom window slowly waking the two children. They chatted for a while and then decided to peep into their mum and dad's room, and leap all over them. Father Baker roared, 'Be still! Go to sleep!' as he tried to grab the last vestiges of slumber, but in his heart he knew it was hopeless; once the children were in bed there was no peace. A fidgety tranquillity set in for about five minutes, but the parents were forced to rise.

'There's no peace for the wicked,' commented Mrs Baker jokingly.

They all quickly washed and dressed and hand in hand they walked to church. The bells were pealing out from many different spires in the area and although they lived in a city suburb, the air was fresh. The daffodils showed their heads within the garden walls in the street, and everything around seemed happy and bright. The children laughed and talked, and very soon they all arrived at the church. The family took part, singing the hymns and generally praising the glories of God.

After the service they all walked briskly home, past the many streets of grime caked houses, Still the bells were pealing out; all around the Sunday morning feeling was in the air and people meandered along the smog ridden terraces and wide pavements. At the paper shop they collected and paid for their Sunday paper, and made their way home.

Mrs Baker got the frying pan out and it wasn't long before eggs and bacon sizzled for everyone. Somehow she had a gift of always keeping it hot and tasty, and the bread was always fresh with a crusty top. The coffee, percolated from ground coffee grains, always left the kitchen smelling like a coffee house.

Andrew ate his breakfast, enjoying every last scrap of it; his father raised his head from mopping up all the bits of bacon and egg with a crust of bread. 'What should we do today then?' he addressed the children at the table.

'Let's go fishing!' shouted Andrew.

'No, that's boring,' yelled Susan.

'Don't shout,' said Mr Baker, 'can't you children speak to each other without yelling?'

'Al right, where do we go?'

Mr Baker spoke up, 'I've got to put up a shelf for your mum, when I've done that we'll have an early dinner and then we will all go up to Heaton Park.'

Father had spoken and that was that, but Andrew and Susan agreed it was a smashing idea.

Heaton Park

As the family alighted from the bus, in front of them, standing majestically were the large entrance gates of the Park. The park keeper lived in the house attached to the gate and all around was the green grass and thousands of jonquils, daffodils and narcissi, poking their sunny heads up and waving about in the breeze, as if to say "hello and welcome" to the many people flocking through the gates and up the central drive.

The children dashed off playing tag in and out of the bushes. A large expanse of turf flanked the main tarmac drive, bordered by groups of beautiful large old, dark green rhododendrons, smothered in purple or dark red unopened flower buds. The shrubs were all about eight to ten feet tall and so big that it was easy for the children to hide in them. Many boys and girls used to play in and out of the bushes and nobody really minded, provided the children did no damage to the beautiful shrubs.

Andrew and Susan ran and ran until they were tired. They were so engrossed with their game that neither of them noticed how far their Mum and Dad had walked. Their parents knew they would find them because the family always had an agreement that if anyone got lost, they would meet by the lake beside the boathouse.

Andrew and Susan got their breath back and dashed off back along the main drive. It didn't take them long to locate their parents, who were strolling along, simply enjoying the scenery. They reached the large folly that dominated the drive and passing through, they caught their first glimpse of the water.

The lake always looked a brownish-grey colour; it was a large lake and green painted railings kept the public from going near to its edge. The other side of the railings was also full of daffodils, waving their heads around in the breeze, accompanied by the gentle lapping sound of the water as it rippled on the stones.

In the distance, gliding gently by, were skiffs and rowing boats their oars dipping in the water as fathers pulled their families through the shimmering water and the children dabbled their hands, much to the annoyance of their mothers who complained about wet cuffs—not that the children ever seemed to mind.

The sound of a little motor boat chugged by, just to let everyone know that something with power was around, if required. The ducks scurried out of the way and bobbed up and down, always a foot or so away from the boats as if held by an invisible arm, the boats never touched them.

'Please Dad, can we go on the boats?' Andrew pleaded with this father.

Susan joined in and asked, 'Can we have an ice cream?'

Their father knew how to settle this little rumpus. 'You can have one or the other, but you're not getting either until we've had a good walk, so there will be plenty of time to make your mind up.'

Susan and Andrew debated on the boat trip or an ice cream. Andrew insisted on the boat trip, and likewise Susan decided that an ice cream was far better than an old boat trip, so the discussion quickly turned into an argument; the argument turned into a row. Susan pushed Andrew. Andrew pushed her back, at which stage mum stepped in, 'Will you two ungrateful little tykes stop this argument? You've been told before about fighting and squabbling? I've a good mind to turn round and go back home right now! Goodness only knows; anyone would think you'd been dragged up, not brought up.'

Susan and Andrew stopped and shame-faced they walked on past the boats and the ice cream, and it wasn't long before they were chatting again, and within ten minutes they were pushing and chasing each other, playing tag and leap-frogging across the grass; the ice cream and the boat forgotten for the moment.

In front of them was a large expanse of greenery, and away to the left Susan and Andrew knew there was a sand pit and some swings. They indicated to their parents where they were going and dashed off to play on the amusements. They took in turns in pushing one another and swung as high as they could. Their Mum and Dad caught up with them and sat down on one of the benches, watching them playing and running around. Other youngsters paddled in the paddling pool fed from a crystal clear stream.

All of a sudden one of the Highland cattle that had been grazing quietly gave an enormous bellow. Everyone turned to look; there was Andrew who had decided to poke the large, shaggy animal with a stick. He thought the beast wasn't worried in the slightest; but Andrew was, as he saw his father tearing across the play area. 'What do you think you're doing?' he asked.

'I was only scratching it,' replied Andrew.

'I'll scratch your backside with the same stick if I find you doing anything like that again.'

Andrew ran off and sat on a stile, waiting for his sister to catch up. The old wooden stile was one of those that looked like a large figure 'A' and had steps that you climbed over. It was quite high because it crossed into the field that kept the herd of large shaggy, Highland cattle together. The inquisitive cattle approached the family as they walked along, but Mr Baker soon shooed them away.

'Oh, Bob!' she called to her husband.

Dad laughed and quickly protected his wife from the cattle. 'They're quite harmless,' he chuckled, 'I think they like the flowers on your hat.'

A few moments later they reached the stile at the other end of the field and climbed over. A silver stream glinted in the sunlight and its path of glittering crystals vanished into a nearby copse.

'That's where we're heading,' said Dad. Andrew and Susan chased the twinkling water into the woods. The little brook gurgled and burbled along and the two children followed, occasionally stopping to float a twig or throw a few stones into the water. Andrew came to an area where the water spread out a little and the stream twirled past on the edge, leaving the backwater to eddy and swirl around gently. It was about two feet deep in places and only six inches in others; instantly Andrew wondered if there would be any fish in this little stretch of liquid tranquillity.

He lay on his stomach on the bank and peered over the sides. The bulrushes, with their sharp leaves, stood like soldiers flanking the water. Andrew watched engrossed in the gently moving water, when a little flash of silver caught his eyes. He moved slightly forward to get a better view of what was happening beneath the surface. Cautiously he peered into the stream and there, just below the water on the edge of the weed, was a stickleback, its large red breast for all to see. This handsome little fish stayed quite still and then Andrew noticed several more beside the thick undisturbed weed at the very edge of the water.

Andrew showed Susan the fish in the water and told her that these little fish made a nest in the weeds. Susan didn't believe her brother, but he promised to show her the facts in a book that evening. Just then a frog croaked and leaped up onto the bank. Susan jumped almost as high and screamed. Andrew chased the frog, eventually throwing his cap over it to capture it. He carefully picked it up; he was delighted and showed his dad who made him promise to leave it in the park before he left. Andrew then chased Susan with the frog it had turned into real fun!

The Bakers all sat down on the grass and eventually Andrew's frog hopped into the water, before he could stop him. They watched him swim into the bulrushes and vanish, happy to be back in his own environment.

Mrs Baker pulled out a huge bar of chocolate from her bag and divided it up, to whoops of glee from the children. Mum always seemed to have little surprises when they least expected them. Contentedly, they sat around munching the nutty chocolate. Andrew made a little boat out of the silver paper and floated it down the river. It bobbed its way along until it was out of sight.

The family sat for a while, just drinking in the happiness that comes from being at peace with the world, and from enjoying the simple pleasures derived from a happy family. Mischievous though they were, both Susan and Andrew were good children, although undoubtedly Andrew had a substantial helping of devilment in him. He always tried to do what his mother and father advised him to do.

Susan and Andrew took off their shoes and socks and tested the water. 'Oooh, it's cold,' squealed Andrew, as he was the first one to paddle in the stream. But determined to play in the bubbling stream, the children floated pieces of paper and twigs, and made little rafts of the weeds, while mum and dad took in turns to lie back in the grass and just generally relax, which after all, most parents do sometime on Sundays.

After an hour had drifted by, Mr Baker told Susan and Andrew to make sure they dried off as he was planning to move on a little further into the park. The children sat on the bank and wiggled their toes; the sunbeams danced between the branches and gently kissed their feet, drying them in the warm rays.

The Baker family meandered through the leafy glade following the stream, eventually coming to a beautiful expanse of lawn. As they proceeded along the path, Andrew spotted a dark circle on the grass.

'What's that Mummy?' he asked.

'That's a fairy ring,' she replied adding 'At night, when everyone has left the park and the sun has vanished over the horizon, it becomes very, very quiet here in the park. The moon rises high in the sky and hangs like a giant lantern.'

The children listened, wide-eyed in awe.

She continued, 'Well, deep down in the leafy glade when the stardust has been sprinkled, out come all the fairies and people of the forest and just as you have danced and played and dabbled in the stream, so do they. That dark green ring is a fairy ring caused by all the fairies dancing in a circle, the grass gets flattened and little bits of fairy dust comes off their boots. In the morning, the dark green circle appears.'

'Is that true, Mum?' asked Susan.

'All I can say,' said their mother, 'is there is the fairy ring, plain as can be for you to see, so judge for yourself.'

The children really had something to think about and very quickly they were lost in their own thoughts on the subject. Meanwhile, Mr Baker found the rose garden and wandered up and down the Hybrid T's, which were his favourite. The large brick wall provided shelter to the garden adorned with *Albertines* and *Paul's Scarlet*; two varieties of rambling roses that flower profusely. The family wandered through the gardens enjoying the surroundings, as did other families. It was indeed a beautiful Spring day.

Just around the corner, the Bakers came across the Lion House; formerly the residence of the owner of the estate park, but now it had become a café selling light refreshments. The family sat down on the two bronze lions, which guarded the entrance to the café. Mrs Baker bought tea and cakes, fizzy drinks and packets of crisps with little blue bags of salt, which the children sprinkled on the crisps, then shook violently to make sure they were well salted. People hustled and bustled all around as tables changed hands with feeding groups of people coming and going.

Mr Baker didn't like this place; after the serenity of the rose gardens. The café was noisy and undignified. He quickly drank his tea and hustled his family to do the same.

'Let's get out of here and back into the open spaces,' The family obediently followed suit, the children carried their bags of crisps as they vanished out of the noisy café.

Further along the pathway was a large golf links, where they paused to watch the players display their talents. Mr Baker laughed as one unfortunate golfer sliced his ball, which landed with a resounding plop in the middle of a small lake on the course. Mr Baker had never been a golfer, but the picture of the golfer jumping up and down was quite a funny sight.

Further round the pathway they came to the tennis courts. Once again, they paused for a moment and watched the players while their Mum told Susan and Andrew the names of the strokes and how to score. Their mother had played tennis previously and loved to tell of her backhand stroke and volley, which apparently had given her much pleasure in the past.

Susan and Andrew ran on down the path again and up to another stile. Andrew decided to sit and wait for his parents. When they arrived, they all climbed over the stile and found themselves in an area full of more rhododendrons. Once again, the bushes gave great cover and the children hid from their parents amongst the large predatory shrubs. As their parents passed by, the children jumped out from either side of the path shouting 'Boo!' Mr and Mrs Baker pretended to jump and Mr Baker chased Andrew down the pathway, but he wasn't as fast as his son and the fleet-footed youngster quickly lost him.

As Andrew rounded a corner in the path he stopped in his track. There right in front of him was a great lake, slightly overgrown around the circumference with large rhododendrons stretching out to kiss the water's edge; the sun winked on the surface and glistened as if accepting the bushes above.

The family caught up with Andrew all of them amazed at the beautiful lake, which none of them had ever seen before. They had not walked along this old pathway and over the stile, even though they had been to Heaton Park many, many times before. They had never thought to explore beyond the usual walkways.

Andrew's thoughts immediately flooded back to his fishing rod, but his hopes were quickly dashed when he saw the sign 'NO FISHING'. Undaunted, he peered into the water and located a few sticklebacks. There were also minnows and undoubtedly this would turn out to be a good place to fish—with a net and jam jar. In amongst the weeds Andrew found a newt, lazily drifting with its legs outstretched, and across the surface of the water, speedy little water boatmen used the lightness of their bodies and the elasticity of the water to paddle across the surface.

A mechanical noise on the opposite side of the lake disturbed the serenity and tranquillity. Crows, perched in a nearby tree, rose as a black cloud chorusing their disapproval. The high-pitched noise continued and a little red powerboat skated across the surface of the lake disturbing all around it. The craft skimmed backwards and forwards creating ripples that ran across the surface and gently lapped at the perimeter. The frog engine, powering the nautical dart, started to splutter and the invisible hand guiding it gently manoeuvred it closer to the bank to retrieve it.

The Bakers walked around the lake and watched the man refuel the plastic tank; the smell of octane permeated the air. He held the boat with one hand and flicked the propeller mounted on the transom, like an aeroplane. It plopped around, but refused to start.

Suddenly the engine burst angrily into life making a terrible noise. The man set the rudder angle and placed it on the water to tear across the lake in an ever-decreasing arc. The boat operator had a little black box of tricks with a large aerial and a few switches and dials. As he moved the dials the craft performed a large figure of eight across the surface of the lake for its audience. We all watched with great interest and even the crows decided to settle down again.

By this time, the sun was lazily starting to dip its head and Bob Baker announced that it was time to start making a move towards the park gates. 'Three hours from now,' he said, 'it will be dark, so we'll have a nice stroll back.'

Taking a different route, the Baker family meandered along the pathways, Susan and Andrew darting in and out of the bushes chasing each other playing tag. Steadily they headed back towards the main footpaths, which would eventually lead them past the big boating lake.

Twenty minutes past five, and heading for the Lion House again, the family paused to check the splendour of the ten or twelve kites of different shapes and sizes, flown and towed by puffing fathers or nimble sons. The kites dashed backwards and forwards across the sky, their tails flying and bouncing, dividing the horizon in an effort to get away from their owners. A large box kite slept near a cloud, hardly moving, proclaiming itself king of the sky and daring any of the others to reach its dizzy height. None of the others bothered; they chased each other dancing in a kaleidoscope of colours, thoroughly enjoying freedom for the day.

Andrew and Susan proceeded down the hill; a little band was playing military music in a cast iron and concrete shelter surrounded by bushes. The volume of the music got louder as the children approached closer. Surrounding the shelter was about fifty seats; people sitting, some dozing, ladies knitting and old men snoozing or moving their walking sticks in time to the music.

Andrew eyed a Labrador tethered and sitting quietly with a middle-aged man, undoubtedly about to drop off to sleep. The dog raised its eyebrow as Andrew took out the caramel he was chewing and threw it towards the animal. Unfortunately the sweet stopped short but the dog, determined to have the delight, jerked in the direction of the masticated toffee.

Crash!

The deckchair folded with the man in it; he roared angrily, disturbing the surrounding tranquillity. The band played on regardless. As Mr and Mrs Baker appeared on the scene the area was in general disarray. A lady's knitting wool had rolled away and the dog was still attempting to get at the toffee while towing the deckchair. The gentleman lay spread-eagled on the ground with legs at right angles to the sky, and people around looked exasperated. The dog barked to show his approval as he chewed the caramel, which stuck to his teeth and Andrew ran on laughing at the disturbance he had unintentionally left behind him.

At this moment, Susan established her advantage. She knew they would soon be at the boating lake and didn't want to argue with her brother again. 'If you agree to have an ice cream, I promise I won't tell Mum you caused all that commotion at the bandstand.'

Hesitantly, Andrew agreed as he knew there was no chance of getting a boat now. Besides, it would be getting dark soon and when they went on the lake, he liked to stay there for a long time.

The Baker family, along with many other families, walked on down the long path towards the main gate; all of them hurrying towards the great monolith that marked the exit of the park. The park keepers checked the bushes for anyone likely to be hiding in the undergrowth, as the sun sank rapidly behind the oaks and the beech trees. A chill came into the Spring air.

The children caught sight of the ice cream van. 'Can we have an ice cream, Dad? You did promise before.'

Mr Baker produced some coins and said, 'Make mine a choc ice please.'

The children dashed off and waited in the queue with the other people. Susan held the money and Andrew held the ice cream. He had a large cone with splashes of raspberry all over it. He gave one to Susan and went back to his Mum and Dad with theirs, carefully licking his Mum's around the edges of her wafer, as it threatened to drip on the floor. There was little danger of this with Andrew around!

The children made noises of enjoyment as they stood at the bus stop waiting for the bus to take them to the Halfway House, where they had to change and catch another. They were still noisily enjoying their ice cream when the bus arrived. The Baker family went upstairs and settled themselves down for the journey home. The bus conductor came round to punch the tickets and hand them back as the bus rumbled off.

The light was fading as the family got off the second bus; dusk was closing in fast. They walked down Bradshaw Street, the cobbled road where they lived, and were soon snug inside their terraced house. Mr Baker raked the fire while Mrs Baker made the tea. The family all had fun and Andrew had found another place to go fishing.

After tea, Andrew and Susan played draughts and read books before heading off to bed. Tomorrow was a school day and for that they had to be up bright and early.

Meanwhile the BBC announced "*Journey into Space.*" It had been a good day and Mr and Mrs Baker settled to enjoy the warmth of the fire and listen to the radio.

The Canal

The week passed quickly as each day turned into the next, Susan and Andrew went to school and returned after their lessons. Susan always walked back with her friends down the High Street, but Andrew would kick a ball or a tin with one of his pals over the cobblestones of the back streets, until they came to the Croft, a patch of ground that lay derelict and used as a general play area by all the local children. Occasionally an old tramp would sit there and if he was lucky, he got a cup of tea and a bun. When it rained wet and muddy puddles appeared around the top end of the Croft and Andrew and his friends delighted in digging bridges and dykes out of the clay to trap the water.

While they played they planned their next adventure. Eddy had recently learned the whereabouts of the canal, and all the lads knew it was a great place for fishing. So they decided that was where they would go on Saturday. The boys knew it was dangerous to go there by themselves, but the urge was very strong. Eddy, Stephen and Andrew decided that at nine o'clock Saturday morning they would all go to the canal.

Stephen lived a few doors up the road; both his brother and his father were keen fishermen and Stephen had all the best equipment—a beautiful split cane rod and two different types of reels, hooks, weights and spinners, plus a box full of assorted floats. If Stephen came, they both knew there would be plenty of equipment to borrow and the fishing would be good.

Friday night came and Stephen rapped at the door.

'Would you believe our luck, Andrew? My Dad has offered to take us on his motorbike.'

'Wow, that's great!' replied Andrew, thankfully relieved. Now he wouldn't have any trouble telling his Mum and Dad.

Nine o'clock the following day, Andrew was up bright and early. Dad gave him his pocket money and told him to be a good boy and not do anything daft. His Mum gave him some sandwiches and cake, and with his accumulated fishing tackle and his home made rod, Andrew walked up the street to Stephen's house. A few moments later, Eddy arrived. He, like Andrew, had only a home made rod, but the boys were proud of their efforts and just dying to try them out.

Outside the house stood a big BSA motorbike, with a shiny black Watsonian side-car. Eddy and Andrew climbed into the side-car, and Stephen sat on the pillion seat with a crash helmet on. The boys in the side-car looked after the fishing tackle; Stephen's dad jumped on. With an almighty roar, the engine leaped into life. The whole thing started to shake as the vibrations went through the frame. Andrew could hardly contain himself and secretly smiled with excitement. He knew he loved fishing, but this was a different sort of excitement; he'd never been on a motorbike before.

The combination pulled away and headed down the street, out into the traffic and down to the traffic lights. Off they went, the boys were on their way. They passed rows of terraced houses, the shirt factories, the gas works and many different streets; some with bright red bricks, but mostly the bricks were fairly dark, covered in grime, where years of soot from the factory chimneys had left their mark.

The motorbike sped on its way. Fifteen or twenty minutes went by and the boys found themselves looking at a large red brick wall, which seemed to go on forever. Then they saw a sign 'Racecourse', but all the entrances were locked up as there was no racing on that day.

The motorbike pulled off into a side street and spluttered to a halt right at the top of the street. To all intents and purposes it looked as if there was just a blank wall surrounded by terraced houses. Mr Youngman led the way and then they saw a little wooden door in the wall; they all passed through and immediately in front of them was the canal.

A few men could be seen sitting quietly, rods in hand; a little orange or yellow float bobbing motionless on the still water. The canal was very straight with a timber strake running along the top of it. For as far as you could see, large black metal bollards sat on the bank, every hundred yards or so, with metal rings anchored to the ground in between them.

Andrew asked, 'Is it still used for ships and barges?'

'I don't think so,' replied Mr Youngman, 'possibly the odd barge, but not much else comes up here now.'

The boys started to get their fishing rods set up. Andrew was nearly ready; all he needed was a few maggots for the end of his hook and a couple of pieces of lead shots. He cast out and sat patiently, half-watching Stephen set up his split cane rod which had a cork handle with two brass ferrules to support the reel to. It was a three-piece rod and the sections joined together with brass fittings that slotted into one another. Stephen put on the reel and started to thread the nylon. He attached a hook and baited it, put on a couple of pieces of lead shot and ... *Swoosh!*

Andrew was so busy watching Stephen get his rod ready, he'd forgotten about his father. Mr Youngman had cast; the line hovered for a moment as it soared into the distance and made the noise of a whip that echoed in the air, *plop!* The tackle hit the water, right in the middle of the canal.

Stephen cast, and his float bobbed about ten feet closer. Andrew and Eddy could only manage to get their floats a few feet off the bank, but Mr Youngman said it didn't matter. What mattered was quietness and patience, and he told the boys that after fifteen minutes they should adjust slightly the depth of their lines, if necessary. Patiently the boys waited. Occasionally they were compelled to draw in their lines and recast, carefully checking each time that the bait was still intact.

A gentle breeze, like the breath of an angel, moved Andrew's float closer to the canal bank. Suddenly the float bobbed, Andrew felt the line in his fingers tighten. Carefully he watched his float—it bobbed again. This time he couldn't contain his patience. He struck the line as if fishing for a whale; the float leaped out of the water as he reeled in the line as quickly as possible. His yell had attracted the whole group, but on the end of his hook—nothing!

'But I could have sworn I caught it; honest I did.'

Mr Youngman baited the disappointed lad's hook again. 'Listen Andrew, when you see the float bob up and down that's the fish just having a little nibble. You would have to be very lucky to catch a fish by snagging at the line. The fish may do that several times, he may even go away and come back in a few minutes. This is where the skill comes in. After playing with the bait the fish will take it right into its mouth and that's the time to strike, but only strike gently. Remember quickly, but just enough to take all the slack out of the line. Don't forget, it's not a shark you're trying to catch!'

Andrew listened intently, grateful for the advice. He recast and settled down to wait. Stephen got a bite and expertly brought the fish to the surface. His dad put a landing net under it and passed the handle to his son. Stephen retrieved the fish from the net and took the small hook from its lip. It was a rudd; the boys all looked at the six-inch fish. Mr Youngman explained that the fins were a little darker red than a roach. He flipped the fish into the keep-net tied to a nearby bollard. Well, at least that was a start!

Eddy was next to announce he had caught a fish and quickly reeled in his catch; the line looked heavy, and as it broke the surface the boys hooted with laughter. Eddy had caught an old sock. After the amusement died away, Stephen told Eddy to lower his float down the line, because he must have been scraping along the bottom to catch that sock.

During the next half hour, the father and son team pulled in another three fish, all of them a similar size. Andrew and Eddy thought their luck was out but just as Andrew was starting to get restless, he saw his float move; he watched intensely, then it did it again, and again. It bobbed beneath the surface very gently and returned. Four seconds later, it jerked downwards, Andrew struck.

'I've got it!' he said, and carefully reeled in the fish, proving that his home made rod and the advice previously gained was just as effective as any other. The fish broke the surface, splashing and dashing from side to side. Carefully he placed the landing net underneath it raising it out of the water—a fine roach; eight or nine inches long.

Andrew caught the admiring glances of his friends; removed the hook and gently placed the fish in the keep-net. His first fish! He wouldn't forget this day in a hurry.

He baited the hook again and cast out, happy with his achievement and delighted that he had listened to the advice given by Stephen's father.

The morning passed quickly. The pals ate their sandwiches and chatted, occasionally stretching their legs to go and ask the other fishermen if they had caught any. The time gently rolled by, when suddenly a large clap of thunder signalled the change of weather. What had been a lovely sunny morning was going to turn into a rainy Saturday afternoon.

The boys quickly put their gear away and prepared to make a dash for the motorbike. Some of the men simply put up umbrellas and changed into oilskins, the mood of the fishing not to be disturbed. But the boys weren't quite that enthusiastic yet and they'd had a good few hours fishing with ten fish caught between them—not including Eddy's sock.

They emptied the keep-net into the canal, just as the first large plop of rain started hitting the water; the fish vanished instantly into the inky darkness of the water, none the worse for their capture.

The group ran down the canal bank and through the door in the old brick wall, out into the street again. The rain began to fall now. Quickly they got into the side-car and closed the top, the windscreen misted up almost immediately, but at least they were in the dry and not too wet.

Stephen and his father had bright yellow oilskins on to keep out the weather. The motorbike roared into life; click, the gear engaged and away they went. The rain streaked across the front of the wind shield; the bike bounced and vibrated along, slowing and stopping at traffic lights. Everything looking different now, as the rain settled in for the afternoon.

'Thanks a lot, Mr Youngman!' Andrew and Eddy chorused as they took their fishing tackle,

"See you later Stephen."

The boys made their way back to their homes, a little wet, but delighted with the day so far.

Andrew's Mum got him out of his wet clothes and he went upstairs to the bathroom to dry his hair and daydreamed as he looked at the green plastic curtains with little boats on that stretched across the window.

Going to the Cinema with Nanny

"Andrew,' his Mum shouted,"
"Are you coming down? Your soup's on the table.'
Andrew placed his leg over the bannister and slid downstairs. A large bowl with different painted animals all around the circumference was sitting in front of him, full to the brim with dark meaty soup. Large chunks of crusty bread were on the plate.

"Eat up," said his Mother,

"I want to go to the Maypole this afternoon and collect Nanny on the way back."

Susan, who had been sitting there quietly, piped up 'Can I come?'

'Yes,' replied Mrs Baker.

'Can we both come?' asked Andrew,

'Al right, but you've got to be good,' she said.

Andrew liked going shopping; there was always a chance of a few titbits at the Maypole. Andrew drank the soup and ate the bread, then got ready for the trip to the shops. He put on his dark blue jerkin and zipped it up.

'Bring your pack-a-mac Andrew,' his mother called.

'Okay,' he replied as he slipped it into his pocket. Soon they were all walking up the road. Susan gave a little 'kangaroo hop', which was a habit of hers at the time.

'Oh do stop that Susan!' said her Mum sharply.

'What?' said Susan, hardly aware of what she had done.

Andrew imitated her and Susan chased after him to give him a clout; she didn't catch him. The two children chased and tagged each other up the street. Mrs Baker walked quickly behind, hoping the rain would not start again.

They arrived at the Maypole general store and went inside. As soon as they entered, as always, a delicious savoury aroma greeted them and if the storekeeper was in a good mood, he'd give out little bits of cheese or meat to taste. Andrew pressed his nose up against the glass and prayed to be offered a bit of cheese. He was in luck, a curly haired man, who had just cut a wedge with a thin wire on a board, flicked the crumbs onto a plate and put them on the counter. Like greased lightning, Andrew's hand shot out and accurately selected the largest little nugget of cheese.

'Do you like that, lad?' the curly haired man asked.

'It's beautiful,' replied Andrew, 'but I like the biscuits better.'

The man laughed and went to a tin and offered Andrew and Susan a biscuit; which had the shapes of athletes on one side and icing on the other.

'Delicious!' said Andrew.

Meanwhile Mrs Baker had been doing the shopping, collecting bacon and eggs, and cheese and ham for Sunday tea and of course, a few biscuits.

Andrew asked, 'Can I buy a pennyworth of broken biscuits please, Mister?'

The man laughed again and went to the square tin box with a tight lid. He weighed out a few and put them in a bag.

'There you are son; let's see your money.'

The boy handed his money across the counter and he took the biscuits. 'Thanks Mister!' he said and followed his mother out of the shop, leaving the delicious smell behind.

They all held hands and crossed over the main road heading for their grandmother's house; she lived just a couple of street away. 'Hello Nanny!' the children yelled as she answered the knock on the door and let them in.

'Do you want a cup of tea, Celia?' she said to their mum. A pot of boiling water stood on the old black grate.

Nanny always had the curtains drawn, and piles of paper laid around the place. A general air of mustiness permeated the air. Nanny was seventy-three and she had been by herself for a long time; a real warrior of a woman, who feared no one, but lived each day remembering the past. Her long white hair swished around her face. She found a scarf and promptly tied it up.

Mum had decided to go straight home, 'It might rain Mother, let's get going.'

Mrs Baker checked everything, to make sure the gas was off and the windows closed and they went out. Nanny pushed the door hard after slamming it and off they went.

Nanny and their Mum chatted as they waddled down the flagged pavement. A watery sun threatened to burst and soak them all. The family headed for the sweet shop. Nanny always had a few sweets, probably the only luxury she had in her daily life—that, and the occasional trip to the cinema. The doorbell clanged announcing their arrival.

'Hello,' the man said, 'what can I get you?'

Andrew giggled and glanced at Susan crossing his eyes, which made her laugh. Unfortunately the sweet shopkeeper had a squint; Andrew could never work out whether he was looking at him, or at the toffees twenty degrees to the right.

Nanny asked for a quarter of nutty toffee. She mentioned the trade name and he got out the steps because the jar happened to be on the top shelf. He climbed the steps and tipped the glass jar towards him. Down he came, weighing the sweets and replacing the jar on the top shelf again. This exercise happened quite naturally, the shopkeeper was obviously used to this.

Nanny continued, this time she wanted sweets that were on the second shelf at the opposite end of the shop. The shopkeeper obliged and poured and weighed the sweets. Susan decided she would spend some of her pocket money and chose the nutty toffee Nanny had just had. Out came the steps again, and up went the man.

Mrs Baker bought some chocolate, and then Andrew decided he would like some sweets from the top shelf, but he couldn't quite make out the name of them so he asked the man to climb up and get the jar down, which he did. Andrew didn't want those. 'Please may I have a look at the next jar?'

The man got it down.

'I'm afraid they're too expensive. You see the jar, right at the end; can I have a look at those?'

By this time several people had entered the shop and were getting quite agitated at the little boy putting the shopkeeper through his paces. The man struggled to get the sweets down and when Andrew saw the price, he thought, 'I'll only be able to get two ounces of those,' so logically he said 'No thanks!' and dodged out of the shop. The man was certainly glad to see the back of him.

Andrew giggled; he had a pennyworth of sherbet from the shop on the corner of Fenny Street. Whoever heard of spending nine-pence on a few sweets anyway! Nanny gave him a piece of nutty toffee and chuckled to herself. Andrew's mum pretended she wasn't amused, but she could see the funny side of it really.

Susan and Andrew went on ahead down the back entry, past the brightly coloured painted backdoors. Tigger, the black dog, hit the door with its paws in an attempt to get out. It barked; always scaring the children half to death whenever they went by. Andrew banged the door again and the dog went crazy, leaping and barking.

The children ran on down the cobbled entry. Andrew and Susan went round to the front of the house. Andrew climbed the railings and sat on the pillar at the entrance, waiting for his mum and Nanny to arrive. Just then the front door opened.

'Hello Dad,' said Susan.

Andrew jumped off the pillar, just as his father yelled at him. 'We didn't know you were in Dad,' as he dashed past into the hallway.

'Where's your mum?' he asked.

'She's coming with Nanny,' they chorused. Andrew then told his father of the fishing trip that morning.

Nanny and Mrs Baker came through the front door. 'Hello Bob,' said Mrs Baker.

'Hello love,' he replied.

Nanny said 'Hello' and they all sat down. Andrew proceeded to tell his Dad about the motorbike and the canal and he went into all the detail about the fishing and how he'd caught the biggest one. They all had a cup of tea and Dad told Andrew of the time when he used to fish for eels on the River Ouse at Sutton Bridge. Dad used to tie a bunch of worms onto a line, which was placed in the water, then the eels would swallow the worms and the line, and they would carefully draw them out of the water and shake them off the line, into the bottom of the boat.

Mum said all the talk of food was making her hungry so she went into the kitchen and started making the tea. The kitchen looked out over the backyard.

A solitary rose was struggling to grow in a bit of soil beside the wall. *'Lady Godiva'*, a climbing rose, had been given to Andrew as a present the year before for his birthday. At the time Andrew thought it most odd as a gift, and would rather have had a slab of toffee or a Dinky toy, but although he didn't know it at the time, rose-growing was the start of a love affair, which would proceed with him into later life.

Next to the rose was an old table with Andrew's fish tank and a red Oxo box with holes in the lid that contained his frogs, collected from Broughton

Park. Andrew fed them on local grass, plus whatever bugs he could find and gave them a swim in the goldfish tank, which was green with algae from being outside. A piece of wood floated on the surface which the frogs always clung to, like men on a life raft. Another box, next to these, housed a horny old toad, which Andrew occasionally carted in his pocket. The clothesline passed backwards and forward, and a pile of coal lay in the corner, next to the toilet door.

Mrs Baker cooked some scones in the gas stove and kneaded some dough to make bread in the old black range in the living room. The children had squashed banana sandwiches, which were their favourites, followed by scones and éclairs. But what they all wanted was the fresh bread, which their Mum was just about to bake in the hot oven, a knob of butter on the hot bread and a bit of strawberry jam. Absolutely delicious!

Nanny asked, 'Can the children come with me tonight?'

'Yes, why not?' said dad. 'Where are you going Nan, to the pictures?'

'Wow!' said the children and jumped all over the floor.

A few minutes later Mrs Baker put a piping hot loaf on the table and with a sharp knife, butter and jam, they all tucked into the simple food that was a true mouth watering delicacy.

'You'll be good tonight, won't you Mister?' she turned and pointed to Andrew.

'I'll be good Mum, I promise,' he said.

'You'd better go and have a wash and get changed then.'

The children clattered upstairs. Nanny drank her tea, while chatting to her daughter and son-in-law. 'That place will be the death of me,' she said, referring to her employment. 'I spent four hours on my knees cleaning yesterday.' Nanny had worked hard all her life, she knew no other way.

Soon Nanny, Susan and Andrew were walking slowly down the road heading for the Rialto cinema. Nanny carried a big blue handbag that contained a hundred miscellaneous items, including the sweets. A few minutes later they queued, waiting to pay to get in. 'One adult and two halves, please.' Nanny paid for the tickets and they walked towards the usherette, taking their coats off as they went.

The Rialto always had a certain smell of its own; not unpleasant, but distinctive. They followed the lady who ushered them to their seats. The place was full of adults, very few children were around, which made Andrew and Susan feel very grown up. The cinema reeked with smoke curling from nearly every second adult sitting down, nanny told the usherette to find them a seats near a non smoking area

The lights dimmed slowly. Nanny popped a lump of toffee into Andrew's mouth and a large cock crowed—*The Pathé News*. The cock crowed again and someone a few rows up did the same. The news had begun. Some student from a university had run a mile in under four minutes and the crowd had gone mad at this, proclaiming him the greatest thing since sliced bread. Andrew thought, 'bet I could run as fast as him!'

He dropped his cap on the floor creating a disturbance while trying to find it, only to be dragged by one ear by Nanny. 'Find it when the lights go up; sit still now!' she whispered sharply. Nanny could have commanded a Sergeant Major—little boys were no problem to her!

Very soon the feature film came on, all about the Canadian Mounted Police but with a lot of singing in it, which Andrew didn't particularly like. Susan however, thought it was beautifully romantic. *'Oh Rosemary, I love you,'* sang the Mountie, but then it had several good fights in it and a canoe on the great river; so all in all Andrew agreed it wasn't too bad for boys, as well as girls.

Towards the end, Andrew started to fall asleep but once he stepped into the night air it quickly brightened him up. The attendant had opened the doors and together, en mass with the crowd, they spilled onto the pavement to the traffic lights and up the road. The air was chilly, even though it was Spring. The stars shone brightly, people waited outside the fish and chip shop; the smell drifted down the road drawing people like magnets. Nanny scuttled by, anxious now to get home.

She saw Andrew and Susan to the top of the street and watched them run down to their house, once safely in she toddled off home to bed herself. Their parents listened as the children told them of the film. They made and drank Ovaltine, and then the children mounted the stairs, cleaned their teeth and rolled into bed.

'It's been a terrific day today,' Andrew whispered to Susan.

'Goodnight, Andrew,' she said.

The two young siblings closed their eyes and drifted of to sleep.

The Attic

Sunday morning came and it was tipping down with rain. Nobody stirred in the Baker household.

A while later, Andrew decided to make a tent. He tucked the sheets in tightly at the edges and took two of the dark brown wooden stair rods and used them as tent poles it worked beautifully. Andrew lay there thinking about the film the night before reliving every moment of it.

Susan came across and got into the tent beside him, together they talked.

'Do you think Dad will paint the attic today?' asked Andrew.

'I don't know,' replied Susan.

'I hope so, will you help?' asked Andrew.

Susan said she would, so they decided to ask their Dad again. He had been promising for months to give Andrew his own bedroom. He said they would decorate the old attic room at the top of the house, but first all they must move all the junk to the cubbyhole at the top of the stairs.

Andrew and Susan decided that when they came back from the service that morning, they would set to work and move everything into the cubbyhole, so that dad could start.

They played a little longer in the tent, and then pretended that the cupboard was a boat. Andrew had once locked Susan in the cupboard and got his backside tanned for the pleasure! He thought about doing it again because it really made her scream, but decided against it remembering his mother's right hand.

Andrew's Mum and Dad lay dozing, when the children crept into bed beside them. They whispered to their Mum about the plan to clean up the attic and would she mind telling Dad, as they didn't want to disturb him right now.

'I heard that, you two little devils!' he said, 'can't you ever let me rest?'

They knew he was in a good mood. As he rubbed his eyes he said, 'I suppose we could have a go at it today. It's absolutely bucketing outside.'

The Baker household rose, washed and went to church, but this time the sound of the bells at St James', didn't seem so enticing. The dampened stones meant that all and sundry walked quickly, caped in pack-a-macs or similar rain wear, seeking what protection they could from the weather conditions. They straggled into the service like drowned rats; a thousand people in the church all looking the same. Father Riprap, as he was known locally, played merry hell with his late arrivals as they trailed in.

Back at the house Mum prepared the most bountiful breakfast of bacon and eggs, fried potatoes and home made bread, the early morning meal went down a treat. Afterwards the children went upstairs to the attic. First they collected things together There were bits of bric-a-brac, old uniforms, pictures to hang on walls, old mirrors, old curtain rods, more stair rods, lots of carpet and an old bed. An hour went by and with everyone helping, several items were thrown out and some re-stored in the cubbyhole.

Mr Baker took Andrew and Susan down to the decorator's. Although it was Sunday, in this district several businesses were open for trading because they were owned by people of the Jewish faith, who have their Sabbath on a Saturday.

The door chimed as they pushed it open. All around there were little stacks of wallpaper and different shaped tins of paint. They pulled out various rolls and looked at them, until they found a simple little pattern that was easy to join together and not too expensive. Mr Baker bought the rolls of paper and some wallpaper paste, a brush and some magnolia paint.

The shopkeeper wrapped them up and put them in a large polythene bag so that they wouldn't get wet. Andrew carried the paint and off they went again, back out into the rain.

Once home, they took off their shoes and left them near the range. Mr Baker displayed the paper for the approval of his wife. Meanwhile, during the time they had been out, Mrs Baker had been cleaning and brushing the woodwork, the skirting boards, the window ledge and the bannister. The place was looking different already.

Andrew helped his Dad measure the paper and they pasted and hung the first strip. This was great; it meant that he would get his very own bedroom and Susan could have the one they usually slept in.

Susan was given a paintbrush and she happily painted the skirtings and the window ledge. Mother came upstairs with an onion on a piece of string to collect the smells, or some such reason, and the boys hung the paper. By lunchtime, two walls were complete and the place was really taking shape.

Sunday lunch was a ritual with the family. They washed their hands and Mr Baker removed his overalls before heading downstairs. Mrs Baker went to the large ornately carved sideboard and took from the cupboard a decanter of sherry, carefully poured two glasses, allowing the children a taste, before handing a glass to her spouse.

'Cheers Bob,' she said and sipped the amber nectar while roasting the potatoes. Mr Baker took out the carving knife from its case and the sharpening strop, and proceeded to systematically hone the edge of the blade. This done, he called for the meat, which was placed before him. Susan had set the table, the napkins were all in place and all the knives and forks set out. Mr Baker proceeded to cut the piece of roast beef and Andrew and Susan brought the plates in.

Cauliflower, peas, Yorkshire Pudding, roast potatoes and roast beef, topped off with lashings of gravy made from the juices in the roasting tin. The four ate heartily, forgetting for the time being about the attic decoration.

Sunday lunch was the best meal of the week, it was the one thing they all agreed upon. Tinned peaches and cream came next, followed by a share of the block of chocolate.

The dishes were cleared and washed while Mr Baker put his feet up and promptly fell asleep for an hour. This was a very definite signal to be quiet. The children went upstairs and played in the bedroom. Susan had a book of ghost stories, so the pair of them created their own atmosphere by sitting in the cupboard. Susan read to Andrew *Black Coffee*. This was really scary especially when read by the light of the torch.

'That was really eerie Sue, do you think it's real?'

'Of course it's real, it's in the book isn't it?' she said.

'I don't think it's real.'

'Bet you won't drink black coffee again for a while,' she said.

Andrew thought about it, but said nothing. It was still pouring with rain outside. They heard a stirring on the stairs and pushed open the door to see their Dad coming up towards them. They all made their way up to the attic again and started work. It didn't take long for the other walls to be done, but then came a tricky little bit, because the attic was situated immediately under the roof. Part of the ceiling section was on a slope.

'I think I'd better have your Mum up here for a bit,' he said. Andrew went downstairs to fetch her.

'Hold this Celia, while I paste this end on.' Mr Baker had a long piece of wallpaper all covered in paste and was systematically sticking it to the slope. He just got it into position, when it decided to slowly unfold. However, he wasn't looking at that moment, and two seconds later, the paper had come down wrapping itself all around his head. Mr Baker let out a roar; he was furious.

Everyone else burst out laughing, but one look from him and everyone scarpered, leaving him to sort out the mess. Twenty minutes later the children ventured back upstairs to see their dad. This time he laughed, but still protested that it was not funny. The attic ceiling was slowly getting finished. Mr Baker decided to let everything dry before moving Andrew's bed upstairs to the attic.

The little boy pressed his head against the pane of glass; rain was still pouring down the outside. In the distance he could see the giant crane gantry on the docks. All of this was silhouetted against a background of dark thunderous clouds, magically lit up by streaks of fork lightning. He watched, captivated by the natural fireworks, but slowly his mind drifted back to his fishing.

His Dad brought him back to reality with a shout, 'I hope that paint's not wet.'

Andrew checked his clothes but it all appeared okay. He gingerly felt the woodwork, luckily for him it had dried.

A few days later, he moved in. Dad had fixed him up a light over the bed, so that he could read at night. At last he had his very own bedroom.

The Anniversary

The weekend crept round again and the boys were pleased to be out of school and into the fresh air. Andrew and Eddy caught a bus up to Heaton Park. They decided to take a better look at the big lake Andrew had discovered a couple of weeks previously. The two lads made their way through the park enjoying the sights amusing themselves by firing a catapult at tin cans or bushes. The boys arrived at the first boating lake and watched for a while. They then meandered on up past the Lion House and over the hill, through the golf course to the annoyance of the golfers and into the adjoining field, climbing fences and swinging through trees, but not causing any damage; just two boys, out for a ramble. Andrew remembered what his father had always said, *'the shortest distance between any points is a straight line'*. With this in mind, the boys crossed the hills and anything else that got in their way. An hour later, they arrived at the lake. There it was, stretched out before them.

'Well Eddy, what do you think?'

'It's smashing! Andrew, let's walk around it and find the best bits.'

The boys skirted round the perimeter; in some places the rhododendrons were so thick they couldn't get to the water's edge. They wondered what sort of fish were in the lake, but the sign very clearly said 'NO FISHING'. They knew they would not be able to fish with their rods.

By two o'clock, several men had gathered with model boats and the boys spent a good hour watching them skim backwards and forwards, with the yachts gliding along their sails adjusted to complete a semi-circle still managing to come back to the side of the pond a little further on. Various powerboats chugged backwards and forth with their noisy engines, others flitted and darted across the surface of the water.

Andrew looked for the newt he'd seen on his previous trip. Sure enough he saw some, and the sticklebacks were still there; little minnows darted about too. The boys found an old jar and tried to catch some, but decided now they were fishing with the rod and line, they would leave the jar and net fishing alone.

Later they made their way back through the park, past the café where they bought a bag of crisps between them, and down to the rose garden and over to the big boating lake. As they walked along, looking at the boats, Andrew remembered his Mum saying it was their Wedding Anniversary tomorrow and, as if by magic, there in front of him was a field full of daffodils and narcissi. Andrew looked on this as a gift from God. He looked around and quickly vaulted over the fence. Eddy kept watch on the outside, keeping a lookout for 'Parkies'.

It wasn't long before Andrew returned from inside the bushes with two immense bundles of daffodils and narcissus. He handed them to Eddy while he climbed back over the fence. The two boys made their way down the main path, many people stared at them as they walked along with the flowers, and they started to feel uncomfortable. So they took to the verges and crept along the perimeter beside the big rhododendrons. They could see the entrance gates in the distance and reckoned that once they were through that, they were safe, but a park keeper had spotted the boys and gave chase.

'Come here, you boys,' shouted the Parkie.

The boys ran on, trying not to drop any of the flowers. The park keeper started to close the gap and forced the boys to run at an angle to the gate. Yelling and shouting, and waving his stick, the Parkie got closer, then the door of the gatehouse opened and another one came out right in front of them. He grabbed for the boys and Andrew ducked under his arm but he had grabbed Eddy, and as he swung him round Eddy lost most of the flowers. Andrew's foot caught the park keeper's ankle.

'Run, Eddy run!'

The boys dashed off while the Parkie clutched his ankle. Eddy was holding four broken flowers but Andrew still had a very big bunch beautifully intact. The boys kept going; they decided to run past the bus queue even though a bus had just arrived. They looked around anxiously, the men had stopped chasing them, but they decided not to let up. They arrived at the next bus stop just as the bus drew up; they boarded clutching the daffodils and hoping they'd escaped.

As the bus gathered speed up the road, the boys saw the Park Police Van fly past with its flashing lights on. They stayed very quiet, cautiously getting off the bus at the place they had to change, quickly catching the next bus until, at last, they arrived at the top of their street. The boys split the flowers up and took a bunch each, and headed for their respective homes.

Andrew's mum was delighted with the flowers and filled every vase in every room downstairs. The parlour came to life with the blooms everywhere, contrasting with the maple table and the Bergère suite. While she put them in the vases she asked, 'Andrew where did you get them?'

'I saw them growing on a bit of wasteland and the man sort of let us have them.'

His mum didn't believe the story and queried it with him, but decided not to waste them anyway. When his father arrived home, he got a lecture about taking other people's property off allotments.

'They didn't come from an allotment, Dad, honest they didn't.'

He decided that doing good turns wasn't such a good idea as everyone was so upset with him. All he was trying to do was make his mum happy on her wedding anniversary. Even Dad forgot to buy any flowers.

The postman came to call.

For the next few days general school life and the backstreet way of life took over. One day rolled into the next. Andrew, Eddy and Stephen played on the Croft; digging holes, filling them with water, floating lollipop sticks and bombing them with chunks of mud.

Every evening they went round collecting bottles to get the return money on them from the shop. Sometimes they would get as much as six-pence, which would buy them ice lollies and aniseed balls. They begged red-headed matches from passers-by and built little fires on the Croft, which was always a cause for amusement and most importantly they made guiders.

Andrew acquired two sets of old pram wheels, a piece of plywood and an old van seat. He fixed the axle to the wood and cut the body to his own length so that he could sit on it. The front axle was nailed to an individual piece of wood, which was used to steer it and lastly the seat was fixed with six-inch nails and a rope attached to the front.

The three friends all had a guider, each of their own design. They held races taking it in turns and pushing each other across the Croft with the other sitting on the guider steering the course. Each evening Andrew's mother would come to the edge of the Croft and call him in from play.

But not all evenings were such fun, occasionally on the way home from school, boys going to the flats or estates would start fights and the only way to hold your own was to fight back. And so Andrew learned to hit hard and hit fast because it was the only way to save oneself from a beating.

Sometimes when he came by himself through the entries, he would come across a group of five or six boys, all happy to take on one little boy. So not only did he learn to fight, but also to run. When four or five of them chased him down the entry, he could find the crack in the wall by his gate with his foot, place his hands on top of the six-foot gate and vault over the top. Andrew quickly learned to be a survivor. The backstreet's were a consistent and relentless teacher. Like many things that happened, his parents didn't seem to be aware of the jungle within the cobblestones which surrounded them.

One day, through the mail a large brown envelope arrived. Susan and Andrew were soon to find out that their parents may not have been aware of the details, but had a very definite desire to have a chance of a life style with their family in a very different environment. The envelope was marked for the attention of Mr Baker and it had come from Australia House. Mr Baker opened his letter, it contained many little books on Australia; housing, jobs, countryside, taxation, schooling and hospitals.

'What have you got all this for, Dad?' asked Andrew.

'Your Dad has a notion to go to Australia son,' his Mum replied.

'Where exactly is Australia, Dad?' asked Andrew.

His father showed him on a map. 'I won't be able to go fishing at Broughton Park if we go there,' said Andrew.

'No, son, you'll fish the river Murray for *'real fish'*,' he said and produced a picture of a man holding a large trout as if it was a tiddler.

'Isn't that what you call fishing now?' he asked. Dad was excited. Mum and Dad read the leaflets all night, somehow Andrew's Mum wasn't all that keen and she didn't say a lot—not then anyway.

Andrew and Susan ate their tea and listened to the radio until it was time for bed, occasionally looking at one of the booklets that their Dad had put down. They kissed their parents goodnight, and went to their bedrooms.

Andrew looked out of his attic window and watched the stars twinkling in the distance. He could see the derricks of the ships at Salford Quays. 'I wonder if I'll ever go on a ship like that,' he thought.

The rain had started again; he pushed his nose against the glass, watching the little rivulets running down the window. A car splashed through a puddle up the street and stopped a few yards up the road to talk to a young woman standing under a street lamp. The rain spat on the pane of the glass, and all the lights outside seemed to sparkle brightly as he eyed them through the water running down the window.

Somehow he'd never thought of moving anywhere else. As far as he was concerned, the street was his home; the street was his life. He thought hard and soon found himself climbing into bed, where he drifted away into the night.

The usual rituals took place on Sunday morning and in the afternoon Andrew and Eddy went up to Broughton Park with their fishing tackle.

'What did your Mum say about the flowers?'

'Oh, she was pleased,' replied Eddy.

'Didn't you get a grilling then?' asked Andrew.

'No,' said Eddy, I told my Mum you gave them to me.'

'I got a real ear-bending; they kept on accusing me of stealing them off some old allotment, but I didn't say they came from the park.'

'I don't think I'll do that again, that Parkie was mad. Cor, I thought we were in for real trouble when he grabbed you. Do you think he'll recognise us again?'

'I don't know' said Eddy, 'but I don't think we'd better go there again for a while.'

'They've got millions of flowers in there that nobody can see because they're in the bushes,' said Andrew, 'Never mind, I'm glad we got away just the same.'

The boys chatted away as they walked up the road towards Broughton Park. They walked all around the park, stopping occasionally to see if anyone had caught any fish and asking if the man had been round to check the fishing permits, which the boys hadn't as yet managed to acquire. They jumped over the railings and crept through the bushes until they came to their secret hideaway. From this spot, they could look out over the lake, but the large reeds and bulrushes disguised and hid them from view. On either side there was a gap about ten feet wide where the reeds hadn't grown and the water lapped right up to the bank. The boys kept low, not wishing to be seen because they were on the wrong side of the fence. It wasn't that they wanted to break the rules, but they just didn't have the six-pence required for the fishing ticket and so this was the only other way.

They put their equipment together and cast in, using a crust of bread for the bait. Andrew used his quill float. He lay on the bank watching the float and thinking hard, his mind started to wander about the things his Dad had said and those little books on Australia. All around was peaceful, the moor hens scooted across the water. The boys watched a frog swim to the reeds. Eddy's float drifted close to the edge of the reeds. The boys didn't say much, they were just happy to be there. Andrew thought about taking a few bulrushes home to his Mum, then dismissed the idea remembering the nagging he's had about the daffodils.

He drew a ladies stocking out of his pocket.

'Where did you get that?' asked Eddy.

'Off the clothes line, said Andrew.

'Your Mum will kill you,' exclaimed Eddy.

'No she won't—I took it off your line.'

'Oh no!' protested Eddy.

Andrew put a stone in the toe of the stocking and tossed it into the water. 'This will do to keep the fish in until we have finished, and then you can hang it up when you go home. No one will ever know the difference. Don't worry about a thing.'

From that point onwards Eddy hoped they didn't catch any fish that day, but just as he thought about it, Andrew got a bite and what's more, he brought it into the shallows and landed it.

A beautifully marked perch; it was not very big but it was attractive. Its fin was arching; rising and falling. Andrew gently wrapped his handkerchief lightly round its back and removed the hook and put it into the ladies stocking tied to a twig pushed into the bank. The perch didn't move much after its initial rush at the nylon.

Andrew was pleased as punch, and with a big grin on his face he cast his line out. Eddy sensing disaster for his Mum's stocking, gently removed the bait from his hook determined that he wasn't going to catch any fish that day, but the boys stayed and fished on a while enjoying just being beside the water. Andrew caught two roach to go with his perch and true to his plan, Eddy didn't catch anything.

As time went on, their stomachs started to rumble and that was the signal to pack up and go home for tea. Andrew handed the stocking to his mate. 'There you are, no harm done, providing you don't tell her you kept fish in it.'

He handed over the wet stocking to his friend who eyed it with anxiety, hoping it would dry a bit before he arrived home. Eddy eyed the newt at the bottom of the toe and tried to rinse it in the water. His Mum would murder him if she ever found out. The boys retraced their steps through the bushes, looking right and left, and then hopping over the fence they made their way back towards the red brick entrance and out onto the road.

As they reached the main road a bus came along, the two boys hopped onto the running board; they could see the ticket collector upstairs collecting fares. The bus proceeded down the road, every minute carrying them closer to home. They saw in the mirror, the Clippy had finished and was making his way towards the stairs just then bus jerked to a halt at the traffic lights. Perfect! The boys looked at each other, knowing that neither one had the bus fare and jumped off at the lights, dodging in between the cars to the pavement, just as the Clippy arrived at the rear deck of the bus.

The boys smiled at each other, knowing that it had probably saved them a mile walk and no harm done. The bus pulled away and the boys walked on. They chatted amicably about school and the prospect of the Summer holidays that were looming up. It didn't take them long to reach home, where they went their separate ways to tea.

Eddy told his Mum that he had found the stocking in the entry. She proclaimed it must have blown off the line and promptly washed it.

That evening, Andrew asked his Mum and Dad, 'Where are we going this year for our holidays?'

'I don't know son,' said his dad, 'why don't you get the railway book and have a look, then you can tell us where you would like to go.

Susan rushed into the lounge and took the book from its shelf. The railway book had sepia pictures of all the trains and the places they ran to. The pictures were different shades of brown and stood out from the pages very clearly. The children went through the pages one by one, picking the places with little harbours in Devon and then passing them by for the bulb fields of Lincolnshire, only to return to the funfair of Blackpool and its great big Tower. They all chatted excitedly about the prospects of a holiday.

Later that evening, when the children had gone to bed, they heard their parents discussing the cost of having a holiday and how much they could afford. Eventually it was decided they would try to get away somewhere for a week, at least. The next question was, where? The choice seemed to be between Southport, Lincolnshire and Blackpool, and eventually Blackpool won.

The children jumped for joy at the thought of long sandy beaches and rides on the donkeys.

And so it was decided.

The Frogs

Andrew had a money box with a smiley face; this had a black hand and when you put a penny in its hand, it took it up to its mouth and swallowed it. Soon the children were doing everything they possibly could to save money for their Summer holiday.

Andrew went up to the park after school in search of frogs, as it happened, he came across a glasshouse that had been broken near a fairly stagnant pond. Cautiously he lifted a piece of asbestos sheeting and there, sitting underneath, were about fifty little frogs. They hopped and jumped all over the place as soon as their peace had been disturbed. But Andrew was quick and he had come prepared.

He picked them up, one by one, careful not to tread on them as they hopped and croaked in all directions. He put them in his Oxo tin, which had holes punched in to allow them to breathe, and then he quickly ripped up some grass in little tufts and put that inside. The frogs croaked and hopped around the box. He had a small tea chest at home in the back yard; that would do nicely to keep them happy. His toad resided in it at the moment, but he was sure the toad wouldn't object to a few lodgers.

When he arrived home he tipped the frogs into the tea chest with the toad in it. Andrew took the little box and went to the Croft. He dug up some tufts of grass and carefully laid it in the bottom to form a green bed and then he took a bowl of water and set it into the tufts so they would have something to swim in. He put a piece of metal grating on top, just to keep the cats out.

Feeling a sense of achievement, Andrew then went in for tea. Monday's tea was always good; cold meat from Sunday's joint, mashed potatoes followed by rice pudding and about four cups of tea.

After his evening meal Andrew went out to play with the boys from his gang. There were four friends who played together; Stephen, Eddy, Andrew, and Malcolm. Malcom had a pet snake and when Andrew told him of his frogs; Malcolm asked him how much he wanted for them.

'I'm selling them for four-pence each,' said Andrew.

So it was settled; Malcolm bought three frogs which he fed to his snake. The snake thought this was a real treat as he only used to get a mouse about once a week, and Andrew was delighted because this was money towards his holiday; so everyone was happy.

News soon spread about Andrew selling the frogs and during the next few days, the backyard turned into a trading post with boys coming to swap possessions or purchase one of the little green frogs.

One evening, at about six-thirty, there was a knock at the door. A man and his son stood there with a dead frog, demanding his four-pence back. Mr Baker turned to his son, 'What do you have to say about that?'

Andrew said 'It's not true, the frog was alive when he bought it, it's not my fault if he doesn't know how to look after frogs. All my frogs are alive.' He offered to sell him another at half price, just as a gesture of goodwill. But the man got very upset and started saying he would call the police if he didn't get his money back. Andrew told him he couldn't have it back; he only sold live frogs and not dead ones.

Andrew's Dad told the man to clear off, but then he turned to Andrew and told him off for selling frogs, 'You know son, I don't like you selling frogs. They are wild creatures and as such, should be free. So before I come home tomorrow night, I want you to go down to the Croft and let every one of those frogs go.'

'Oh Dad, that's not fair!' Andrew protested.

'Don't answer back now,' said his father, 'You do as I say!'

The following evening, Andrew let all his frogs go only to see some of the other local children trying to catch them, but at least he had done what his father had asked. But the thing that really upset Andrew was that his father had not backed him up when he needed it.

The model Boat

Three or four weeks went by without anything special seeming to happen; school every day, a bit of fishing at Broughton Park. The boys still didn't venture towards Heaton Park. They played with the guiders on the Croft, chasing each other round the home-made track and had the occasional battle with different gangs from a few streets away. The Summer evenings were starting to draw out.

The children were preparing for bed, although it was still light outside, in through the door came their Dad. He had been working overtime. Andrew ran to greet his father as he always did, but this time dad couldn't open his arms and swing him into the air because this time his arms were full.

'What have you got there Bob?' asked Mrs Baker.

'What do you think it is Andrew? It's for you.'

Andrew's eyes nearly popped out of his head. He started to unwrap the newspaper, but he could see immediately that it was a boat completely made out of wood, shaped into a cabin cruiser and heavily varnished. A compartment at the stern lifted to display an engine and two batteries. The cabin cruiser was about three feet long and had a stand.

Dad explained that his friend Tommy had brought it in and he had swapped it for a packet of Woodbines. Andrew was ecstatic! It was without doubt, the best present he had ever had in his life and his father had given it to him as a gift for no apparent reason other than the situation had presented itself.

'Can I try it in the bath, Dad?'

'Go on then, but don't forget you're going to bed in fifteen minutes.'

Susan and Andrew dashed upstairs and quickly filled the bath. They watched the boat settle itself on the water. Then Andrew lifted the box on the stern and switched on the engine. There was a little stop-start switch on the engine, which put the engine in gear. Andrew pushed 'start' and the little bronze propeller immediately started kicking water up behind the boat, pushing it along.

Unfortunately the bath wasn't long enough to give the boat a real trial but at least the children could see its potential. Mr Baker came upstairs and watched the boat chug up and down the bath. 'Okay now, that's enough. Let's have you both in bed.'

Andrew took the boat out of the water. 'Thanks Dad, it's a fantastic present!'

Andrew rubbed the bottom of the craft dry and then carried it upstairs in his arms to his attic bedroom. Carefully he rearranged his chest of drawers and positioned it there, on its stand, without a doubt taking pride of place within his possessions. He switched his light out and fell asleep looking at his boat.

The weekend came and went, unfortunately the weather was against taking the boat to the park and so the boys went to the county matinee on Saturday afternoon with a bag of sweets and a peashooter and, as usual, made a nuisance of themselves, but then half the children in there were doing the same thing.

That evening they all played Chinese Chequers; the rain poured all weekend and stopped any outdoor activities. Andrew, once again, found himself with his nose pressed against the windowpane watching the rivulets of water running down, blurring his vision.

Susan had crept upstairs and together they looked out of the window; brother and sister, making secret plans with each other. 'Do you think we will go to Australia, Sue?' Andrew asked.

'I don't know; it's an awfully long way away. There won't be any rain there either,' she said.

'I quite like the rain,' declared Andrew. 'Dad seems very keen to go, doesn't he?'

'I suppose we'll have to wait and see what happens.'

The children chatted quietly, down below they could hear their parents talking in slightly raised voices. Susan crept back down to her room and the voices stopped. The only sound remaining was the pitter-patter of the raindrops and occasionally a car light would throw weird patterns of light across the room. Andrew fell sleep.

Nanny

The next morning, the children went off to school as normal, but when they arrived home their mother was in a very distressed state. Nanny had had a stroke and was in hospital. Their Mum was extremely distraught. Andrew and Susan knew that something was wrong, but the extent of the emotion just didn't register in their minds.

Mr Baker arrived home from work and was told of the situation. Bob and Celia went off up the road to the phone box. Susan and Andrew promised to be good until they got back. Not long afterwards their parents arrived back with fish and chips to save on the cooking, as their mum didn't feel up to it. The news was that Nanny was stable.

The doctor arrived at the house about seven o'clock. 'Just popped in, Mr Baker, knowing you must be worried. But she's as strong as an ox. Another person, it might have killed—but not her, she's made of sterner stuff. I know she'll pull round al right. But I don't think she should be left by herself any more in that house.'

Mr and Mrs Baker thanked the doctor for his concern and as he finished his tea, agreed that they would give the situation some thought. He told them that Nanny would be in hospital for at least another week and so they had until then to make arrangements. The doctor said goodnight and Mr Baker let him out.

'Well Celia, there is only one thing for it; she'll have to come here when she gets out of hospital, but the main thing is she's okay, she's going to be all right, so don't worry.'

The Football Boots

That evening, after school, the boys went down to football practise at Manly Park. They all played football every day at school, but this was the first time Andrew had been asked to attend the official school team's practise. He felt slightly honoured, but unfortunately he didn't have any football boots. All the football boots were brown leather, with leather studs nailed to the soles and a new pair cost about thirty shillings. He knew there was no way he could get that much money from his parents.

One of the boys had a second-hand pair for nine shillings; maybe he could buy them, they'd do perfectly well. He borrowed them for the practise and they fitted fine. After the practise, the coach asked him if he would like to play a game on Saturday.

'Yes, certainly Sir,' Andrew replied.

'Make sure your boots are clean.' The teacher had told the team what time to arrive, including two substitutes. Andrew was picked as one of the team. He gave the boots back and, like a dog with two tails, he ran home to tell his parents his exciting news.

His Mum and Dad were pleased, but didn't seem to take a lot of notice of him. The boys were forever kicking balls around and it seemed as if they were always in some team or other.

'But this is different,' he insisted, 'this is the official school team.'

Andrew asked for ten shillings to buy the football boots.

"NINE SHILLINGS you must be joking."

'Sorry son, We haven't got nine shillings spare for football boots, we need all the money we get. I mean I think it's great you playing football, but I am sorry, there is no money for football boots.'

Andrew felt really downhearted; he didn't know where to turn. For the next three days, he tried to sell things at school; his marbles, his cigarette card collection, his stamp album, unfortunately most of the boys were in a similar situation, the most anyone ever had was six-pence.

He had two shillings and even with his pocket money of one shilling and three-pence, he would still need six shillings and nine-pence. He asked his Mum several times if he could get the money, but she stuck to what Dad had said.

That day Andrew went to the sports master and told him he couldn't play in the team; he made up some excuse but he didn't give the real reason, he was too upset. He went home and in the privacy of is room he buried his head in the pillow and cried his eyes out.

He'd heard his parents arguing about money before, but he never really appreciated its true value until that day. The sense of loss after being chosen for the team was heart breaking. It was a cruel world he lived in, and a cruel lesson he'd learned that day.

Saturday came and he couldn't even go and watch because the sports master would see him. He privately made up his mind that he would try never be without money when he grew up.

Nanny comes home

When Nanny came out of hospital she came to live with us and took over the parlour as a bedroom. At least mum could look after her. Dad wasn't too happy, but he accepted the situation.

The days turned into weeks and apart from a lot of study at school for the end of term exams, nothing else much happened. The school nurse came and gave the whole school Polio injections. The school went quiet and all the children sat their exams. Teachers marked the papers feverishly for the next few days, prior to the school summer holiday break-up. Two days before the end of term, the school sent reports home with the children, and many didn't return to school after that.

At last the Summer holidays had arrived. The gates opened for the last day at school and everyone had cakes and pop, and then it was finished—freedom for six weeks!

The bell went. The children cheered loud enough to wake the dead and a stampede of children left the school, streaming in all directions, all of them happy. Twenty minutes later, only the janitor and the cleaner remained; peace and quietness had come to that particular closet of learning.

The Summer Holidays

Excitedly, the children climbed the stairs to bed that night. Mr Baker had read the school reports and although neither of them glowed academically, at least their general standard was acceptable. He was reasonably pleased.

Bob Baker had also just told the family that his holidays had been agreed at work and in three weeks they would all be sitting on Blackpool beach. As the children climbed the stairs, their heads full of fantasies; they made plans for the holidays.

That night Susan crept up to Andrew's room and the pair of them got in bed and chatted about Blackpool. Their Dad had said they would go by train, which was always a cause for excitement. From the attic window, Andrew could see the trains in the distance, clouds of white smoke drifted into the sky to signal their departure from the station. Soon, very soon, they would be travelling on one; only twice before had the children been on trains, so this was a real novelty.

They quietly chatted about how much they could save by that time and where they would stay, which end of Blackpool they would go to and pondered upon whether their parents would take them up the Tower. Although they were too keyed-up to sleep, Andrew found himself nodding off and quietly Susan slipped out of bed and into the sanctuary of her own little nest.

The children woke early as normal but decided, out of rebellion, just to lie in bed until after their normal school time. Breakfast eaten and ready to go, mum was taking them into the city to buy a pair of shoes for Susan and get her new uniform ordered. Susan was going to grammar school after the holidays and Mrs Baker was determined that the uniform would fit and that it wouldn't become a last minute rush.

They jostled their way off the bus and up the stone stairs out of the bus station. A man playing a barrel organ with a brightly dressed monkey on his shoulder greeted everyone as they swarmed past him. Occasionally someone would drop a penny into the monkey's cup. The man played on, the crowd surged forward. Up the street they walked all keeping closely together and pushed along with the crowd. The Bakers reached Market Street and into the shoe shop.

'Yes, Madam, what can we do for you?' the lady asked. Susan and her mum sat down. 'A pair of brown shoes please; flat with laces.'

'Oh Mum!' protested Susan, 'that's not fair. I am growing up now.' Mum compromised a little, 'let's make it a court shoe with a baby Louis heel.'

Susan was pleased when the assistant brought out several pairs of shoes, but none of them were to Susan's liking, apart from the ones with heels larger than mother wanted, and so they moved to the next shoe shop. This time they started off by asking for a brown shoe with a baby Louis heel. Andrew ducked out of the shoe shop and hopped into a model shop next door to gaze at the yachts and model aeroplanes. The balsa wood caught Andrew's attention because they had just started playing with model aeroplanes. Out of the corner of his eye, he saw his sister and mother leaving the shoe shop and quick as a flash, he was out on the pavement beside them.

'Where were you, my lad?' his Mother scolded.

'Just in here Mum, looking at the balsa wood,' he said. She pretended to ignore his excuse and they walked on. Susan held her shoes tucked under her arm in a box. They passed the tripe shop and Mum asked if they wanted some for tea.

'I'd like some cow-heel,' said Andrew.

'Al right then, we'll get some on the way home,' said mum. They reached the top of the street, all around them the people jostled in and out of the large stores on either side of the road. In front was the large green expanse with lots of flowers in bloom, park benches and statues. This was Piccadilly Square.

Many buses were parked on one side and cars rushed by, affected by the Summer madness, everything was busy and the crowd hustled and bustled; everyone seemed to be in a hurry. The young family went into the big shop; they headed for the escalator. The moving staircase took them up to the gents department where Andrew was to have a haircut.

'Ah, no Mum! I don't need a haircut,' he argued.

'You have two choices; it's here, or a bowl on your head tonight and your dad will do it. Your Dad won't take you to Blackpool with hair over your ears you know.'

Andrew had a bright idea. 'Listen Mum, if I don't get a proper haircut today we can use the money to go the pictures instead.'

'Where will you get a proper haircut?' she asked.

'I promise, I will Mum.'

'Al right, you've got two days and if you don't it's a basin over your head. Got it young man?' the voice of authority had spoken.

'What about the flicks then?'

'We'll have to see what's on and only if it's suitable.'

'Or we could go and see the *Lady and the Tramp*,' said Susan.

'But it's my haircut money!' retorted Andrew.

'We'll see what time they start,' said Mum, putting an end to the quarrel before it got going.

The smell of ground and percolating coffee invited them into the Kardoma, a well known coffee house, where they sat and ate Cornish pasties, chocolate éclairs with coffee for lunch. Mother bought some Blue Mountain coffee grains and had them ground for Dad. She paid the bill and headed upstairs to get Susan measured up for her new uniform. Mum totted up the cost of all the new clothes and wondered just how they were going to pay for it all. The holiday was going to cost a lot, but she'd budgeted for a while and had some money put by. The little family headed out into the sunshine, but as they walked down the road, a few drops of rain started to fall

'Come on,' said their Mum, 'let's go and see when this cinema opens.'

Captain Blood was starting in ten minutes after they arrived, so that was that, the other film would have meant an hour's wait. 'Two shilling seats and an adult,' Andrew piped through the kiosk glass.

'That will be three and six young man.' His Mum gave him the money and he paid it through the slot in the window. The lady punched a lever and the tickets flew out of a flat metal desktop. She handed them to Andrew.

'Thank you,' he said. 'Thanks Mum.'

They all took off their coats. Mrs Baker bought them a packet of popcorn and they made their way into the cinema. The lights were still on, so they had no difficulty in locating their seats and making themselves comfortable. A few minutes later, the lights very slowly dimmed, until the whole area was an inky blackness. Once the preliminaries were over, the music demanded attention and Captain Blood sailed and plundered backwards and forward across the oceans. The children enjoyed every moment of it; Pathé news followed and a cartoon followed by a 'B' rated cowboy film. When finished they made their way out into the damp street

After being in the darkness, the children were surprised to find it was still light outside. A large queue had formed as people waited for the next session. Out on the street people hurried and scurried along, anxious to get home after their day at work. Mrs Baker made her way along to the tripe shop which was still open. She bought some tripe and cow-heel sprinkled with vinegar and wrapped in white paper. Later they made their way to the bus stop and the short trip home.

'Bob will wonder what has happened to us,' she said.

'Oh he won't mind, he knows it's the first day of the holidays,' remarked Susan. The children sat together on the bus which was crowded with workers and shoppers. Sure enough Dad was in the house waiting for them to arrive. He put a pot of tea on the table.

'Where have you been?' he asked, 'I've been working hard; I want my tea!'

'Well, you'll just have to wait a minute, I've only got one pair of hands,' their Mum said. 'Five minutes later, tea was on the table; tripe, cow-heel pickles, bread and butter. Mum fried up some chips to go with it.

'We've been to the pictures, Dad,' said Andrew, 'and I've been measured for my uniform,' said Sue. The children both agreed it had been a good day for the start of the holidays.

The next few days proved to be fairly mundane with Andrew's little gang playing on the Croft at the end of Bradshaw St., and chasing each other with the guiders down one side of Fenny St., and back up the other onto the croft. The four wandered for hours on end up and down the streets, and across to the flats a mile away, gathering pop bottles bringing them back and washing them and collecting the money on them from various local corner shops. Two-pence on a bottle meant lots of good bottles had to be collected for a few bus fares or lolly money.

'What about your haircut, my boy?' said his Mum.

'I'll get it done today, really I will.'

Mrs Baker reckoned she'd end up cutting it herself, but she gave her son the chance to make good his promise. Andrew occasionally played with a boy whose Mum had a hairdresser's shop on the corner of a local street.

Knock! Knock!

'It Paul coming out?' said Andrew to the lady.

'Paul, it's Andrew at the door for you.'

'Come in Andrew, fancy a cup of tea,' she asked.

Paul came to the door

'Yes please,' said Andrew and soon the brew was presented.

Mrs Evans' first customer came and she vanished leaving the boys alone, they played together for an hour with toy soldiers and a canon that fired matchsticks, the customer went and then the shop was empty. Paul swept up the hair on the floor. Andrew picked up a pair of scissors and gingerly trimmed the end of his hair.

Just then Mrs Evans came in, 'What are you doing Andrew?'

'Oh! Come here, I'll soon straighten that up. Whatever possessed you to cut a piece of your hair?'

'I just wanted to see what colour it is.'

'Oh you boys,' she said, and sat him in the chair. Soon she was busily snipping away. Andrew was very happy. He got his hair cut without any problem and the devious little boy had made good his promise to his Mum.

Andrew introduced Paul to the rest of the gang later that morning and Andrew's Mum was delighted with the haircut, though she wondered how her son achieved it, she really hadn't believed him when he said he could get it cut himself prior to them going to the cinema.

Malcolm's Snake

Malcolm dashed around to Andrew's back door. It was about four o'clock. 'Quick get the boys, Andrew, I've lost my snake. He's disappeared.'

Andrew dashed off to get Stephen and Paul; Malcolm went off to get Eddy. The boys had only just left each other and gone home for tea.

'What happened, Malc?'

'I was feeding him and I let him out in the backyard, my mum called me and when I got back he'd gone.'

'Why didn't you put him back in the glass tank?'

'I just didn't think,' said their worried friend. The boys searched everywhere but the snake was nowhere to be found, certainly nowhere obvious. Two hours later, the boys gave up looking.

'Maybe he will turn up when he's hungry.'

'That won't be for a week, he just had a rat my uncle brought home from the tannery. All he will do now is sleep for a bit.'

The boys went out on the Croft for a while. They gathered some sticks and paper, begged a couple of matches from a passing bus driver and lit a fire on the Croft. The boys sat on the brick wall. Eddy told the boys of the latest sign his big brother had taught him. 'You put your fingers like that.'

'That's the Victory sign,' said Stephen.

'No it's not, it's the other way round,' insisted Eddy, 'you try it and see! Just flick your fingers up as a car goes by.'

Just then a taxi came down the road; its yellow light was on indicating it had no passengers. Andrew jerked up his fingers in the way Eddy has shown them. The taxi driver jammed on his brakes and leaped out of the cab hurling abuse at the boys. They all scattered in every direction, not wishing to be caught by the cab driver.

'Cor, that was effective, what does it mean?' said Andrew.

'Don't know,' said Eddy, 'but it certainly works.'

That night Andrew asked his father what it meant. His Dad was angry and told him it was a bad sign with a vulgar meaning. Andrew was forbidden to use the sign again. Eddy had tried it on his father to see what effect it had and received an almighty cuff round the ear, which knocked him to the ground. The boys decided they would keep that sign for very special occasions—it was obviously bringing a lot of trouble to them.

One day drifted into another; the boys sat on the top of the air-raid shelter at Malcolm's house firing a catapult at the stray cats that wandered around the yards or in the back entry. Mrs Thompson, Malcolm's Nanny, went to the toilet adjoining the air-raid shelter; the boys took no notice, preoccupied with firing pebbles at cats. All of a sudden an almighty scream shattered the tranquillity. Mrs Thompson emerged from the toilet, dark brown stockings around her ankles, dashed from the toilet screaming, 'A snake! A snake!'

Malcolm looked at the other boys and they quickly slid of the roof of the old air raid shelter down into the backyard. There was Malcolm's snake happily coiled around the pipe coming from the cistern.

'Cor, what a stink! It smells like a dead rat!' said one of the boys.

'Good job she didn't flush it,' said another, 'you might have lost him for good!'

The boys laughed. Mrs Thompson had come out and was standing beside them. 'Get out of here you little horrors, and Malcolm, make sure that thing doesn't escape again.'

Malc put the snake in its glass tank and went to find his mates, who had scarpered up the back entry. Mrs Thompson had seen the snake in the mirror hanging on the back of the door; she went back to finish what she had started. This time she could relax.

A Trip to the Swimming Pool

The days were warm and sultry; Andrew had played with Paul a little more recently.He only lived one street away. That afternoon Paul's father took the boys to the swimming pool. Mr Evans had a black Ford Consul; he was the only person around them who had a car. Paul, Eddy and Andrew piled into the motor having asked their parents' permission and away they went.

Mrs Baker was happy she knew where her son was and it got the boys off the streets for a while. They cruised up the road until slowly they left the shops behind them and the larger houses came into view; all of them surrounded by shrubs and trees flanking the entrances. Then without any notice, the open fields and the hills rolled down to greet them. Mr Evans pulled the car up a shingled driveway and before them, a beautiful swimming pool.

He parked the car and the boys got out. They could hear laughter coming from inside and squeals of delight penetrated the country air. Mr Evans paid for all of them and soon they were inside changing into their swimming togs. It was a glorious day. None of the boys could swim, although they all said they could. They changed quickly and all headed for the shallow end. The next ten minutes saw all sorts of one foot-on-the-bottom attempts at swimming and a hundred and one excuses why they couldn't swim in this pool. Eventually they stopped trying to show off and simply settled down to enjoy the water and the fact that they were there.

The boys played on the grass surrounding the edge of the pool and, like lizards on a rock; they dozed in the sun after a spell of using muscles not normally brought into everyday use. Young men dived from the boards at the deep end, and families frolicked together in the water. All around was an air of gaiety and laughter, the true spirit of the Summer holidays. The sun shone down and the boys got a little suntanned, although it was difficult for them to stay still for long. As fast as they warmed in the sun they jumped into the water to cool off. The friends picnicked on the grass and after lunch spread their arms and basked in the sun; and so the day continued until the long rays kissed the families at play and the afternoon drew to a close.

That evening, after arriving back at their homes, the boys thanked Mr and Mrs Evans for a super day and with their togs thrown over their shoulders, sauntered up the back entry to home.

'That was absolutely fantastic,' said Andrew when asked by his Dad, amazingly though, he didn't even know where he'd been. He enjoyed his tea and listened to Walter Gabriel on *The Archers*, croaking away to Doris. He wondered what tomorrow would bring; he certainly hadn't bargained for today.

Watching Television

The two children were invited next door to watch the television on special occasions. Mrs Hooper was a kindly lady, who had taken a shine to Susan and used to let her watch the TV occasionally. Andrew sat down where he was told and promised not to move a muscle. Mrs Hooper was a Justice of the Peace and she and her husband, Duke, were good friends as well as neighbours of the Bakers. Mina had a very serious attitude, and when told to sit you knew that if you wanted to watch TV then you had to be good.

Mrs Hooper picked up a large glass jar from the shelf and passed it round. The children's eyes lit up as they reached into the jar and pulled out toffee in golden paper or shining green triangles of chocolate.

'Oh! Quality Street!' exclaimed Andrew.

'Thanks, Auntie Mina,' the children whispered, so as not to drown out the television.

The rule was that Andrew had to leave early, because he was the youngest. This always struck him as being unfair, but just the same he had enjoyed the television and said his 'Goodnight' and 'Thank you', then left his sister behind, for another hour. Once safely indoors, it was straight up to bed, but there was no problem getting up, he could relax in the morning and simply pull the covers over his head and drift off to sleep. He got a book off the shelf and read for a while, quickly getting engrossed in the *Adventures of Robin Hood* and it was while fighting a battle alongside Robin that he dropped off to slumber.

Two hours later his mother picked the book off the floor and tucked his hand back under the clothes before she switched off the light. She looked at her son for a minute and bent over and gently kissed him before going downstairs.

A Surprise for Andrew

The next morning dawned bright; daylight had managed to ease itself thought the gap in the curtains and brighten the room. Andrew slid his body out of bed, put his foot on the book and decided to read for a while before going down for breakfast. His Mum climbed the stairs. 'Still got your nose in the book I see,' she said.

'Yes Mum, it's Robin Hood,' replied Andrew. 'Come on my lad, up you get now. It's time for breakfast. Your Dad went to work two hours ago.'

'Okay Mum,' he said and made his way down to the bathroom to wash and clean his teeth. Andrew played with the soap, shaped like a diver, squeezing it under the water and allowing it to shoot out from between his hands, splashing back into the basin.

Susan came in, 'Stop splashing you little horror!'

'I'll splash you if you say that again,' replied Andrew. The children tussled for a moment then went and got dressed. Soon they were sitting at the table, eagerly eating their cereals.

Andrew went into the yard and put a snail and a slug into the toad's Oxo box. He checked his fish in the big tank and put a little fish food on the surface. The water had gone green, but the fish didn't seem to object at all. He decided that he would get a few sticklebacks to add to the tank. So with a project in mind for the day, he put on his shoes, pulled his jerkin up and told his mother he was going to fish for a tiddler to give the perch in the tank some live food.

Stephen and Andrew wandered up the street. The boys caught a bus that took them past their school, to a demolition site in preparation for a new housing scheme. They walked down the road, fishing nets in their hands and jam jars with string around the neck as a handle.

The boys came to the old corrugated iron fence and pushed a sheet to one side, making their way into the enclosed derelict site. Many years ago, a factory had stood there but during the war this had been bombed and the craters and bombed-out brickwork formed little ponds, which had always been good for tiddlers and tadpoles when in season and the occasional sticklebacks which seemed to grow to a good size in the green weed-ridden ponds. The boys fished happily for a while, catching tiddlers and sticklebacks until the jam jars were brimming with fish. They then decided to look around for a tin can to transfer the fish to, and they played amongst the old brickwork, Andrew slipping off the little brick island and got one foot wet.

'My Mum will kill me!' he cried in despair.

'No she won't, you will be dry by the time we go,' said Stephen.

'I hope so,' replied Andrew.

The boys played on for an hour or so, the morning quickly went by. Eventually they found a gallon tin that was spotlessly clean. The notice on the front of it said that it had once contained fresh olives. The boys rinsed it out and transferred the fish, weeds and fresh water to the container, which they proudly carried across the old site through the fence, carefully replacing the corrugated tin panel, and off down the back streets towards their homes. They took in turns carrying the tin, trying hard not to slop water over the sides.

An hour later, tired out and dishevelled, the boys reached the back entry, and they went in through the door and filled the glass tank up by pouring the fish into it.

The little sticklebacks darted around happy to be free from the olive tin. Little did they realise that this was a situation of survival of the fittest. If they managed to keep in the thick garden weeds they would be safe, but if they ventured out into the open water, within the tank the hungry perch would eat them. Andrew had swapped some comics and a catapult for the perch some days before and made the mistake of putting them in with his goldfish. Unfortunately, the perch ate the goldfish.

It had taken Andrew ages to work out just where they had gone. Eventually he managed to get two of the four goldfish out of the water and into a bowl so the perch didn't eat them all. For some reason it didn't relish bits of cake and perch only eat when they feel like it, so live fish was the best food for it. Besides it was the natural way that these fish existed. It always amazed Andrew that he never actually saw the perch eating the sticklebacks, but each day there were a few less swimming around. Still his food system worked and he reckoned that was about a week's worth of food, so he didn't have to fish for tiddlers for at least that period of time.

'Andrew,' called his Mum, 'Come in and get changed. I want you in your smart clothes in half an hour. Go upstairs and get washed and don't forget to comb your hair,' she instructed.

'Okay Mum, where are we going?'

'I am taking you down to the Johnston's, she replied. 'I am leaving some tea for your Dad in the stove.'

Quickly Andrew changed. Susan was already dressed up. The two children went off to the bus stop with their mother and caught a bus down the road. Andrew was busy eating the last of a lemon curd butty that he had slapped together rather rapidly.

They got off the bus and walked up the road. The Johnson s lived in a flat on the ground floor of a large Victorian house. Mrs Johnson was a nurse and was a long-term friend of Mrs Baker. Dr Johnson, her husband, was a professor of philosophy and taught at the local university. His hobby was making model boats.

They greeted the family warmly when they arrived and invited them inside. Mrs Johnson chatted to Mrs Baker and the children went out into the garden to hunt for the tortoise. Eventually they found him under a bush. Andrew gently picked him up, careful not to turn him upside down. The children were fascinated as he pulled his neck slowly in and out of his hard shell. Andrew placed the tortoise in the wire netting run that had been set up for him. Inside the ladies enjoyed tea and biscuits. Dr Johnson had joined them with a large plateful of sandwiches, which they ravenously tucked into.

Afterwards, Dr Johnson asked Andrew if he would like to see his workshop. The two males went down to the basement. There, to the amazement and awe of Andrew, were three model yachts under construction. The little lad's eyes nearly popped out of this head. He'd never seen such beautiful boats and he was promised a boat ever since his mum had accidentally dropped and broken the ketch that Dr Johnson had made for him a year before. Andrew wasn't counting the cabin cruiser his Dad recently came home with because that was an unexpected surprise.

The kindly man looked down at Andrew, 'Which one would you like, Andrew?'

The boy was speechless. He couldn't believe his luck. 'Can I really have one, sir?'

'If you like to choose one of these three, I'll finish it off for you. Maybe we could finish this one,' he said pointing to a little sloop-rigged yacht. 'Would you like to help?'

Andrew beamed with delight.

Dr Johnson clamped a piece of lead pipe in his vice and cut it to the width of the keel. Then he shaped the ends and flattened the pipe to fit the keel smoothly. He filed the lead balance to the wooden keel which gave it stability. They went upstairs and tested the yacht in the bath to make sure it floated upright correctly. Everything looked fine.

Dr Johnson gave the boat to Andrew and showed him how to operate the sails. He also gave him a little paintbrush and some red paint to paint the new keel with. Andrew was over the moon. This was indeed an unexpected gift. He thanked Dr Johnson many times that evening before he left.

Later on, when they got home, he showed his father the new yacht. Together they admired the beautifully made vessel. Andrew spread some newspaper on the dining table and carefully painted the keel of the vessel, as instructed by Dr Johnson. He placed the boat on the shelf to dry and tidied up the newspaper, carefully washing and cleaning the brush.

His father got out more documents and booklets about Australia and passed a magazine, with a yacht on it, to his son. 'There you are Andrew, you could sail a real yacht if we went to Australia.'

Andrew spent half an hour looking at the brochure while his mother and father discussed the situation. Soon it was time for bed. The children kissed their parents goodnight and Dad chased them up the stairs, pretending to catch them but careful not to let them slip at the top. Susan and Andrew snuggled down in their beds and quickly fell asleep.

The following morning, Andrew was up early. He had breakfast, put on his windjammer, collected his boat from the shelf and headed out of the back door to look for his mates. He soon located Eddy and Stephen and proudly showed off his new yacht.

The boys headed off to the park to find somewhere to sail the boat. An hour later they were walking between the pillars of Broughton Park and they slipped over the rails to select a spot and gain the advantage of the bank and the prevailing breeze on the lake and away she sailed. The little red yacht bobbed to the leeward and raced away at an angle, scattering the ducks and drakes while parting the water. The yacht threatened to capsize, but fortunately the wind was kind and it didn't blow too hard. An angry swan chased the boat and threatened to sink it. Fortunately the boat kept sailing and the swan decided not to pursue it.

With all this excitement the boys hadn't noticed that the little yacht had gone beyond the positions they had all stationed themselves at. She was heading at the rate of knots for the centre of the lake, scattering ducks and birds of all descriptions and weaving and dipping, pushing its stem through the water. The boys leaped to their feet, clambering one after the other over the metal railings towards where they thought the boat was going to end up. They ran all the way round the perimeter of the lake. Andrew hoping all the time that the Parkie who they knew must be patrolling somewhere, wouldn't see the little red yacht in the middle of the lake.

Just then a gust of wind pushed the boat like a giant hand, and instead of it dipping its bow and racing heading towards its goal, it change position and started to race away. The boys were dumbfounded. Anything could happen now; maybe they would never get it back. The lads ran along the bank watching the boat cutting and dipping on the water, passing the giant banks of weeds and rushes that threatened to engulf it and trap it forever.

The hand of fate pushed it continually towards the centre of the lake, guiding it past obstacles below the water on and on she went, ploughing through the ripples of the lake. However the wind changed and the boys watched in amazement as it pushed the boat towards them slowly from the centre of the lake. She came closer and a few ducks scattered and squawked and the yacht raced on. Andrew had found a large stick which he intended to use to pull the boat in.

Minutes later the little yacht was heading towards the bank. The boys had positioned themselves to catch it and good as gold and as if by magic, she steered herself into the bank of weeds just beside where the boys stood. Andrew clambered over the fence and with the help of the big stick, extracted the boat from the weeds.

'Wow! That was some sail and a bit of a fluke that it came back to his part of the bank!'

Time after time she had threatened to capsize but somehow the little boat made it safely to the shore. Andrew wiped her dry along his jacket sleeve. For twenty minutes the yacht had darted around the lake chasing the ducks and defying the rudder, before deciding to come back to dry land. He knew it needed a few amendments. He decided he would talk to Dr Johnson as soon as possible.

The boys spent some time playing on the swings and climbing a big old yew tree that was sympathetic to the needs of young lads. The boys played happily for an hour or so.

'I'm really hungry,' said Eddy.

'Yes, so am I,' the others chorused, 'shall we head home for lunch?'

The three lads set off towards their homes. Halfway down the road a bus came into sight, the boys jumped on knowing at the next stop they would have to get off as none of them had any money. Lady luck shined on them as the bus raced along; the Clippy was upstairs and two stops passed by and the boys still sat there. They decided not to push their luck any further and alighted at the next stop just as the Clippy came downstairs.

They dribbled a tennis ball along the road. Andrew clinging on to the yacht to make sure no harm came to it. The streets passed by and soon they turned down the road that led to their homes.

Andrew pushed open the back door and a beautiful aroma came from the kitchen. 'Hello Mum,' said Andrew.

'You're just in time,' said his Mum, as she pulled a big meat and potato pie out of the oven.

'Oh boy! That looks delicious,' gasped Andrew.

'Wash your hand then, goodness knows what you've been doing with them,' she said and proceeded to serve up the pie.

'When do you think we will be going down to the Johnston's again?' asked Andrew and he explained to his Mum that the boat needed a few adjustments to make it sail better. Andrew's mum agreed to phone Mrs Johnson within the next few days and promised her son a trip to their friends in the near future.

Three days later the Bakers found themselves down at the Johnson house. Andrew told Dr Johnson what had happened on the trial sail. Dr Johnson recognised the problem and set about putting a heavier keel on the craft. Unfortunately Andrew had to leave his yacht behind this time, but Dr Johnson delivered it round to Bradshaw Street a few days later completely finished and brightly painted.

Nanny – A Sad Moment.

The giant lorry rolled down the road, the weight of the vehicle causing the enormous wheels to squeal and draw attention to itself. 'Wow!' Andrew rushed out of the window and gasped. 'It's Dad,' he said, 'in a great big lorry.'

Andrew rushed for the door just as his Dad jumped out of the cab onto the pavement. 'Hello Andrew!' he said in a cheery voice.

'Is that yours Dad?' Andrew asked.

'Well, I drive it, son.'

'Can I have a ride Dad?' He carefully lifted Andrew into the cab to sit in the seat.

'Don't touch anything now,' said his father as he went inside.

'What are you doing with that lorry here,' said Celia.

'Oh I was just on my way back to the depot so I thought I'd call in for lunch. Did you get any post today? He asked.

'Yes, there's a big envelope for you from Australia House. So that's the reason you came home!' said mum.

He opened the envelope and checked the contents, various forms spilled out onto the table displaying the State of South Australia to be the finest and most welcoming place for people to migrate. Andrew came in from the lorry and saw the pile of books. 'Is this somewhere else to go Dad?'

'No son, Australia is many times the size of Great Britain and it is divided up into different states. Western Australia, Northern Territory, South Australia, Victoria, New South Wales, Queensland, Tasmania and the capital is Canberra.'

Andrew looked at the booklet on South Australia. 'Enough of this!' said Mrs Baker, clearing the table for lunch and she set out a large plate of mashed potatoes and onions. Mr Baker cut the meat left over from the Sunday joint. The Bakers tucked into the lunch and it wasn't long before Mr Baker was kissing his wife goodbye and heading back to work.

'Can I have a ride to the top of the street Dad,' asked Andrew. His father lifted him into the cab and turned on the engine which then burst into life. Mr Baker pulled the large lorry away from the kerb and slowly drove it up the street. The vehicle dominated the little road, dwarfing everything around it. Andrew jumped out at the top of the street, waving to his father as he drove off towards Eccles and the depot.

Mrs Baker sat pondering for a while, wondering if they would ever reach Australia. One thing she knew, they'd never leave England all the time her mother was alive, and if that meant waiting for a long time then wait she would. They had discussed this and it was agreed, but what disturbed her was her mother's health. She hoped that this wouldn't happen for many years, but deep down she knew that all was not well.

Nanny came to live with us at Bradshaw Street after her stroke and over a relatively short time she had several more strokes. She was 73 years of age and had spent her life working very hard, mostly as a cleaner. One fateful day the ambulance was called and she was taken to the hospital.

At the bottom of the steps, just as she was being helped into the ambulance she opened her purse and gave Andrew and Susan a ten shilling note each. With a tear coursing down her cheek and her white shining hair blowing in the breeze she said, 'I don't expect I'll see you again, be good and enjoy every day of your life.' Moments later the ambulance door closed and she was driven away. Nanny died in hospital a few days later.

Delamere Forest

Knock! Knock!

The sound came from the front door. A cheery man stood there. 'Dandelion and burdock lady?'

She said, 'yes, why not?'

The man went back to his cart and siphoned out the locally made drink into a stone jar. Mrs Baker took the jar and paid the man a shilling.

Andrew and Susan pushed the cart up the road to the next stopping place and were rewarded with a drink from an old tin cup. They were happy and this was the tradition in the cobblestone street.

The days rolled by steadily, then one morning Mrs Baker made a surprise announcement. 'How would you like to go to the country for a few days?'

Susan and Andrew jumped for joy, with a big 'Yes!'

Their Mum qualified it 'but only if you're good. Alright! Alright! Now calm down and I'll tell you about it. Do you remember a friend of mine, May Wright? Well, she has a caravan in the country near a place called Delamere Forest, and if you promise to be really good we've been invited to go down there for a couple of days and the real surprise is that we are going tomorrow.

'Wow!' exclaimed Andrew, 'That's fantastic! Can I take my fishing rod?'

'Oh Andrew, must you always connect everything with fishing?' she looked at him quizzically. 'No! And that's that! There will be plenty of things to do when you get there. See if you can find your swimming trunks; I understand there is a large pool nearby which Anthony uses every day and I'm sure if we ask him nicely, he'll take you down there.'

Andrew was satisfied and didn't pursue the issue regarding his rod. The two children dashed upstairs in search of their swimming togs. Both children got out the things they wanted to take. Andrew's consisted of a comb and toothbrush, towel, trunks and a change of clothes. But Susan's pile was as high as a mountain on the bed. 'You can't take that lot!' exclaimed Andrew.

'Yes, I can, I'll take what I want,' argued Susan.

Mrs Baker soon settled the matter, 'whatever you decide to take, you carry!' she said.

'That's fair,' said Andrew, but Susan wasn't impressed. Excitement engulfed the pair and they chatted about the caravan and the woods and speculated about how big it was going to be.

That evening after tea, the children were packed off to bed early, their Mum and Dad discussed plans for the future. Andrew and Susan drifted off into the land of nod, full of excitement about the trip the next day.

Mr Baker, as usual was up early in the morning. The first the children heard was the old fire great being poked and raked around to establish if there were embers glowing. Bob Baker placed a few sticks on the fire and went to the kitchen to put the kettle on the gas stove. He brought a bucket of coal and carefully selected where to put them to gain the best advantage. Soon the fire was burning brightly. Mr Baker sat down for a moment in his overalls, a mug of steaming tea in his hand.

Celia, his wife, came in through the door in her dressing gown. 'It's still nippy, Bob, even though it is the middle of Summer,' she said.

'Don't worry love, you will have all the warmth and sunshine you want when we get to Australia,' chuckled her husband.

The rain trickled from the door as she made her way in from the outside toilet.'

'Ooh, it's not very good weather for this trip to Cheshire today.'

As if by invitation, the rain tapped on the windowpane. Mrs Baker put a few rashers in the pan and soon they were sizzling along with an egg or two. Bob Baker tucked into breakfast, the door burst open and Susan and Andrew spilled through into the living room.

'Cor that smells good Mum, I'm sure you're the best cook in the world,' said Andrew.

Susan collected the tea and sat down on the table, 'it's a shame it's raining' she said, 'but maybe it'll be brighter in Cheshire.'

Their Dad felt in his pocket and reached out two half-crowns; he gave one each to the children.

'Thanks Dad,' they chorused.

The children, overwhelmed with excitement, kissed their Dad as he said cheerio to his family. 'Have a nice break,' he called, 'it's time I was off to work.'

Mr Baker went to his wife and they said their farewells and off to work he went. Their Mum served up the breakfast of bacon and eggs with a cob of bread. 'We will have a long journey in front of us, so eat up now and you won't have to eat until we get there.'

They all ate heartily. Susan helped her Mum with the dishes. Andrew collected the bags from upstairs and half an hour later they were all in the street with the door locked.

The rain still came down. Mrs Baker complained about the weather as the family headed up the street to the bus stop. On the bus all was wet and miserable, but the children were excited. Twenty minutes later they arrived at the railway station.

'One and two halves to Mould Cross please,' said Mrs Baker.

The collector gave his instruction of where to change and which trains to catch.

'Keep together now.'

The children carried their luggage through the station. Susan's case started to feel heavy. People milled backwards and forwards, pushing and shoving as they hustled to and fro to work. The steam from the giant locomotive filled the station dispersing like a cloud into the high roofs. Andrew stopped to look at the engine as they walked towards the carriages; it belched and hissed like a giant steam dragon as it dared the driver to allow it to escape. A man uncoupled the carriages from the engine and the buffers took up the slackness of the safety chain as he uncoupled the hissing beast. Task complete, the rail man climbed up and signalled to the guard—the train was free.

'Are you coming with us or having an excursion on your own?' his Mum called anxiously. Andrew quickly chased up the platform and once inside they settled themselves down. Mrs Baker had put the baggage up on the rack and closed the window; the carriage smelt smoky although there was no trace of any around. A brown picture stared down at them from the wall, depicting a train crossing a bridge in Devon.

'Is this where we went to Torquay Mum?' asked Susan. 'Two years ago wasn't it?'

'Can I go to the toilet again?' Andrew cried, already grabbing the door.

'Yes,' she said, 'but don't get off the train and don't talk to any strange men.'

Andrew vanished up the carriage, meanwhile the train continued to fill up with passengers. 'Mum who is Kilroy?' Someone had written Kilroy was here on the back of the door.

Andrew was back again 'Oh you are a wag.'

'I hope you remembered to wash your hands.'

Suddenly all the doors began to slam. Andrew leapt for the thick leather belt that held the window in position, releasing it so that he could look out.

'Watch your feet Andrew,' cried Susan as he clumsily trod on her toes. Smoke belched out of the engine. The guard waved his flag and got on the train and, at precisely that moment, the carriages rattled together and pulled taut as the engine spurted steam towards the roof of the station.

Slowly giant chuffs of smoke came from the funnel; chuff, chuff, chuff. They gathered a little speed and there was a piercing scream from the engine whistle as the train moved slowly along the platform.

'Close that window or you will fill the place with steam,' Mum shouted. Already the steam was circulating around the platform. The engine wheels skidded on the tracks as it sought to gain traction and pull away from the platform, clanking over the tracks it settled into a motion all of its own.

The rain still fell but the children were full of excitement, their noses pressed tight against the window as the rains streaked by along the glass. Outside was the industrial rear of the factories; dirty, dark, dank brickwork enclosed the chimneys and slate roofs, broken display boards advertised the names of the products for sale. It didn't seem to matter that they might fall down. Occasionally a plant of buddleia with its long purple spikes would brighten up the walls or yards. The train rushed by allowing only a glimpse of the commercial depravity. No one seemed to care about the rear of the factories, or the accumulation of debris, no matter how or under what circumstances it had gathered. The engine rushed on shrieking its whistle and telling everybody it was on its way.

The factories slowly vanished behind them and the terraces of suburban houses. Back gardens and playing fields; one after the other came into view and quickly vanished, but just for an instant held the attention of Susan and Andrew. Little puffs of smoke engulfed the carriages occasionally, just to remind them that a steam engine was dragging them swiftly along.

Mrs Baker settled back with a newspaper, allowing the train's motion to relax her, soon the newspaper slipped forward and Mum settled for forty winks. Andrew got out his *'Topper'* comic and Susan read the *'Girl'*. The train shrieked again as it rattled over some tracks heading in a different direction.

The Bakers were on their way.

Twenty minutes later the train was nosing its way into a station. The doors opened and slammed shut as the people alighted on to the platform, while others scramble through the doors. Passengers shuffled into the carriages, 'Two more stations children and then we change trains.'

Once again the monster sent forth its steam and let out a scream as the wheels raced, and then settled for a slow pull as the inertia built up.

The big black engine chuffed out of the station. The sound of people closing the windows could be heard up and down the carriages. Soon green fields started to carpet the landscape. The factories and office blocks, houses and brick walls all drifted away and as if by magic the train had stopped as well.

'Hey Mum, it's not raining and look it's even dry on the roads. Look Susan, there's a rainbow. Wow! Just look at that!'

The children peered out of the window, the train raced on through the morning air breathing its fire and smoke, clattering along the line deeper and deeper into the countryside. It wasn't long before they heard the squeal of the brakes and the train slowed down, chugging very slowly as they entered into the little station. Nasturtiums hung from the boxes threatening to brighten up the smoke darkening woodwork. A porter in a uniform was painting the door of the left luggage office. A few pansies and lobelia hung out of a basket.

'Isn't this pretty?' said Susan, 'just look at those lovely flowers and what a lovely idea Mummy. It's a pity a few more places don't brighten themselves up.'

'Yes Susan, they're very pretty. I expect we'll be seeing a lot of flowers now we're in the country.'

The guard waved his flag; only one person had got off the train at this station although a few got on. The train lazily pulled out of the little station covering all with a belch of steam and the smell of anthracite smoke. On they went, the children counted cows in the field.

'How do you tell a cow from a bull Mum?' Andrew said.

'A cow has got udders Andrew.'

'You mean that set of bagpipes under its legs?'

'Don't be silly,' said Susan, 'that's where it stores its milk.

'A bull has one of those too,' quipped Andrew.

'No it doesn't, just try milking a bull's tassel then, my smart little lad, and it would chase you all over the field! A bull is a male, it doesn't have udders at all,' Mrs Baker said, at which point the two children were looking out of the windows in search of bulls and cows so that the difference could be well and truly established.

Trees and rivers came into view and just as quickly vanished. They saw farms and all over the countryside bright yellow fields of rapeseed lit up the hillside in a blaze of sunshine and now, only occasionally, did they notice the noise of the train going over the joints or the puffs of steam clouding the view.

In no time at all the engine was pulling into the station where the Bakers were to depart. Andrew was first off and took the luggage from his mum. Susan closed the door with a slam, by which time Andrew was half way along the platform. 'I'm just going to see the engine".

'Don't you get too close to that thing,' she replied.

The large black engine sat squarely on the track. The driver, with an oily rag in his hand, leaned casually on the chequered plate occasionally polishing a piece of brass.

'Hello young 'un,' he called.

'Hello Mister,' replied the boy, just as the guard waved his flag, which the driver acknowledged. He pulled the cord and the whistle screamed, making Andrew jump.

The driver released the brake and opened a valve; smoke and steam seemed to come from everywhere. It covered Andrew from head to foot and slowly the engine moved forward. The driver gave Andrew a cheery wave as his head slowly emerged from the clouds of steam.

'Bye, bye,' said Andrew and waved his hand.

His Mum patiently waited on the platform. 'Come on Andrew, we have another train to catch now. Just look at you, you're covered in soot.' His mother clipped his ear and ushered him along the platform to a small two carriage electric train which looked very modern and clean.

They settled themselves in and soon the little electric train pulled out of the railway halt and clattered down the track. The guard came down and punched the tickets.

'And where are you two going?' he asked, looking at the children. 'We're off to a caravan in the forest,' said Susan.

'A forest eh? That'll be Delamere Forest,' said the guard. 'You'll be able to see it soon as we go right by it for about five minutes; you can't miss it,' he said.

'Next stop, Ma'am,' and touched his forelock.

'Thank you,' she said and took the tickets from his hand.

In the distance the forest came in to sight; it seemed to go on forever and ever. The little train chugged by and soon was starting to slow as the railway station came into view and welcomed the passengers getting off. Anthony Wright was there to greet them.

'Hello,' he said, 'good trip then?' he asked, as the train pulled out of the halt.

'Well not bad,' said Mum, 'a bit damp to start off, but we made it.'

Anthony was sixteen and in college; his Mother was a close friend of Mrs Baker. He led them up the road carrying Mrs Baker's bag. The two children trailed behind. Andrew had decided to kick a tennis ball up the little lane and promptly kicked it into a bunch of nettles, which stung his leg.

'Ouch!' He let out a yell and everyone stopped.

'What on earth has happened to you?' asked his mum.

'I've been stung by a nettle,' Andrew retorted.

Anthony laughed, 'that will teach you not to treat them with respect! If we look around you will always find a dock leaf nearby " Look there's one."

Anthony bent down and pulled a couple of broad green leaves and then he rubbed it into the sting, which had come up on Andrews's leg in a group of little lumps. He placed the other leaf in Andrew's hand and told him to hold it on the sting. The little party started off again up the lane to the caravan site.

Susan was dragging behind a bit, what with carrying a case with all her bits and pieces and occasionally to give a little bunny hop—a habit she acquired and did for fun. Andrew was still hobbling, keeping well clear of the nettles and hoping there wasn't going to be lots of them all over the place for a chap to fall into.

Mrs Baker and Anthony arrived at the gate; they went through, closely followed by the children carrying their cases. Up the path they went. The caravans sat happily on pieces of concrete which were all spread out, some of them under trees, some of them in the open, occasionally surrounded by flower boxes, but all of them brightly painted and in good condition.

Anthony went up to a caravan parked beneath the tree and pushed open the door. 'Here we are, make yourself at home.'

May Wright stood in the entrance to greet them, 'Hello Celia, how are you? Hello children. Did you have a good trip? Would you like to have a cup of tea?" The words all seemed to come out together. May was bubbly and happy to see her friend.

'Yes please, I would love to have a cup of tea. In fact we all would,' Mum said looking at the children and nodding. 'The trip was good but, my word, how it rained this morning! This little boy of mine got himself covered in soot from the engine and stung by a nettle in the last two hours, so goodness only knows what he is going to be up to in the next two days.' She looked at him and smiled.

'Where are we going to sleep, Mum?' asked Susan.

'I don't know as yet. Aunty May will sort this out a little later.'

Andrew went into the lounge area and sat in a seat next to Anthony. A small stove sat in a corner framed by a copper surround. The mantelpiece above was covered in shining bric-a-brac. On the other side of the kitchen there was a toilet and two separate bedrooms. One had a double bed in it, the other two bunks.

'We will share the double Celia, and the children can have the bunks. Anthony will sleep in the lounge in his sleeping bag. Do you agree?' she asked, although she said it as a statement rather than a question.

Everyone nodded, and slurped their tea at the same time.

Ten minutes later Andrew was outside. The sun was shining down through the long thin poplars. He knew he was going to enjoy being at the caravan park. All around was a forest of trees with just the occasional patch of grass to be seen peeping between the erect trunks.

A voice came from behind, 'Come on Andrew, I will show you around.'

Susan and Anthony appeared from behind and the trio set off to establish their whereabouts. Anthony showed them the shops and the amenities block. Then they went outside the gate, carefully crossing the road and making their way along the small pathway which led through the trees.

They arrived at a small cleared area where the grass lay like a carpet. Birds sang and twittered, and squirrels scampered up the bark. Susan and Andrew had never seen squirrels before in their own habitat, and stood for a few moments watching the fascinating little creatures. They seemed very tame and were obviously used to people.

The trio moved on and the woodland area exploded into a large green space; they could hear laughter and splashing coming from behind a wall in the distance. Anthony explained that the Castle Mill swimming pool lay behind the wall. They could see the high diving board clearly towering above the perimeter boundary.

'That's where we will go this afternoon, if your mum will let you,' said Anthony, pointing at the pool.

'Oh I'm sure she will, especially if you are going,' said Andrew.

As they walked back through the leafy glade, Andrew spotted a small stream twinkling in the sunlight.

'It gets bigger further through the forest and eventually finds its way into a small lake about a mile away.'

Andrew made a mental note to explore along the banks of the stream when he could; yes he really was going to enjoy this place!

That afternoon the families made their way to the swimming pool. Once inside, they quickly changed and while the ladies made themselves comfortable on the wooden seats Susan, Andrew and Anthony went into the pool. The youngsters stayed at the shallow end and splashed around amusing themselves and trying to swim. Anthony used the high diving board and impressed everyone with his skills.

A little while later he paddled through the water on an inner tube. The children took turns to be pushed around the pool by Anthony in the tube. The sun shone brilliantly down, it was hard to believe that only four hours before it had been pouring with rain.

Once back at the caravan later that afternoon, the ladies made tea which the hungry children ate greedily. Later, Andrew and Anthony made their way outside.

'Can we go along that stream?' asked Andrew.

'Yes, why not, there isn't a lot to do here apart from exploring and reading,' said Anthony.

The boys made their way along the banks pausing every now and then to admire the water or throw a pebble in. They watched it race and bubble over the stones splashing and swirling into little eddies as it rushed along. Weeds and irises grew side by side in clumps by the bank and occasionally the stream would broaden into little pools.

'You sometimes get some frogs here,' said Anthony, 'and once or twice I saw a man fishing 'though I don't know what for.'

The boys ambled along completely carefree and enjoying the moment of the day. They walked for about half an hour until the stream widened and flowed much faster. The banks looked as if they have been carved out by a giant hand.

They stopped near a rocky pool watching the water cascading at the other end of the pool. A man lay face down watching the water; he hadn't apparently seen the boys or heard them, the sound of the splashing falling stream had drowned their hushed voices. The boys motioned to each other that they had seen the gypsy and crouched down beside an alder, watching, not daring to move in case they spoilt the moment. The man had his hand in the water; very, very slowly he moved it forward as if he was feeling for something. Suddenly, like a flash of lightning, he swept his hand upwards catching his fingers in the gills of the trout and throwing it clear onto the bank. He wrapped his spotted hanky around the fish; a sharp blow with a rock to the fish's head killed it instantly. Proudly he looked at his prize; the fine, spotted brown trout lay on the bank.

'You two can come out now,' he called to the boys, 'I heard you coming five minutes ago, but I wasn't going to miss this beauty by acknowledging you. I thank you for keeping your heads down anyway. Do you want to have a look?'

The boys rushed over to the fish. It lay there with its mouth open looking glazy eyed; its skin sparkled with a group of brown and orange spots on its back, it certainly was a lovely fish.

'I only take what I want to eat,' the gypsy said. 'We live on the caravan park too.' he continued, 'the council moved us a year ago. When you have lived in a caravan all your life there is no way I could live in a house.'

'How do you know where the fish are?' asked Andrew.

'Yes and how do you catch it without a hook and line?' asked Anthony'.

'Al right boys, one at a time. Now then young 'un,' he said looking at Andrew, 'First of all you have to attract them to a spot where you want them. Some places are fairly natural with a fine bank and a natural ridge carved out by the water, but the way I always make sure I have a little supper of fish awaiting for me, is hanging over there,' he pointed to the tree.

The boys followed his direction and hidden below some branches hung on an old bark.

'Whatever is it?' asked Andrew.

'Well now,' he replied, 'first of all I find an animal that had died; a cat or rabbit or similar, then I put some old bread and rice in the sack and punch a few holes in it. I hang it up and leave it for a few months, always careful to put another one together well in advance. You see, by the time it has hung for a few weeks the meat had rotted and the maggots feed and grow. Gradually they wriggle about and now an again they fall out of the holes in the middle of the sack.

'Now, as you can imagine the Hessian rots after a while and the maggots drop in the water more freely. Well, that little ol' brown trout hangs around until he gets his fill and you can see that never really happens because he is always hungry! So you see there are always a few of them waiting for a tasty morsel to drip on the water. There now are you happy young'un, now you know my little secret? And you Anthony, you want to know how to tickle a trout well it's a very old secret.

'There are some who would say it was illegal, but I don't agree. First you slide your hand into the water, but you must never make a shadow in the water otherwise you will frighten the fish away before you start. Then very slowly you work your hand along the ridge until you feel the trout. Now amazingly at this point the trout doesn't swim away unless you try to grab it, which you don't. It's best just to position yourself right on the bank. Once you know exactly where it is, you move your hand very slowly, just occasionally touching the trout's belly until you know you are at its gills. It's at this point you have to be extremely quick. You slip your fingers into the fish's gill and lift upwards in a throwing motion and if you are lucky you have got yourself some breakfast! But as a word of warning, watch out for the bailiff because if he catches you then you will find yourself up before the magistrate for poaching. Now boys, I will have to be going, good luck with your fishing but I suggest you keep to a rod and line.'

With a twirl of his hat he vanished into the undergrowth and was lost to the twittering of the birds.

The boys chatted excitedly. 'I wonder ... could we do that?'

'Well, we can't at the moment; all the fish would have been frightened away by our shadows and the splashing of the water when he pulls that trout out.'

'The reality was quite a trick wasn't it? Somehow though it's a bit like cheating,' said Andrew, 'I think I would rather catch them on a fishing hook.'

'Yes, I know what you mean, but you must remember the gypsy just wanted the fish to eat and for all we know he will be out setting rabbit snares tonight,' said Anthony.

Andrew nodded in agreement, and the two boys made their way back along the bank. The gypsy had made the boys promise they wouldn't tell anyone about their secret, to which the boys agreed. They confirmed this to each other before they stepped over the road to the caravan park. Dusk had fallen.

'I am glad you two are back, it's getting dark,' the ladies chorused at the boys, 'run and fetch some water Anthony, there's a good lad.' He strode off with a container to the tap, returning a few minutes later with a container splashing over the brim.

A beautiful smell emanated from the kitchen; sizzling in the pan was six of the biggest sausages you ever did see! The children sat in the lounge, mouths' watering. The little table had been set and Tony Hancock and Sid James were keeping them in fits of laughter as *'The Reunion'* blared out of the radio. Large plates full of bangers and mash were placed in front of the children, garnished with onions and cooked nettles. The fresh air had done them good and they made short work of the meal.

The Calor gas light was lit and sent out a friendly glow over everybody. That evening the children played ludo and dominoes, the radio provided the background entertainment and the two ladies chatted constantly.

Soon it was time for bed. Susan and Andrew said 'goodnight' and toddled off to their room. The bunk beds were very comfortable and no sooner had their heads touched the pillow they were fast asleep.

The next morning, bright and early, the children rose. The sun had forced its way through the caravan windows. Susan and Andrew awoke to a blaze of sunshine warming their cheeks and announcing the day. They all washed and dressed, hurriedly getting through their breakfast. The children were anxious to get out onto the grass outside and explore the locality.

'Don't go too far away, you two,' their mother called out after them. 'I want to go into Chester a little later.'

The children played tag by the edge of the forest. Andrew saw the gypsy again and said 'Good morning'.

The gypsy acknowledged him with a knowing wink, 'Good morning young 'un.'

Half an hour later their mum called out 'come and get your hands washed.'

The bus pulled up outside the caravan and the two ladies got on and paid the fare as the children scampered past to find a seat beside the window. Anthony stayed behind preferring to go swimming, but promised to take the children later on in the afternoon when they returned. The bus sped down a county lane twisting and turning, and stopping occasionally to collect people. The children chatted about the houses and farms, the animals in the fields, and the compared the differences from where they lived. Soon the bus turned into the large bus station.

Chester was certainly different; the children were in awe at this beautiful city. All the buildings appeared to be black and white; Tudor style. The main street had a balcony of shops running all the way along above the pavement and stretching across the road was a beautiful old clock spanning from side to side.

The ladies enjoyed themselves looking at the shops and admiring the latest fashions. They went into a grocer's to collect fresh food for lunch and tea, and then sought out a corner house to have a cup of coffee and a large cream cake. Both ladies told each other they shouldn't eat them and then promptly devoured the full cream cakes which had been on display. Susan and Andrew had an éclair and a vanilla slice; the custard oozed all over his face but he quickly mopped it all up with his tongue and polished it off.

Four hours passed since they left the caravan camp and soon they were all heading back on the bus making their way along the county lanes again, twisting and turning passing the houses and farms. Mrs Baker leaned over to the children, 'I was born near here you know. My Dad was a coachman to Sir Robert Cunliff, but he died when I was a baby so I never really knew him.'

'I am glad I have a Dad,' said Susan.

'So am I,' said Andrew.

The children nurtured their own thoughts for a while. The bus rounded the corner and then they were home. The caravan was starting to feel like home now; well home for a day or so anyway. Anthony stood at the door, 'Put the kettle on,' said May, 'I am dying for a cup of tea."

Then Andrew asked, 'Do you mind if we go swimming Mum?'

'No, not at all,' she said, 'providing Anthony is going with you. But you can't swim until at least an hour after your dinner, so I suggest you get some food inside you pretty sharpish!'

'Oh Mum, can we have some corned beef?'

'All right then, and I will make a few chips to go with that.'

'Is that all right May?'

'Help yourself Celia, you know where everything is and then we can have a bite when the children have gone.'

Lunch finished, the children played outside for a half an hour or so before making their way with Anthony to the swimming pool. They splashed and frolicked in the water, while being towed in the inner tube by Anthony. The children enjoyed themselves and dried off in the sun.

Later that afternoon they returned to the caravan through the forest and along the path. On the way back the boys saw the gypsy, once again, heading into the forest. They looked at each other but did not say anything to Susan.

Arriving at the caravan with Susan, they left her and headed back down the path to see what the poacher was up to this time, but they could not find him. Half an hour went by and suddenly there he was; he appeared to have come from nowhere.

'Hello there boys, how are you?'

'We're fine, sir,' said Andrew, 'Did you catch another one?'

The man looked around furtively and then opened his jacket to display a beautiful cock pheasant tied by the neck and dangling from a little hook under his armpit.

'Wow!' said the boys, 'How did you catch that?'

'Well as a matter of fact, I just found him wandering around and went up to him and put him in my coat. It makes a nice change from fish you know.'

'Oh come on Mister; please tell us how did you catch 'im?'

Once again the man looked around furtively, 'Well, you promise not to tell another soul?'

The boys said, "cross your heart and hope to die if I ever tell a lie."

'Okay,' said the gypsy 'Now listen carefully, but remember you must never tell another soul, unless you are really desperate for food,'

'Okay,' echoed the boys.

'First, you get yourself some raisins and soak them for a couple of days in whisky or rum so that the alcohol gets all soaked up. Then you put the raisins in a place where you have seen a pheasant feeding, because often they come back to the same place time after time again. Well, just like anyone else when you get full of whisky or rum the old pheasant gets a little drunk and at that point he just wanders around looking for some more. For some strange reason they don't bother to fly away if you are careful and so you can walk up to him and grab him by the neck and take him home!'

'That's fantastic!' said the boys. 'Are you really serious?'

'Well,' said the gypsy, 'you should learn a little lesson from that just like the ol' pheasant, he certainly found out how serious it was. I suggest you boys don't take to drinking until you really are capable of handling it and knowing exactly what you are doing, or you never know something like this may happen to you!'

A little chill went round Andrew's body. 'I don't like the sound of that but don't worry we won't start drinking for many years to come.'

'All right,' said the gypsy, 'off you go and remember don't breathe a work of this to anyone.'

'Don't worry mister, we promised, and we won't say anything,' and with that they dashed off down the pathway and back to the caravan to find a lovely dinner just about to be served up.

That evening they did the usual playing draughts and cards with the radio playing in the background.

The following morning they said their goodbyes to May and Anthony for a lovely two days and made their way to the station As the train pulled out of the halt with the children waving Andrew caught a glance of the gypsy and his bright red necktie heading along the pathway towards the forest. 'I wonder what he's after this time,' thought Andrew. 'I suppose that is something I will never know.' But one thing's for sure, he would never forget the little trick the gypsy had taught him, not as long as he lived.

Heaton Park Boating Lake

On arriving home the Bakers found their dad had been busy during their absence. He had decorated the hallway with a Lincruster wallpaper.

'Wow Dad! That looks nice!'

'You have been busy!'

Celia said to Bob, as she gave him a hug and looked admiringly on, 'Well it needed doing and I have been meaning to get at it for ages. Did you all enjoy yourselves?'

'Yes it was fantastic,' the children chorused.

Mum put the kettle on and they all had tea. 'There is another surprise son, in the back yard.'

'What's that Dad?' he asked.

'Don't ask me, go and look for yourself!'

Andrew went outside and there, against the backyard wall, he saw his climbing rose *'Lady Godiver'*. A little spray of beautiful pink roses had come into bloom.

The thought struck him, as he admired the beauty of the flowers, if everyone in the street planted a rose or two, or something similar, what a contrast this would make against the brickwork. It was like beauty and the beast. The delicate little flower giving off its simple perfume contrasted against the dirty brick walls, which dominated the whole of the back entry and the adjoining yards.

Later that week he told Aunty Mina, the lady who lived next door. She had given him the rose as a birthday present a few months before.

The next few days passed quickly and Andrew told his mates what had happened at the caravan and about meeting the gypsy and seeing the trout caught, but he kept his promise and did not explain the secrets that the gypsy had shown him.

Sunday came around and the routine family trip to Heaton Park. This time they headed straight for the boating lake where they paid the half-crown for the boat and waited in a queue until it was their turn. A few moments later, a family boat came alongside. The men helped the previous occupants, a young couple, onto the landing stage. The Bakers got in; Mum and Susan sat at the stern and Dad in the middle with the oars, Andrew at the bow. The boatman pushed the craft gently away while Bob Baker adjusted the oars in the row-locks.

Steadily with each movement of the oars the boat gathered speed moving through the water. Easing its way from the bank, a little two-seated motor boat chugged past them and the single seated skiffs beautifully balanced slid speedily across the lake. The oarsman, rowing the boat in perfect rhythm, was sliding on a moving seat backwards and forwards in the craft.

Mr Baker imitated the fit young man pulling them in a steady rhythm the boat gliding along, all the craft headed in a clockwise direction round the lake. An island emerged as the boat rounded a corner; the brambles and the trees dipping their bows into the lake. A boat had pulled up and had being tied by the painter to a branch; the occupants long since vanished onto the interior of the island.

The Bakers slowly edged by, avoiding the overhanging branches but going close enough to create an interest. Various types of ducks quacked their way backward and forwards disobeying the clockwise direction everyone was supposed to be going in.

'Can I have a go Dad?' The voice of his son piped up from behind him.

'Come on then, but just take one oar and don't rock the boat.'

Andrew sat beside his Dad. The large oar in his hand felt very unwieldy, but carefully he drew it back and dipped it in the water. The boat slowed and started to turn because of the unevenness of the strokes. Several times Andrew tried again his Dad trying to balance the movements of his son with his own while teaching how to row correctly.

Slowly they gained a motion in time with each other and the little boat moved forwards once again, but this time rather more slowly. The little craft seemed determined to head off in its own direction; it seemed to be going off round the lake in a semicircle until Dad stopped rowing, which gave Andrew a chance to square it up with his slightly ungainly movements. The little craft eased its way around the lake.

Andrew tired of being told to pull together and dip it evenly; in the end he was just plain tired. His dad happily took over again and the boat glided along to an even steady rhythm.

The big passenger boat passed them by, full of happy people waving and looking all round them; the boat was a regular cruise around the lake and was always full and fast, at least in comparison to the rowing boats.

Andrew dipped his hand in the water; his Dad growled at him and that was enough to make him quickly drag it back into the craft. They passed the boathouse totally surrounded by rhododendrons. The doors were open and a gleaming motor boat sat at a mooring inside. The sun caught the brass and made it shine like gold. Then just as quickly the boat had slipped past and the polished spectacle was lost from view.

Mum saw the man holding a card with the boat's number on it. 'Look Bob, it's time to go in.'

Bob Baker guided the little craft into the mooring, deftly slowing it down and turning. Just as he manoeuvred it alongside the landing stage, the man on the landing put his foot in it and held the boat tight to the timber while helping Mrs Baker and Susan on to the staging. Andrew jumped out causing the boat to rock backwards and forwards; his Dad let out a yell as he fought for his balance, but he quickly steadied himself and thanked the boatman. A few minutes later Andrew caught the thick end of his Dad's tongue for not thinking before he acted.

Next the family enjoyed ice creams before walking on up the hill to the pet zoo, which had been recently built. Andrew and Susan stared at the brightly coloured Chinese pheasants, bantams, geese and ducks.

In another enclosure was a fox, which emitted a foul smell, pacing backwards and forwards. At the end of a large fenced-off area was a collection of wallabies. Various rabbits and guinea pigs were nibbling at large leaves and other edible delicacies. In another fenced-off area some kids and a nanny goat frolicked and gambolled backwards and forwards. The animals were certainly fun for all to see.

Mum and Dad quietly discussed the forthcoming trip to Blackpool as the Baker family turned and headed back down the path towards the main gate. The children once again chased each other and played with the ball while dodging in and out of the large rhododendron bushes on the way to the gate.

Tomorrow was the start of the Summer holidays the new day was to bring fresh excitement.

Blackpool - The Annual Summer Holiday

Monday morning, bright and early, the Bakers clambered into the black taxicab. Andrew remembered the 'V' sign the lads had given to the cab driver and hoped this wasn't the one. The cab sped away leaving the little terraced house safely locked up with the neighbours promising to look after it.

Soon they were all getting out at the railway station. Mrs Baker and Susan waited with the big brown leather suitcases, Susan still clutching her bucket and spade to make sandcastles, although these days they tended to be used for burying each other with, instead of the original intention of the implement.

Mr Baker and Andrew walked along the station to the ticket office. 'Two and two halves return to Blackpool,' he said when they finally got to the ticket window.

'It seems as if half of Manchester is going to Blackpool today,' said the ticket man.

Mr Baker paid the ticket man the money and whispered something about 'Robbin' devils' under his breath as he examined his change.

The two males wandered back to where they had left the ladies. They checked the big departure board and went to find out which platform the train left from. All around people hustled and bustled scurrying about their business and heading towards or away from the trains and platforms. Engines hooted and steam bellowed from their funnels; giant clouds of steam belched from the train as the engines coughed their power into the roof of the station.

The Bakers made their way along the station stopping only to purchase a *'Lion'* and *'Girl'* magazine, together with a couple of newspapers.

Once their tickets had been clipped and they passed through the metal barrier at the entrance, the family settled themselves into a carriage. Mrs

Baker checked to see if her hat was straight in the mirror and then sat down. Bob Baker had already put the cases on the rack and tucked his brown trilby on top. Andrew watched out of the window while Susan moaned that she could see nothing. At this point a warning came from their Dad who threatened to take them both back if he got any more nonsense from them.

Suddenly the guard blew the whistle, the green flag was waved and he stepped onto the train. Simultaneously, the train jolted as the engine shrill whistle was blown and a great chuff of smoke bellowed under pressure from the funnel. The wheels raced on the track but did not progress forward. As the power of the engine was unleashed, very slowly the train and the carriages pulled away, the tension on the connecting chains rattled then slowly at first, the engine belching some almighty clouds of steam, pulled away from the platform steadily gathering speed.

It didn't take long for the powerful engine to eat up the miles as it sped along the track, leaving behind the dirt and grime of the city as it passed all the backyards of the warehouses. Soon they were riding through the countryside and small towns came and went. They passed alongside a wide canal with a ship which appeared to be making slow progress. The train stopped occasionally to pick up visitors and set down passengers; their journey did not last long. In fact, from start to finish they were no more than an hour on the train. Slowly the giant locomotive pulled into the station; a large sign had greeted them on the outskirts welcoming them to Blackpool.

'Can't take us home now Dad, we're here.'

'Don't be cheeky,' came the reply from Mum.

They piled out onto the platform and waved to the ticket collector. Hundreds of passengers were carrying suitcases for the Summer holiday. Soon they were through the barrier and were making their way towards the taxi rank. Once again they all piled into the cab.

'Where to boss?' the driver quipped.

'Wellington Road,' said Dad, 'I am not sure of the number but I will tell you when I see it.'

'Okay boss,' said the driver and off he drove. A few minutes later they arrived.

'That's five shillings, boss,' the cabbie stated.

Mr Baker gave him his five shillings and whispered again under his breath 'Robbin' devil!' It was Dads opinion that no one should be paid unless they did physical work for it.

They carried the cases up to the front door and rang the highly polished bell.

A woman opened the door and greeted them with a smile.

'Oh come on into the house,' she said in a wheezing voice, and pulling a half smoked cigarette from her lips, 'you must be tired after your trip. 'I'll just put the kettle on and we'll have a cup of tea in a minute.'

The Bakers sat down in the front room.

A few minutes later the landlady returned and sat down, but before the first sip had been swallowed, she was in full flight again. 'Pots of teas cost an extra two shillings and if you want a bath there is a special meter, which only takes one shilling pieces.'

She reminded all concerned that although the deposit for the rooms had been paid, could we make sure that the full amount was paid up two days before the departure. And it would help all the other residents if we didn't get drunk, except on Saturday nights, which according to her was acceptable. Mr Baker nodded and replied that he had no intention of getting drunk on any night.

She immediately squeaked back 'Oh you are a one! I can see we'll have to watch you! Still, I will show you to your room now.' She stood up and put her teacup on the tiled mantelshelf covered in polished brass. The fire burned in the hearth, even though it was the middle of Summer.

They trooped upstairs one after the other. Mr and Mrs Baker had one room with a double bed, wardrobe and washbasin with a slightly cracked mirror. The window overlooked the backyard and through a crack in the next row of houses you could just see the sea.

The children's room was similar, except that they had two single beds and their room was at the front of the house.

'I put fresh towels out at the end of the week, but if you want any more 'specially, there were a few in the cupboard.' She pointed to an airing cupboard on the landing. The landlady informed us what time breakfast was and then quickly vanished downstairs.

The children got unpacked and pushed the suitcase under the bed. They had each selected a bed and were just in the process of testing the springs when the door was pushed open.

'Come on, you two, we're going for a walk to get some fresh air into your lungs.'

Bright as buttons, the children crept down the stairs. Mr Baker put the key on his key ring. The sun shone brightly, but a strong breeze warned them how cool it was, even though it was in the middle of Summer. They rounded the corner and saw the promenade in front of them.

Just then, a large double decker tram, painted cream and green, rumbled down the track. Susan and Andrew squeaked with excitement they had never seen trams of a domed shape before, even though trams still ran though the centre of Manchester.

The family crossed the road and stood on the promenade, the breeze blew off the sea permitting the seagulls to wheeled around, diving and soaring, always looking for food, always trying to steal the recently bought fish and chips from the holidaymakers

The golden sands swept out before their eyes. Joyously the children found the steps to the beach even though their parents had no intention of walking on the sands. 'We'll wait for you at the next set of steps beyond the pier,' said their Dad.

'Okay,' they chorused, quickly vanishing amongst the people laying scattered between the deckchairs, sandcastle buried Dads and children.

Quickly Susan and Andrew came across the donkeys all tethered together.

A queue of children waited for a ride and a sign indicated that three pence a ride was needed for the pleasure. A donkey called Rosie bent its head and nuzzled Susan who wasn't looking at the time. Instantly she jumped out of her skin with a yell that scattered the poor animals causing the man holding the reins a minor task to control them.

Andrew fell all over the place, laughing. Susan anxious to exact vengeance chased him over the sand. Eventually the children found their way to the steps leading up to the promenade and ran up as quickly as their legs would allow them. Their Mum and Dad greeted them. 'Come on you two, let's go and have some fish and chips.'

The family walked up the windy promenade towards Blackpool Tower eating the freshly made seaside delicacy pondering occasionally at the purpose-built wind shelter to gain a respite from the constantly hungry seagulls.

Most days turned into a replica of the previous. The little family had breakfast then went for a walk, sometimes catching a tram to a different area, and occasionally visiting the arcades but Dad always thought these were a waste of money. Each day there was a trip to the beach and a ride on the donkeys.

Andrew and Dad enjoyed the pitch and putt course at Lytham St Anne's and on another day the Bakers went up Blackpool Tower to see the view for miles in all directions.

Dad was buried in the sand many times and in the evening the Bakers would walk along the piers or visit the fun fair, but rides on these were expensive and money was tight, so only occasionally would dad allow the children a fairground treat.

Towards the end of the holiday the little family would enjoy one visit that they would never forget. Dad purchased four tickets to the circus within Blackpool Tower and this really was special. The children watched the grand parade, the elephants, clowns, acrobats and trapeze artists; undoubtedly this was the finest show they had ever seen. A day or so later, they paid the landlady and the Bakers were on their way home to Bradshaw Street.

It was a good holiday and enjoyed by everyone, but money was always tight as Dad was saving hard for Australia

Autumn –   Chapter 2   Preparing for Bonfire Night

Towards the end of October, the little gang that played together, Malcolm, Eddie, Stephen and Andrew decided it was time to start collecting firewood and anything else that would burn. Bonfire night was only two weeks away; without a doubt, this was one of the precious moments of being a child and especially a child from the backstreet's of Salford.

Eddies Dad allowed him to use the top of their outside toilet, which had a concrete roof on it; a bit of a posh lid for this neighbourhood. Andrew's Dad refused to let any rubbish come into the backyard. Any real rubbish, big stuff, went straight to the Croft and started to build up the bonfire site straight away. The problem with doing this was that the material used to be stolen by rival gangs collecting for their own bonfire, or in some cases, kids would just set it alight when no one was around.

The boys, under the circumstances, therefore used to store the best material in one of the backyards. Occasionally other neighbours would permit their yards to be used for the purposes of storage. After a few foraging parties and trips to the bomb sites, various timbers were dragged out and returned to the Croft; the pile started to grow and other local teams started to help build up the bonfire.

In an old derelict house that the boys knew there was a three-piece suite; it was old marked and stained. Sometimes the lads had seen the girls going in the house with men, occasionally they would throw stones through the window then run away when the older people ran out. This time, no one was about, so they took the old settee and the armchair. It took six of them to get it out; eventually they dragged it through the streets and down the back entry to Eddie's toilet/shelter. With three on the roof and three pulling, they managed to gain a little height eventually getting it up to a safe place for storage. The old armchair proved a little easier; the boys manhandled it into position, turning it upside down and putting a bit of plastic over it to prevent it from getting wet.

Collecting for the fire became the after-school priority. Mrs Baker insisted on Andrew having his tea before he went out and it was nearly always raining when the boys gathered on the Croft. One evening, towards the end of the week, the boys came across a segment of tree that the local vicar had chopped down. Now these boys were never backwards in coming forwards, slowly they approached the vestry door when a voice from behind the gravestones hailed out, 'Can I help you young men?'

The boys jumped back startled by the suddenness and clarity of the vicar, who by now was striding towards them at a pace that meant business.

'Er, yes sir,' replied Stephen who recognised the vicar from scouts, which he attended. Once the ice was broken all the other boys chirped in at the same time.

The vicar held his hands up. 'One at a time, boys, not altogether,' he spoke with authority.

They all clammed up.

'Please sir, can we have your log sir; the one that is cut down in the front of the church garden? My mother always says if you ask for things properly you will often get what you want.'

'Did we ask properly, sir?' Andrew had decided on the honest tactic, after all, this was a vicar and somehow it just wasn't right to steal the log, especially from a church garden.'

'If I say yes to you young scallywags, how will you take it away?'

A short paused followed.

'Go on then, but don't do any damage now and one of your parents has got to help you.'

Another pause followed.

'You know, I don't really agree with bonfire night, but I do have to get rid of the log. I tell you what, I'll give you 'til Saturday to remove the log, but you must bring one responsible parent with you.' With that, the vicar turned on his heel and marched off towards the vestry.

The boys strolled towards the log. Eddie sat astride it as if he were riding a horse. The other boys pushed and pulled it to see how heavy it was. They all knew that if they could get this log burning on bonfire night it would keep going for a long time. Now all they had to do was get a parent to help them. Somehow the task had become huge. That evening around the tea tables, the boys approached their parents.

'Er, Dad, is there any chance you just might be able to help me this Saturday?' Andrew asked in his most plaintive voice.

'Sorry son, I'm working; taking a colliery bucket to Sheffield on Saturday.

Bob Baker drove a low-loader that carried big pieces of equipment which often needed a police escort.

Andrew would have to wait now to find out what luck, if any, the other boys had. That night Andrew fell asleep thinking only of his log and the potential of keeping the fire going for ages.

The following day drifted past at school; one hour merged into the next. The boys all went to different places of learning in the area. That evening they gathered on the Croft to find out who had been lucky enough to gain the parental support.

'Okay, okay,' shouted Eddie.

'My Dad will help us for an hour on Saturday morning,' cried a proud prodigy, pleased as punch that it was his Dad who was assisting.

'My Dad will help as well,' said Stephen.

'My Dad won't, he's working,' chipped in Andrew.

Malcolm said nothing; his Dad was nearly always away somewhere. No one asked where.but all the lads knew he was a regular at Strangeways.

On Saturday morning, they all trooped up to the vicarage; a swift knock on the door brought the vicar to the front entrance, he was delighted to see Mr Youngman, a man he knew from his flock.

'Thanks for the log vicar, we won't take up any more of your time. Stephen's dad was courteous and precise. Stephen's dad had just completed his National Service training and tended to be a bit brusque in his attitude. The boys had dragged the guider up the road. Eddie's dad and Stephen's pulled the log together with about five other lads who had come from nowhere. Slowly and carefully they got the log up the drive, past the headstones, though the gate and onto the road. The little team collapsed on the pavement in a heap, they were all jiggered. The log was proving too long and too heavy for the team, even though they had two adults to help them. Perspiration was pouring off Mr Youngman who was putting in a lot of effort.

Great Cheetham Street is a main road and each day dozens of lorries drive along the road en route to many northern cities and places. Just by chance Bob Baker was driving along this way to collect his giant bucket. In the distance he saw the little group struggling with the tree trunk. Leaning out of the cab he honked his horn. A blast rang out that made the whole street jump to attention. The big yellow indicators flashed out; yellow lights started flashing and Bob Baker cruised slowly but purposefully to a halt.

'What on earth are you up to,' he hollered out of the window.

'We got roped-into this,' replied Stephen's Dad. Eddies Dad came forward and introduced himself. 'Well, I suppose we ought to get this off the road before someone comes and books us,' shouted Mr Baker from his lorry to the pavement. Together the men and the little gathering of kids from the local streets manhandled the huge log onto the back of the lorry. Bob strapped it down, and Andrew and Malcolm jumped into the cab.

'I'll see you at the Croft in a minute,' he shouted out of the window. With that, he tossed a yard broom to Eddie's Dad, 'Give it the once over, mate,' he yelled as he started to drive the giant vehicle slowly away from the kerb, 'and don't forget my broom; thanks!'

With a wave he pulled away, moving very slowly. His first objective was to find somewhere to reverse the giant low-loader. He wasn't disappointed; at the bottom of the road was a big showroom and they frequently had vehicles turning in there. Once again, the flashing lights started and a number of vehicles ground to a halt as Mr Baker reversed his low-loader forward, double de-clutching, as he pulled forwards into the road. The cars gave him a wide berth as he drew into the traffic and made his way one again, into Bradshaw Street and down to the Croft.

By this time the kids, the neighbours and a few passers-by had congregated. Mr Baker pulled the long vehicle as close to the Croft as he could. A pavement cracked as the heavy low loader crawled over it. The rope was undone and a swarm of people heaved the log; first one end was placed on the pavement and then the other was slid off to crash on the side of the Croft. Mr Baker secured his wagon and ropes, collected his broom off Eddie's Dad and with a wave and a shout, returned to his truck.

'Bye son,' he called to his boy as he pulled away, exhaust belching from the giant pipes.

'Thanks Bob,' the men called out and the children cheered and waved as he pulled away.

By this time enough people had arrived to see what was going on and they were roped-in to help move the giant log into position by the bonfire site. It was not an easy task and it took much pushing and pulling, lifting and straining. A few more people arrived to help; ropes were attached and the trunk which slid on the mud, dragged and lifted. One thing was for sure, no one was going to take this log away. It was definitely going to burn on bonfire night. About six men and ten children sat on the log to get their breath back.

'Good job Bob came along when he did,' someone said. The men all agreed, then started chatting for a few minutes.

The boys sat on the old brick wall. This was all that was left of a small row of houses which caught a string of bombs during a German bombing raid. The area all around was decimated; the council covered the bomb sites with soil to make them less dangerous and more presentable

It was now twelve years after the World War 2, this was the one area locally known as the Croft. It was the only outside area in the immediate vicinity the children had to play on.

'You do know about Guy Fawkes?'

'He's the firework man,' interjected another voice.

'No he isn't,' the other two protested.

'Well, anyway we don't have one, okay!' shouted Malcolm, 'we'll have to make one. We learned about him in school, 'cos he's the man with a great big hat. He tried to blow up the Houses of Parliament in London and that's why they put a scarecrow who looks like him on the bonfire.'

'I still don't see why they want to burn him,' said Eddie, 'anyway, if we make one then we can collect a penny for the guy, and then we can get some fireworks.'

'Yep, that's right,' Malcolm came back to life, "I know where there's a good suit. Our old fella still has two years to do in" nick," so he won't miss it. We could stuff it with old newspaper and dress it up a bit. We'll need a mask."

'I'll get that and an old shirt,' said Andrew. Eddie took his Dad's old cap of the peg in their house. The boys got a big turkey feather from the butcher and Andrew found a shirt on the washing line in Fenny Street;

'Well, it shouldn't have been by itself!' someone said.

All the boys met back at the Croft and started to assemble the Guy Fawkes. The girls, Susan and her friend Christine, helped stuff the guy with squashed up newspaper. The boys took the Guy back to the air raid shelter at the back of Malcolm's house; nobody would bother them there and they ceremoniously placed the mask on it. They put on its hat with the turkey feather and declared it suitable for the purpose.

They decided to go in two different places, to get the penny for the guy. They had a cocoa tin and an old baked bean tin for collecting any donations . They set themselves up to do three-hour shifts; one in Great Cheetham Street and four hours at the bottom of Tully Street, that way they didn't look like a gang. The sign was written in the best writing 'PENNY FOR THE GUY'. The boys placed the sign around the neck of the stuffed effigy.

Andrew and Stephen went to the Saturday afternoon cinema, shift; they never missed the matinée programme at the County Cinema and they figured that if they did that shift they might get more money because of the people coming from their shopping or maybe from work. When the picture house closed at four o'clock, the boys made their way down to Great Cheetham Street where they found two friends shouting out, 'Penny for the Guy'. The boys wandered up and down rattling their tins. Soon Eddie and Malc went off to get a rest and have some tea, but not before the little gang had checked the contents of the can. Andrew counted the money; three shillings and eight pence.

'Take the cash out and give us the tin, now you look after the money 'til next time you go collecting with the Guy. Whatever you do, don't spend the money or we'll have none to buy fireworks with.'

Andrew had given the instruction and they all agreed to take a penny piece each to buy bubble gum or lolly as required. The people came and went and nobody made any real comment; some criticised his hat, one man offered to buy the Guy's suit for two and six. The boys declined, 'worth more than that mister!'

Dr Robinson walked passed and recognised Andrew. He was a foreign gentleman who came from Switzerland. Andrew smiled, 'We are collecting for the Guy Sir, so we can buy some fireworks.'

We reckon it was with relief that Dr Robinson was not able to see his own son amongst the local community. With that, he plunged his hand into the back pocket of his wallet and pulled out a ten-shilling note. Quickly folding it and placing it in the tin.

'Wow!' the boys' mouths dropped open, sitting amongst the few pennies this was real money, though Andrew recognised it as a one-off. The odd sixpence was dropped in the tin and a few three-penny bits, but mostly people would put a penny in the tin. Happily the boys were glad of this contribution.

Stephen saw Andrew's Dad coming down the road. Quickly the boys dragged the guider and its content down the back alley out of view. Although the boys had not been told not to do 'Penny for the Guy', they still decided it was the sort of thing their parents might moan about. It seems their Mums and Dads were always niggling them about something or other.

As the hours closed in and darkness started to fall, the boys decided to pack it in for the night. They dragged the Guy taped to the guider, back down the street to Malc's house and more to the point, into his backyard. Quickly they placed a piece of plastic they had found over the Guy's head to keep the rain off then as it started to drizzle, they both stepped into the outside toilet where grandma had had her adventure with the snake several months before.

The boys counted out the money; they were surprised to find they had over a pound. They entered the figure in the little notebook and pushed the book behind the toilet pipe; the money was placed in an Oxo box and placed in a corner by the wall with four bricks and a piece of slate over it. The lads walked home from the Croft.

'I bet we make really loads of money.'

'Yes, but we cannot let our parents know, they will only take it off us.'

The boys discussed the problem as they walked home. They split up, going their own respective ways. A few minutes later, they pushed open their own back doors.

'Where have you been, young 'un? You know you're not to be out after dark.'

'Sorry Dad, but it's only the same time as it was last week, it's just that the nights are getting darker sooner.'

'That's not the point, son, I don't like you being out after dark. Now you mind on, next time I'll give you a clout if you disobey me and you can expect it for sure if your Mum finds out.'

The children sat up on Saturday night and ate fish and chips. This was a real treat. Mum's fish was in the oven waiting for her, *Journey into Space* was on the radio and the two children listened intently.

All of a sudden, they heard the front door bang and they knew their Mum was home. The children threw their arms around Mum and got a kiss on the head for their trouble. 'Have you been good kids?' she asked.

'Of course,' they replied.

Mum delved into her shopping bag and came up with two chocolate éclairs and two vanilla slices. " You can have one each when someone's made me a cup of tea." Mrs Baker did a Saturday job at a large chemists' shop in the city which sold retail goods as well as medical.

'It's bedlam in there every Saturday and you know the store detectives are out all the time. We have to flick a light on if you see anyone lifting goods. I feel sorry for the poor devils,' she said, 'They simply cannot afford the things they need.'

She stayed working there because it gave her the few pounds extra the family needed to make out.

That night when the children went to bed, Andrew crept down to Susan's bedroom. The children snuggled under the bedclothes and Andrew told Susan about making some really good money for the fireworks. They started to try and remember the names of the fireworks. They'd definitely have to have Rockets and Catherine Wheels, Roman Candles and Ripraps. For ages the two children spoke of fireworks when their mum arrived at the door and startled them half to death.

'Off you go now, young man, up to your room and lights out. You get some sleep.' She patted his backside as he scuttled past and vanished up the stairs. Quickly he snuggled down in the bed and within minutes he was fast asleep.

The next morning the children woke bright and early. Sunday was a real family day for the Bakers. First was clean underwear, which had been placed at the bottom of the staircase. Next was the smell of fresh percolated coffee heating on the range. Both Andrew and his father had blue enamel mugs. Mother always insisted on drinking out of a china cup and Susan had a cup with Sooty on it. Coffee drunk, teeth cleaned and hair brushed, the little family set off to church every Sunday morning.

And so it was, Susan skipped up the road; Andrew ran around like a demented Labrador, it seemed everywhere Andrew went, he ran there. The family soon covered the distance up Great Cheetham Street as they grew closer to the church they could hear the choir singing, friends, schoolmates, mums and dads, all congregated at the entrance, feeling their way slowly into the church.

Piously the Bakers moved up the pews to find a suitable seat. They genuflected and moved into the chosen pew. The mass always took an hour and the family settled down to think their own individual thoughts and probably to ask God for advice, or maybe as in Andrew's case, a combination of many things. He wondered if God ever collected for the Guy or had Bonfire Nights or similar. He wondered if God had ever thought about the girl three rows up, or even if God had ever kissed a girl. These weren't bad thoughts, he was just wondering.

The hour passed quickly and soon they were outside, talking to their friends, passing the time of day. One or two had heard of the migration programme and Mr and Mrs Baker were quizzed about going to Australia. Mrs Baker spoke briefly with a schoolteacher regarding the subject. The kids ducked and dived around the talking parties, but soon they were together again, walking down the road towards their own street.

Susan put the key in the door. The coffee smell permeated the hall. The large pan had been left just touching the edge of the hotplate.

'That's what we want first,' said Celia, 'a nice cup of coffee.'

With one voice the children chorused their approval. The big frying pan was placed on the range metal plate. Bob stacked up the fire.

Meanwhile, Eddie and Malc had dragged the Guy down to the bottom of their road calling to all and sundry, 'Penny for the Guy, Missus?' and hopefully thrust out the metal receptacle. When things got a little slow, they moved pitches, hoping their luck would change. The boys stayed for a good session; somehow, though, they didn't make much money. They certainly needed more for a good display of fireworks. Andrew and Stephen took over prior to lunchtime; they didn't fare much better, so they all decided that Sunday was no good for getting people to spend money. They took the guy and the money back to Malc's backyard. The cash was recorded and the Guy was covered with a plastic cover. The boys decided that if anyone wanted to take the Guy they were welcome to do so, all the lads knew where to find each other.

That evening, as they arrived home, Mrs Baker called the boys to come inside. All a little surprised at this, as they thought there were in for a ticking off, but to the surprise of one and all, Mrs Baker had a bowl of apples bobbing in the water. In their haste to get out that morning, they had forgotten it was Duck Apple Day, Halloween.

Now, normally the boys would have been making faces out of pumpkins, but today they had forgotten and being so engrossed with collecting for the Guy, the night of spooks and ghosties had passed them by. Susan and Christine came and livened-up the party, especially when Eddie pushed Christine's head under the water to whoops of delight from the boys. Soon they had all bobbed for apples and Mrs Baker had given them a piece of parkin. It was getting a bit dark outside and she thought the other children's mothers and fathers would be getting worried. She drew the little gathering to a close and sent the children home.

Christine had stopped over and slept with Sue in her bed. The morning came and one and all went for a walk. Christine went home and Mr and Mrs Baker had some business at a solicitor and they kept the children with them, in case they were needed. When this was over, they decided to go for a trip into the country.

Andrew and Stephen sat on the pillars outside their house, the pleasant morning was suddenly disturbed by the sound of a motorbike which had just turned into view at the top of the street. The noisy bike came to a stop beside them

."Hello Andrew," The driver took his helmet and goggles of. It was Roger ,Andrews older cousin,

"Is your Mum and Dad in?" He called out as he dismounted and pulled his bike onto its stand.

"Yes they're both in"

"What type of bike is it?" asked Andrew.

"That's a Francis Barnet", Roger said as he mounted the steps to the front door.

"Ill be out in a minute and Ill give you a ride to the top of the street when I go."

True to his word Roger was only in the house for about fifteen minutes , he had a cup of tea and delivered his message from his Dad ,

"Come on young un I'll take you to the top of the street and back." Roger adjusted his helmet and goggles then mounted the bike turning on the petrol and kick-starting the engine. A very thrilled little boy climbed on behind him.

"Hang on tight now young un" , and with that he selected a gear and throttled away from the kerb. He drove to the end of the street and turned round Andrew clung on to his cousin enjoying the throb of the engine as it bounced over the cobbles.

Roger drove down the road quickly turning at the end and delivered Andrew back safe and sound. With a cheery wave Roger roared off into the distance.

A very happy little boy chatted with his friend and extolled the virtues of his cousins motor bike, which Stephen happily knew all about as his father also had a motor bike and side-car.

A Day Trip to the Countryside

This week they walked down to where they could catch a bus to Broad Moor. There was an asylum built on the moor but it was surrounded by a lovely unspoilt walking areas. When they alighted from the bus, Mr Baker enquired as to the frequency of the service. With that knowledge they turned and headed off down the road, soon arriving at a stile. Andrew was the first there and hopped over the timbers; Susan came next and she too made short work of the stile. Bob Baker helped his wife over and soon they were all rambling down the fields.

'Don't go too far ahead,' bellowed Mr Baker. Susan and Andrew were playing roly-poly down the field. They lay on the side of the long grass and rolled themselves down the hill until they came to a stop, then on trying to stand up, the children were so dizzy they spun round but could not keep their composure and fell over laughing their socks off. Mrs Baker thought this may be dangerous and decided to put an end to this element of the entertainment. The family kept on walking for about half an hour and eventually came to a small fast-flowing stream. Mr Baker took his hanky out and in turn he washed it in the stream and then placed it on the various foreheads of his wife and daughter.

'Can we drink the water, Dad?'

Mr Baker, a naturally cautious man, said, 'Yes, I expect it's probably better than the stuff that comes out of the taps.' Andrew lay face down on the bank and placed his head in the water, getting his head and hair wet.

'Never does anything by halves, that one,' said Mrs Baker, wagging her head from side to side. He sucked in a giant draught of water, enjoying every moment and then he started hunting for newts and frogs.

A packet of biscuits and four small chocolate bars were produced and the

Bakers picnicked by the stream. Mr Baker lay back on the grass and slowly relaxed, just enjoying the sun beating down, even though the morning had been a little crisp and cool. Five minutes later Bob was snoring his head off.

The children moved further away so as not to disturb him; they knew that if he got his snooze he would wake happy. But if he didn't then he'd be like a bear with a sore head. Mrs Baker lay beside her husband, quietly relaxing and slowly dozing herself. The children made boats and raced them against each other, the little sticks bobbing along the brook, bouncing over stones, bumping into ferns, twisting round and coming out the other side as they went further away from the resting parents. The pools were a little larger and the children got a bit wetter. In the end the children decided they should move closer to their parents, treading cautiously not to wake them, where they took off their shoes and socks to dry off. Then in turn a few minutes after sitting down in the sun they both dozed off.

By mid-afternoon the sun's rays had started to vanish and the heat was rapidly diminishing, about this time the family woke from their afternoon slumber. Dad was in fine fettle, he had had a good sleep. The children came round with everyone stirring. Mrs Baker had stood up and was folding the shawl she had been laying on and everyone commented that it was getting cool. With that, they all headed for high ground and the route to the bus stop.

By now it was getting dark as the family stepped on the bus, the vehicle had its lights on. With a series of grates and groans it pulled itself along the country lanes. The bus always seemed to be in slow motion and the driver had an old cigarette lit, which he puffed away at. Every few moments the cab would fill with smoke, then he would open the window and it would clear. After about ten stops, the conductor would stop the bus and join the driver at the front on the outside and jump back on the running board of the bus and carry on down the road for another few stops.

Soon the shop lights, then the semi-detached houses, occasionally a property by itself with a garden. Next a whole group of houses nestling behind high brick walls. Always on the outskirts of Manchester, there were dirty smog covered brick walls to be found.

The bus ground to a halt and the little family got off. It was dark now, a few spivs collected on the corner, hair dragged back with Brylcream, drainpipe trousers and brightly coloured drapes. They were probably going to the cinema. Mrs Baker had always told the children to keep away from them because they carried razors. Dad had always said, 'Don't be so daft woman! They're simply following a fashion cult, 'though the music's a bit loud for me.'

Soon they came to the top of the street.

The Robbery

'We've been robbed! We've been robbed!' Eddie and Malc shouted as they came running towards them. 'Somebody's nicked the sofa and suite from the shelter!'

'Well, blow me down!' said Mr Baker, using his favourite saying when anything surprised him. 'When did this happen?'

Eddie answered, 'I think it must have been last night; I came out of the front door this morning and we noticed it was gone a few hours ago.'

'Did you look up and down the local streets?'

'Of course we did, we looked everywhere,' they replied.

'Well, it's too late to do anything. You'll have to wait 'till tomorrow night to look around. But do you know it would be more effective use of your time if you went collecting more material for the fire. I mean if you did find the sofa, you'd only end up fighting over it and chances are it's in an old bloke's house now, as something to sit on and don't forget not everyone's as lucky as we are.' Mr Baker had said his piece and with that he opened the door and went into their house.

'See you tomorrow after school, I've got to go in now,' Andrew waved and went indoors.

That night he lay in his bed thinking about that had happened. He remembered the hard work of getting the sofa down the streets, he recalled the trouble they had of lifting the chair onto the roof, of Malcolm's left boot on his ear hole when they were lifting; struggling to get the furniture onto the shelter and now it was gone!

Andrew felt angry and he wanted to vent that anger on someone or something. He wanted to find the thief; the more he thought about it the more he knew his dad was right; don't get mad, get even. The whole object of what they were doing was to get material for the bonfire, so that they could all have a good Bonfire Night.

Andrew's brain was buzzing; an idea was forming, not necessarily a good idea, but none the less an idea that could at the worst replace the old sofa and chairs.

The boys sat around in their den in Malc's backyard; a candle flickered on the little central table , all eyes turned to Andrew.

'Now listen everybody, we've been robbed and we all know that's not nice. But we're not going to let it spoil anything, 'cos we are going to get back an old sofa for our bonfire and no one is going to worry about it, okay?'

In a chorus they asked where was this magic sofa coming from.

'That's for us to check out, now does everyone here promise on the gang's honour that they won't tell, whatever we do next.'

They all agreed.

'Okay, now you remember that big warehouse down the street? The one that was bombed a few years ago?'

'Yes,' they all chorused.

'Then we'll take an old suite from there and put it on the bonfire, I expect we'll be doing them a favour anyhow, they must have loads of old sofas in there, some of them might be damaged, so we'll only take an old one, maybe with the springs coming through. I reckon it will be doing them a favour if the truth be known. Okay, so we all agree?'

The boys closed the back gate softly, it was as if they were on a mission now, everyone was quiet. The light rain came down, a street lamp glistened on the cobblestones; the boys walked along the back entries and down the road to join the main street. Malc and Eddie had found a piece of plastic to cover their heads, to stop them from getting wet. It was only a ten-minute walk; the boys wanted to have a look first and find out if anyone was around, or maybe if there was any old broken ones outside.

The first two boys went round the back. A few minutes later the other two vanished over the wall. There was rubbish everywhere; broken bottles, old bikes, rusty oil drums, old tin cans, the place was a real mess and it looked as if no one was there, even the bottom windows were broken.

Suddenly the boys came across an open door; slowly, stealthily they pushed it. The dust had a peculiar smell to it. As they entered they let out a shout, a flock of pigeons darted and scrambled for air as they made their way past the opening door, which had disturbed their slumber.

The other boys hearing the commotion decided to investigate and quickly charged like a herd of elephants around the corner. A few minutes later the boys had composed themselves and decided to check out the interior – after all that's what they came for.

The remains of daylight illuminated their way, even though it was murky, everywhere smelt damp as if there was permanent water lying around. Inside small groups of furniture were roped together with the sisal passing through the handles; a piece of card with a name, a date and a number neatly drawn on it signified the only hint of private ownership. The boys split up and walked about the giant warehouse, each of them looking for furniture that could be described as rubbish. They wandered idly round, casting their eyes backwards and forwards eventually meeting back by the front door.

'Well, did you find an old sofa?'

'Yep,' came the reply, 'there are several real old ones round the back, that look really damaged and torn. I bet they would really thank us for getting rid of this one; it's got big holes in it and bits of furry stuff handing out of it. I reckon it would be easy to get out as well, 'cos it's only got little arms at one end and a curly bit at the other.'

'That's it, then, we'll get it on Friday night then it only has to sit on the Croft for one night before it gets burned and we can guard it on Saturday.' They all decided this was a great plan. The boys walked slowly up the main road, talking about what a great Bonfire Night this was going to be. Eddie and Mal ran on and got the 'Guy Fawkes' out.

For a while they did some collecting at the bottom of the street – 'Penny for the Guy!' they yelled, running across the road to collect the money, chatting up all the old folks and annoying the workmen scurrying home after the hard day at their toil. Steadily the kitty built up, along with every scrap of wood or debris they could haul towards the bonfire site.

The Fire

Four young lads made their way down the street. They towed behind them the home-made guider. The intention was that the sofa could be balanced across the central section and supported on either side. It was already going dusk.

In November it was dark by four o' clock. In the evening the chill had come into the air and drizzle had started, but the boys were on a high. As far as they were concerned this was a daring raid to equal the theft of the sofa. Steadily they made their way towards the warehouse; it was a bit darker than the previous visit. One of the boys had his dad's lighter and another had his torch. They often carried a torch so that they didn't tread in dog dirt while walking up the entry.

The little team arrived at the store. Once again they circled the building, just to make sure they were alone. They pushed on the door; gradually they became more accustomed to the dark. Slowly they made their way down to where the sofa had been; to locate it was easy because it had sat at the end of a long straight aisle opposite the first big tied up square of furniture. At this moment, they noticed another group of lads in the building. Quietly they boys decided to get out and abandon their plan. The boys headed back up the road.

One of the other gang of lads picked up a newspaper, pretending to read it. The boys giggled and joked with each other. They told a couple of jokes and then together they tried to lift a sofa; it wasn't too heavy, but the boys knew they had to carry it a long way.

'I'll get the old pram,' one of them called and headed off towards the door.

The others sat down again—the newspaper was picked up again, only this time one of the boys lit the bottom edge. At first it wasn't noticed, but suddenly it caught alight. The boys dropped the newspaper turning to each other and accusing each other for lighting it. In turn they all denied the accusation, but meanwhile the burning paper had landed on an old horsehair sofa.

They tried in vain to put out the fire, but it seemed to be gathering momentum, the spurting and spluttering was growing more intense and now smoke was coming from the burning piece of furniture. The boys backed off, turning, they ran down the aisle, the light from the flames now clearly illuminating the way.

At the entrance they met a small scared boy with a pram. It took no time at all to bundle him out onto the path. They made their way up the road a few yards towards the flats and stopped. The boys looked round; they knew that they should not be around here now. They told each other that the fire would probably go out, but almost as they said this to each other, little curls of smoke started to swirl out of the door.

'Let's split up and meet back a bit later.'

'I think it would be wise to go straight home, then at least our parents will know where we are.'

By this time, the original group were nearly home and knew nothing of the disaster that had befallen the other gang. The boys were heading away from the warehouse. They had already turned up the side street and steadily made their way up Fenny Street. From the Croft smoke could be seen starting to spiral into the night air. Occasional sparks could be seen challenging the darkness rising. The distant bell of a fire engine broke the traffic silence.

'It looks like a place is on fire!'

'God! Now we're for it.'

'But we didn't do it.'

'It can't be the same building, must be one nearby, maybe the other boys started it.'

The boys were all talking at once.

They got in a little huddle, 'Whatever happens now, no matter who asks you, just remember you know nothing about it. There is nothing to link this to us, no matter what anyone says. So let's get home so our parents can see all of us and when you can hear more fire engines we can come onto the Croft and have a look with our Dads.'

As the boys vanished up their back alleys a red glow could be seen lighting the sky. In the distance the wail of the fire service could be heard and smoke was really starting to billow. By now the first floor was burning like an inferno. Appliances were starting to arrive; police cars wailed and sirens screamed up the road. A crowd had started to gather Great Cheetham Street was blocked off, diversions were set up.

Just then Mr Baker came in, 'There's a hell of a to-do going on out there,' he cast a glance at his son. 'Nothing to do with you, I hope.'

'I'm here aren't I?' he answered, 'can we go and have a look Dad?'

'Not yet, after tea, maybe,' he replied.

Andrew tried not to shake during teatime. No one noticed but he was genuinely scared stiff. All the boys were simultaneously going through the same emotion and eventually sons and fathers stood side by side with dozens of other curious neighbours watching the floors of the massive partially bombed warehouse burn.

Fire appliances came, one after the other and worked long and hard into the night at the brigade fought to contain the blazing warehouse. By the morning, the place was nothing more than a pile of ashes. No one was hurt, but the place was in ruins and four appliances were standing by. Police were still measuring up.

The morning press heralded the story of the mystery blaze.

Because it was Saturday, the boys met on the Croft as soon as they had their breakfast. There was only one topic to talk about and unfortunately it did take up at least an hour of their time as they discussed the warehouse blaze, but soon they were feeling brighter and after all this was their very own Bonfire Night.

The first thing to do was to get the Guy out and do a bit of collecting. They positioned themselves at the bottom of the side street and started collecting, all the time they were there they could watch the police and fire brigade sweeping and cleaning the roads. The giant pile of debris continued to smoke occasionally. The hoses would come out and the brigade would douse it down again. Meanwhile the boys collected.

A policeman wandered across to them. 'You boys didn't see anything suspicious last night did you?'

'No sir,' they replied, 'we were all in having tea when we heard the fire engines, then later on we came onto the Croft with our dads to watch. The policeman walked on a bit further. The boys turned and looked at each other; they had all gone a bit sheepish now, but in fairness they genuinely knew nothing about the blaze.

Fireworks

The little group decided to head for home. Malc took the Guy back to his backyard and Andrew went home. They agreed to meet on the Croft in about half an hour. The intention was to decide how to split up the money and what fireworks to buy. Eddie went with Andrew and they opened the back gate to be met by a very irate Mrs Baker.

'What's the meaning of this?' she exclaimed in a loud voice. 'I've never been so ashamed in my life!' The boys stood there thinking the worst. 'Mrs Grant has just been to see me and tells me you were at the bottom of Fenny Street begging. Yes, my son begging! Whatever next?'

'We weren't begging, Mum, it was a penny for the Guy. Everyone does it at this time of the year.'

'That's not the point, asking other people for money is begging and you should know better.' Mrs Baker was cooling down a bit now.

'We only collected a few shillings, Mum.' Andrew had mentally split the money up. He didn't see why the others should be penalised just in case he was going to have to hand it over. He held out the tin can with the last two hours money in it. 'See for yourself,' he said as he turned to Eddie, 'that's all we've got, Eddie, isn't it?' Eddie pulled out the lining of his pockets to show they were empty.

'Well how much is there?' she leaned forward and pushed the money around. It was gradually dawning on her this was a mountain out of a molehill situation. She counted seven shillings and four pence. Standing upright she declared, 'I think you should give the money to the Boys' Home at Cheetham Hill.'

Andrew thought quickly, 'The money was to buy fireworks. If we give the money to the home, all that will happen is it will go towards some piece of equipment of something else, so why can't we buy fireworks and give some to the Boys' Home?'

Mrs Baker agreed that this was a suitable punishment and also agreed not to tell Eddie's Mum. The boys had a cup of tea and a biscuit.

A few minutes later, they were out on the Croft relaying to their mates what had just happened. The others were annoyed that Andrew's Mum had hijacked the last bit of booty the boys had secured for their fireworks night, but just the same understood it could have been any of their parents. They also knew that they had four pounds, fifteen shillings to spend that only they knew about.

The next bit of the plot was hatched; Malc would go and get the Guy and with Steve, they would go to a different place and see if they could secure a few more shillings to spend. Andrew and Eddie would head up the road to purchase fireworks for the Boys' Home. However, Andrew's Mum decided that as she had to go to the Maypole for a few groceries, she would accompany the boys to make sure everything went smoothly.

It only took a few minutes for the boys to buy the fireworks, they did this with amazing enthusiasm and a knowledge of the names and prices. The boys quickly spent seven shilling on fireworks for the Boys' Home. Mrs Baker allowed them to spend the other four pence on bangers for themselves. Little did she know the boys had nearly five pounds to spend on fireworks.

The trio walked up to the Boys' Home. Mrs Baker stood behind them as they knocked on the door. A cheery fellow answered in a long brown robe. 'Good morning one and all,' as he looked at Mrs Baker.

She nodded politely. 'The boys have something to say to you Brother John,' she thrust her son forward, clutching the bag of fireworks.

'We bought these fireworks for the boys, so that they could see some fireworks tonight, sir.'

'Well, that's very kind of you. Thank you.'

Mrs Baker decided to chip in. She told the monk about the boys begging and the penalty was that the boys had to surrender the money to a worthy cause. The monk pleasantly recognised the irony of the situation and decided to be a mediator, to Mrs Baker he said, 'thank you for your thoughts in permitting the boys to bring the fireworks to us, so that many people can enjoy them.'

He turned to the boys and said, 'in days gone by begging was an honourable profession, but I don't think your intention was to beg and didn't those people put the money in your tin of their own free will?'

He winked at Mrs Baker, 'Maybe later you would like to join us later on and see the fireworks go off?'

Andrew quickly jumped in and told the monk about their own bonfire and the effort everyone had put in. He thanked him for his offer. Mrs Baker extended her hand thanking him and expressing that they would meet again at church in the near future. With that they all marched out of the gate, closing it quietly being them and they headed off down the road.

'Mum, seeing as you've taken our money off us, are you going to make some toffee and maybe some treacle toffee as well?' Andrew asked his mother.

'We'll call in the Maypole as we are going past and we'll see if they have any condensed milk. Then maybe, if you're good, we can make the toffee.'

When they arrived at the Maypole, Mrs Baker sorted out her business and the boys headed for the biscuit tin.

'A pennyworth of the old broken biscuits, please?' asked Andrew. This was his favourite because he didn't have to share with anybody if he didn't want to. Eddie and Andrew took three biscuits each and then passed the bag to his mum for safekeeping, that way they knew they had some for later.

The boys walked on down the road with Mrs Baker, when they came to the top of the street they split up. Mrs Baker went home to make some treacle toffee and the boys went on their way to look for Malc and Steve, who were by now would be trying to recoup their losses with the Guy.

It didn't take long for the little team to catch up with each other and, true to form the boys had made some extra cash. After a little discussion, they decided to take the Guy home and go and spend the firework money, just in case the firework shop ran out of the fireworks they required. Fortunately the boys has previously been in the store and set aside a large number of Rockets and Bangers, together with Ripraps, Catherine Wheels, Roman Candles, Shimmering Cascades and Mount Vesuvius. Collectively the lads had selected the fireworks; the only reason the manager had kept them for the boys was because he had seen the Guy Fawkes and he knew they had collected some money.

The boys sprawled across the counter. The old tin was turned upside down; pennies, sixpences, three-penny bits, shillings, two-shilling pieces and half-crowns scattered in a heap. They had already taken the notes out, not that there were many, just one pound note and one ten shilling note. The shopkeeper was amazed at the amount they had collected.

'My godfathers! You have been working hard,' he exclaimed and with that he placed his fingers in the coins and started to draw them towards him counting as he went and putting them in piles of twelve. Eventually he came to the mathematical conclusion that the boys had eight pounds, ten shillings and sixpence. He took out six pounds for the fireworks; the children had already spent and said to them, 'and what do you want with the other two pounds, ten and sixpence?'

While the boys were making their minds up, Mr Ellis the shopkeeper was putting the fireworks into bags and boxes. The boys still had the two notes so they decided to add the ten-shilling note to the kitty and divide the one pound note amongst themselves and keep that for some time in the future when they had little or no pocket money. The remainder they spent on whizz-bangs and rockets.

Four little boys walked out of the shop loaded up with fireworks, big smiles on their faces and the feeling of success in their hearts. They headed to Malcolm's backyard; their place of sanctuary.

The trauma of the night before was behind them, somehow the problems and horrors of the fire was something in the past, even though it was the very recent past. The Manchester Evening News thought otherwise and kept the story running. No one had been hurt, but this was a big fire and many appliances were in attendance. The forensics department wanted to know how it started, not to mention the police investigating the scene.

Bonfire Night

The boys secured the fireworks in a safe place and scampered off to the Croft to assist the bigger boys rebuilding the bonfire. From every angle, boys young and old could be seen pulling logs, bits of old furniture, old garden doors, planks, building debris and Grandad's old armchair. The little group danced around the chair. Andrew sat in it pretending to be the Guy. They told the big boys that they had made the Guy Fawkes to sit in it. Everyone agreed not to place the Guy in the position, in case it was stolen before the fire was lit. Some of the local men had shown their faces by now and a time of six o'clock was agreed as the light up time.

Two men agreed to stand on guard 'til the main group ate their tea. People still kept coming down the back entry carrying good and bits of debris; this was an occasion when everyone cleaned out the backyards and old sheds, in some cases even the old sheds were burned.

Every now and then a bang could be heard as children found they could not contain their enthusiasm any more and let off a few private fireworks. In many places on the skyline, rockets could be seen coursing through the sky to erupt in a cascade of colour and illumination, only to fade into oblivion and melt into the background, leaving a sparkling trail until it fizzled out and vanished in the gloom. Time after time, the same occurrence would happen only the occasional swoosh of the closely let off fireworks signalled their proximity. The light-up time was drawing near.

In the house, Susan and Andrew were so excited they could hardly contain themselves. Mum had made parkin, ginger cake and treacle toffee. The evening meal had been consumed at a rate of knots!

The few fireworks the children had were on display. Andrew played the deaf mute regarding the grand collection whey had stored at Malc's yard. He knew the boys would bring them out when the time was ready. Mrs Baker was aware the weather was turning damp; she always claimed her corns were playing up when it was due to rain. Streams of light bounced out of the kitchen window, rays of light lit up the coal heap and the toilet door little specks began to sparkle as the light rain started to fall. Andrew and Susan danced around the place pulling on jumpers and raincoats and generally getting ready.

'Have you got a "gamp", Celia? I reckon it's going to be damp out there,' Father had spoken.

The family stepped outside the back door. The light from the kitchen window lit their path to the back yard door. Andrew was first out; silhouettes of other people were heading towards the Croft. Torches were slicing arcs in the night sky. The light rain continued but it wasn't too bad. Dad helped mum up the slippery grass verge on the perimeter of the Croft. Susan had already clambered up the bank shrieking with excitement.

Four men were in a huddle holding rolled up pieces of paper. The men were trying to light the slightly damp material. By this time the local boys had got together, the Guy Fawkes was sitting on the chair with about six fireworks pushed into different places. Just as the men lit the paper, Eddie reached forward and lit two of the fireworks one of the Roman Candles was pointing towards the rear of the chair until eventually they set fire to the seat. The men plunged the burning torches into the pile of debris and slowly the damp pile of debris started to burn; little by little, section by section the damp fire started to catch. The men had previously thrown a few buckets of diesel onto the pile of bonfire material. Every now and then a flash would erupt into the sky.

The rain was silhouetting on the wet cobblestones, the drops of rain were falling heavier now, as the flames lit up the night sky. They danced higher and higher towards the stars, reaching and crackling, bellowing and blazing, smoke billowing, forming clouds. The initial height started to burn away, but the large tree trunk was just getting started.

A group of lads and an old man came onto the Croft, they were pushing and pulling an old three-piece suite; they yelled out for a bit of assistance and three or four people rushed to help them. Eventually the settee and two chairs were bundled onto the burning pile and a mass of sparks climbed into the wet night sky competing with the fireworks for the best Vesuvius look-alike.

The boys were lighting giant rockets; now everyone was watching each other's fireworks. all around the fire parties of people, some families, some groups from neighbouring streets, some that had never been seen before – it didn't matter, everyone was helping and all the community were having a good time.

The weather eased off after half an hour; the large drops had gone and only the slow light drizzle hung around. Even this was easing. Some areas of the fire were taking on a real glow. The mothers had several potatoes already wrapped up in silver foil paper, carefully the ladies placed them in the hot ashes on the edge of the fire. Mrs Brown with her ample proportions sidled round all the men with her ginger cake. The children found it hard to get near to her; she was such an attraction one way or another. Eddie's mum was smashing up treacle toffee and cinder toffee, which the boys were stuffing into their mouths as fast as they could. Mrs Baker had a giant flat tin tray cut into squares of parkin, which the locals were all reaching forward to acquire.

The men produced the odd stone or earthenware pitcher which was passed around as they had a swig and passed it on. A good few of the young women sank a drop or two too and very soon they were all giggling and laughing – a real party atmosphere emerged. More of the women wrapped sausages in silver paper, but sausages were hard to come by, so not too many went in the fire, but certainly the potatoes made up for the lack of meat. Soon most of the smoke-faced bonfire revellers were standing attacking a hot potato with the kids stuffing treacle toffee. Fireworks exploded towards the sky from all the little groups gathered around the flames.

Bonfire celebrations reigned supreme; for another two hours smoke poured from the firework giant Vesuvius spewing magnesium cascaded and crackled spurting white flares and the humble Rip rap did its best to annoy folks as it jumped around in a frenzy. Roman Candles continued to shoot coloured fireballs of kaleidoscopic proportions high into the night air.

The rain subsided; the fire had burned its bulk into a comfortable pile of white ashes, full of embers and glowing hot. At its height the furniture that created the blazing inferno which was evident just after it was ignited but then quickly burned away. Slowly the families drifted off heading for their slumber. All the fireworks were gone. The little gang had saved a box of bangers for the Croft game of making dams from the puddles and then blowing them up with a demon banger.

Such was the busiest night in England for the fire brigade another one was over.

For Andrew and Susan, this was the last bonfire in England they were going to have for a long time. By the time they had said their goodbyes and wandered back to the house, Mrs Baker had the kettle and the cups of tea poured out. Mrs Baker looked around and started laughing,

'You had better go and get some soap and water on your face." Andrew stood looking at his mother, 'you look like you've just come out of a coal miner's convention!'

Andrew and Susan laughed. They said their goodnights and scampered up the stairs to bed. The children took turns in the bathroom cleaning their faces and scrubbing their teeth.

Mr Baker had gone outside to the bonfire to make sure it was correctly attended to; most of the people had left, but a few like-minded locals were just tidying up the debris and running a yard brush around the perimeter. During the night it rained which had the effect of dampening it down, but not putting it out.

Dad's Birthday

Susan dashed down the stairs throwing her arms around her Dad. 'Happy Birthday!' she cried at the top of her voice.

Andrew clattered down the staircase using an upturned tray as a sledge, arriving at the bottom bundling head over heels into the lobby. Father rose from his chair turning in annoyance. 'What on earth are you up to now, you young rascal?'

Andrew beamed, 'Morning Dad, Happy Birthday.' He thrust out his hand to give the token to his father. 'I wrapped it properly Dad.'

Mr Baker extended his weathered tanned hand, 'thank you son,' he said as he took the present from his youngest. He tore the wrapping off and exposed the gift for all to see. Mrs Baker stood in the doorway with a plate full of hard-boiled eggs.

'A giant box of matches; well they will come in very handy, thank you son,' and he reached forward and pushed them safely on the shelf over the hob. Susan crept forward to where Dad was sitting in his big wooden chair. 'I hope you like it Dad,' as she gently pressed the square present into his hand.

'Thank you, my darling,' he spoke in a quiet voice and smiled at her as she looked on. 'A handkerchief,' he waved it around for everyone to see as he took it from the carefully wrapped tissue paper. 'I think I'll keep this for best,' he said as he beamed at his daughter.

Susan's girlfriend had left the house early that morning; she had music lessons to attend to and that meant catching a bus to get there on time.

The Shambles

A letter had arrived from the solicitor. It contained the details of Nannies Last Will and Testament to which Mum had to attend. She found herself with a very small amount of money, just a few pounds, from her pension. She turned to Andrew and Susan and told them they could have ten shillings each to spend on whatever they wanted. Susan decided to save hers.

Andrew's burnt a hole in his pocket. He couldn't wait to go to the fishing shop in Manchester. First he asked his Dad if he could take a fishing rod to Australia. After much discussion it was agreed that provided he carried it and looked after it then this was okay. The next Saturday, Mum took him into town. They climbed the rickety old stairs in the building known as *The Shambles*; a very old Tudor style building, which stood in a square in Manchester.

Andrew told the man of their impending trip to Australia and that he wanted a general-purpose type rod for most fishing.

'Just the thing for you young man,' and he pointed to something expensive.

'I've only got ten shillings to spend mister, and that has to cover everything, rod, reel lines, hooks, floats, everything,' bleated Andrew.

'I see,' said the shopkeeper, 'that's not very much for a shop like this, but we'll see what we can do.'

The man found a fibreglass rod that had been around for a while, quickly he dusted it off with a cloth and matched it together with a wooden, star cross reel. He eventually cobbled together the whole ensemble of kit needed to equip a young man to go fishing properly, a couple of floats, some fishing line, a packet of weights and a packet of fishing hooks size14, which had a nylon line with a loop on one end. Andrew paid his ten shillings and thanked the storekeeper; this was a really good day for the young fishing mad boy.

As he was leaving the shop the storekeeper gave him two spinners, 'that's a present from me,' he said and wished him well.

Farewell to the Toys

The morning was cold; there was frost on the leaves of the privet hedge. The slate entrance was slippery as we stepped out of the door. Mum had wrapped a scarf around Andrew's neck which tucked into my tank top. I'd promised Eddie I'd meet him by the edge of the Croft. I still had two red matches in my pocket. Pucks would always light when rubbed against the local brick. My fingers had automatically delved into my pockets. The matches, together with the Minto toffee had been the first targets.

Andrew marched on, covering the cobbles in no time. Eddie was waiting, blowing warm air into his cupped hands. 'We must be crazy being out in this cold,' he said.

'I know, but you cannot waste a good Saturday morning doing nothing,' Andrew replied.

'Well, what are we going to do? Shall we go to Steve's and see if he's got any pellets for his air gun?' Eddie suggested.

'You remember what his Dad said about taking the gun outside?'

'Yeah,' they both answered simultaneously.

'Billy is coming down at lunchtime from school,' said Andrew.

The boys started to walk down the street. No one had said anything but it was as if a secret hand was guiding them towards the old bombed-out buildings a few streets away. The boys had been told time after time not to go there, because they were dangerous, but they were always an attraction and it was a place where, if they lit a fire, nobody seemed to care. Occasionally a tramp would sleep there. The boys could throw stones and nobody bothered.

This morning the old buildings were looking bleak. The brickwork was tinged with crispy frost and the little bits of glass that remained had patterns we all used to call 'Jack Frost'.

The two boys started throwing stones at the buildings, just to relieve the boredom. They were making for an old air raid shelter previously designated as their 'den'. Eddie pushed open the old green wooden door; no sound came from within. The boys waited for a minute for two to let the strange smells come from the depths. The boys threw two or three half bricks down the concrete steps and waited for a possible response, but none came.

'Come on Eddie.'

Andrew made his way down the steps, pausing after three or four paces to allow his eyes to adjust to the darkness. With a bit of stumbling and tripping, Eddie and Andrew reached a flatter section. Apart from the few half bricks which had been tossed in, the place was quite bare. Two old bunks were still there with a wooden base; the mattress had long since been pilfered. The floor was damp and the air smelt, but it wasn't as cold as the outside temperature. The boys gathered the stones together kicking them into a pile in the middle, sat down and started to tell yarns to each other about what it must have been like with the bombs falling around them.

After a while the boys' eyes become more accustomed to the dim light of the interior. An old Army coat was hanging at the rear of the shelter. The boys approached it. The coat was damp and a bit tatty; it had definitely seen better days. Andrew checked to see if anything was in the pockets, but they were empty; probably the coat had been plundered many times.

While scouting around, Eddie picked up an old army knife from the back of the bunk. It had a black heavy handle, a blade, a spike and a tin opener. It was badly rusted but eventually they got the blade half opened. Now the boys had something to do. 'Let's go to Youngman's and get some oil.' The lads knew that if they went to Stephen Youngman's, the older brother would have some bike oil to clean the old knife.

Just as they were about to depart a shadow crossed the entrance; two other boys could be seen in the silhouette of light. The boys tossed a couple of stones, which seemed to be the common practice, but before the boys could come down the steps, Eddie and Andrew had thrown the half bricks out through the entrance, letting out a roar as they did so and dashed up the stairs shouting at the tops of their voices.

The new visitors turned on their heels and ran as fast as they could. By the time the lads had reached the entrance of the shelter, the newcomers could be seen scampering across the broken down debris. Andrew and Eddie made their way towards Stephen's.

'Great find, Eddie!'

'Yeah, wasn't it? I wonder if it will clean up okay?' he replied.

The boys quickly walked down the streets. The soon found themselves knocking at Stephen's door. Mrs Youngman answered. 'Is Stephen in, Mrs Youngman? Can he come out?'

'He's not up yet,' she replied. 'I'll tell him to meet you on the Croft in half an hour; is that okay, Andrew? Alright then?' She'd answered her own question and withdrew back into the warmth.

The smell of the coke fire had drifted through the air. The boys commented it was a lot warmer in there, than it was out here. They kicked an old bean can down to the Croft, gathering up paper and sticks so they could make a bonfire. Bits of debris still lay around from the bonfire, which was only a couple of weeks previously. Soon the boys had a respectable little fire burning and still had one match left.

The time soon drifted by and Stephen took the lads up the rear of Bradshaw Street to where his brother lived. Eddie showed the rusted up knife and soon it was being expertly manipulated. 'It will take a while to do this properly now, you do realise that?' The brother had spoken and everyone nodded. He soaked the blade in Plusgas and placed it in a Robinson's jar telling the boys to come back in two weeks.

'Two weeks!' chorused Eddie and Andrew, 'that's for ever!'

The boys were bundled unceremoniously out of the back door, while the brother took a large spanner to the Watsonian side-car sitting in the yard.

'Thanks Eddie,' Stephen said as the lads turned to walk down the cobbled back street. The motley collection of boys drifted down the alley. Andrew banged on the back door where he knew the bad tempered black dog was. True to form it threw itself at the back door, barking and jumping, trying to get at the annoying children. They jumped back laughing but they knew it was safe with the back door between them.

The women had started putting washing out along the back entry, despite the cold weather, which showed no signed of letting up. A bookies runner together with a mate in a cloth cap rolling a fag chatted about the action they anticipated in the afternoon.

Andrew climbed over his gate into the backyard; he opened the gate and instantly there was a rush for the 'lavie'. He tapped the perch tank to make sure there was some movement, then dropped a ball of cat food into the water. I suppose the fish had got used to eating many new things now; it had bread a lot and occasionally a cut off of meat, if Andrew got to it before it was cooked. The boys came inside.

'You're not playing in here me laddies,' Mum stated.

'But Mum, the only reason we've come in is because you said I've got to give the rest of my toys away before we go to Australia.'

It's true, she had said that.

'Okay then, but don't make a mess now.' Andrew brought his chemistry set from upstairs and put it on the table. A small train set which ran by clockwork followed; two boats; at least half a dozen board games; a framed picture of the Busby Boys, many of whom died in the Munich air crash; this was just too big – Dad had said it had to go. Just then Billy Davies arrived; he was a friend from school.

The boys chose the toys and sports equipment Andrew was giving away. Billy had the chemistry set and a leather football; the boys split up the other toys and managed to save something for Malcolm who wasn't there.

It was truly a sad day for Andrew giving away his toys which had taken years to get together; the larger items had only recently come into his ownership. The big motor boat he had given to his cousin, John in Lincolnshire.

Billy had given Andrew a *Beano* book which was light to carry as a gesture of friendship. All the boys spent the afternoon playing with the toys and later went out on the jacko skates. Two other lads, Eddie and Stephen had metal skates so they all headed off to the Ford Factory which had a smooth concrete yard. Later on the boys collected Andrew's toys and headed for their respective homes.

At teatime Andrew told his Dad what he had done. 'I hope this old Australia place is worth it,' he said feeling very disgruntled. 'I gave away most of my favourite things today.'

"When you get to Australia we'll get you a few things, which will be more appropriate. You'll see, son. It will be near to your birthday, one month after you get to Oz. By then you'll be settled in and there'll be many different toys and pieces of sports equipment you'll be looking for.' Dad was trying to reassure his son this loss won't be in vain, but Andrew knew his father was a very cautious man when it came to spending money.

Benediction

Later that evening the family walked up the road to church, to the service known as Benediction. It was a popular service and only lasted fifteen minutes. Tonight there was going to be a speaker from Ireland that Mum wanted to listen to. He turned out to be a missionary priest and had a great sense of humour.

Benediction was sung in Latin and the priest and altar boys walked up the main aisle blessing the congregation with holy water. On another occasion he would walk up the aisle and bless everybody with the incense burner which wafted the smoke from frankincense and myrrh. Eventually the church would smell of this fragrance. The whole ritual was very pleasant. The congregation sang their hearts out and at the end of it a feeling of well-being was happily achieved.

Andrew enjoyed it because he saw a couple of girls he liked and later had a chat with some of his mates outside the church. It was not unusual to find that the area immediately by the entrance was blocked off with talking groups of people.

The Winter was starting to grip; it was cold outside and the gathering congregation did not stand about too long. After shaking hands with the priest and wishing everyone well, the Bakers headed down the road, past the eight-foot red brick walls which surrounded the church and away into the fog which was just starting. Andrew gathered his scarf around his neck.

'Cor it's blinking' cold, Dad' his little voice squeaked.

'You just watch where you're going, son, and don't forget to wait at the railings.'

The railings he referred to were at the corner and many cars came around the bend too quickly. Most cars were painted black and so these were harder to see in the dark, even though they had lights on; the fog dimmed the ability to see them. The family together with a dozen others people waited in the void between the rails for the road to clear, then all at once they surged across to the other side, everyone went off at their own pace. Andrew and Susan dashed off together, Susan stopping every few steps to give her little kangaroo hop, a habit she didn't get out of until we left England.

The little family plodded on into the cold, murky night air. The chill was forcing them to walk faster, the lights dimly shining through the fog which seemed to be getting denser by the moment. Soon the Bakers turned down by the familiar street sign saying 'Bradshaw Street'. Andrew and Susan ran on down to their house near the bottom of the street. An old gas light light shone outside; it was cast metal and painted black; the light shone around. Mrs Baker fumbled with her knitted bag and eventually she found the Yale key. The key made a rasping noise as she pushed it into the keep.

The hallway was decorated in dark; brown Lincrusta. Mum pushed the door open and the heat from the grate rushed out. The old Wilton carpet was welcoming to the feet.

Dad placed the coffee pot onto the hot plate while Mum got the four mugs ready with a spoonful of sugar. The radio was switched on and Hancock was just introducing his *Half Hour*.

The Baker family undid their clothing and huddled by the fire. Mother was collecting the gabardine raincoats; Andrew's was dark navy, Susan's was brown, the colour of her school uniform. Mum reached up to the coat hook at the cellar entrance and hung the coats up.

Bob Baker reached forward clasping the hot coffee pot in his hand; the smell permeated the room. It really was a welcoming smell. Andrew had a mug with animals all around the perimeter; he lunged forward and Dad filled the mug with steaming coffee, immediately he moved to the table. Mum was placing a plate full of strawberry jam sandwiches in the middle. A moment later Susan joined him on the other side.

'Did you hear Christian Battersby singing tonight? Wasn't he loud? It was like he was singing by himself,' Susan had commented.

'Yes, he was like a boy inspired,' their mother replied. 'Some say he's going to be a priest.'

'Priest or no priest, he was a right little devil at school as I remember him,' Susan commented.

Half an hour went past and mum caught the attention of the children. 'Come on, boys and girls; time for bed.' The children had heard the same phrase time after time from their mother.

They kissed their Mum. Then Dad chased them up the stairs as normal, catching a leg of the children as they went. Everyone giggled and the children vanished into the bathroom to clean their teeth.

That night Susan whispered to Andrew, 'I'll creep to your bedroom later.'

Although they used to fight like cat and dog they were very close to each other and Susan knew Andrew was feeling down about giving away all his toys Somehow it was as if their parents didn't place any real value on the moment. But because toys were few and far between and only came on birthdays and Christmases, both Andrew and Susan placed enormous value on these items.

Andrew went up the stairs to the attic room, which was his bedroom. A few minutes later Susan crept up to join him. The children placed two stair rods under the light dust cover on Andrew's bed and formed a tent. They had a torch which lit the area once the main light was switched out. The two children chatted and consoled each other on the items which had been given away. Susan had to do the same thing; she lost her big dolls house and several dolls. Mum and Dad had said she could take one, but no more, the little pram she had was given to the church raffle. After a lot of chat and a few tears, the children fell asleep. Eventually Dad came up and carried Susan down to her room and mum tucked Andrew in, removing the stair rods at the same time.

Soon the family was all asleep in bed; the fire had been built up and this was dampened down with tea leaves so it wouldn't burn too quickly. It provided great heat within the old Victorian house.

Snow

A strange brightness filled the room as Andrew awoke on Sunday morning. As he threw his legs over the bed, he searched for his Noddy slippers; they were blue with an illustration of Noddy stitched on the front. His toes wiggled into the void and with a little jump he made his way to the window, at which point he was greeted with whiteness everywhere. During the night it had snowed.

The little boy looked out with awe. As he peered through the window the street's pavement, the garages opposite, the tops of the walls, the edges of the roofs; everything as far as he could see was covered in white crisp snow. Wow! What a day this was going to be.

Andrew dashed downstairs to Mum and Dad's room; they still had the curtains drawn. He bounced onto the bed yelling 'Mum, look outside, the whole place is white. There is snow everywhere! Last night must have been a snowstorm. All the roofs are white; the street is dazzling.'

Susan hearing the commotion came into the room. 'Just look outside, Sue,' cried Andrew, 'it's snow white!'

'Dad, can we make a sledge, Dad – please Dad, can we? We don't normally get proper snow around here.'

Mr Baker agreed to see what wood was available downstairs. He knew the snow would soon melt away, but for the moment there seemed to be enough snow lying on the ground for a day or so.

Mrs Baker was the first up; once her slumber had been disturbed there was no point in lying in bed. She quickly poked the fire and built up the grate, throwing a few bits of wood just to coax it along, before putting the coal and coke on to bring it to life. By the time all the rest of the family were down, the flames were dancing brightly. Andrew dashed for the back door as he opened it snow fell from above and covered him. He squealed with delight and felt its coldness go down his neck. His mother rebuked him.

'Come in here, you little monkey, you'll catch your death of cold.' She caught the back of his Fair Isle jumper and pulled him inside, but not before he'd made a snowball and thrown it over next door's wall. The backyard was two inches deep in crispy snow. Andrew was looking forward to finding his mates, but he also knew he needed a sledge.

The bacon and eggs were placed on the table and Dad had promised to make a sledge if he had the timber, but not until the family had been to church. On Sunday the little group always walked up to church, today was no different.

Andrew and Susan kicked the snow in little flurries as they walked up the road. They had a hard time concentrating on the service. The mass, which took about an hour, concluded and the family quickly found themselves on the way home. The most important thing for Andrew was to make a sledge and play with it on the Croft before the snow vanished.

Eddie came round and his Dad was making a sledge. Stephen's Dad was making a sledge and so Bob Baker was embarrassed into creating an effort of something for his son to play on. He vanished down into the cellar and two hours later Andrew and Dad had cobbled together a fairly heavy but plausible looking sledge. Now the moment of truth came as the duo dragged it towards the Croft.

It was surprising just how many father and son teams were out there, dragging and pushing all sorts of wooden contraptions across the snow.

'I'm too old for this,' wheezed Andrew's father as he pushed both boy and sledge across the slippery snow.

'We'll be al right once we get on the slope,' the happy little boy shrieked.

'Hiya Andrew!' yelled Eddie. The two boys reached the slope at about the same time and both fathers were happy to see their sons career off down the snowy glide. The two men breathed a sigh of relief as they watched their sons bounce over the rutted incline. At the bottom the pair got off and dragged their snowy contraptions back up the hill, only to do it again and again.'

Mr Whitaker lit up a *Craven A*. 'You don't smoke, do you Bob?'

'I used to,' he replied, 'but I gave them up when I realised how much I was spending on cigarettes. I haven't smoked now for two years. We need all the money we can save now for our Australia trip.' Bob was proud of the fact that he was going to Australia and he was happy to tell anyone about it.

Another flurry of snow fell around lunchtime and after dinner the family wrapped up well and went for a walk along 'The Cliffs'. This was an area that went down to the River Irwell. From here there was a big old house in the grounds; somehow it all looked different covered in snow. Everyone was getting tired so the walk didn't last too long and the snow had made the ground wet and boggy.

The following day on the way to school, the boys kicked the snow around and soon the black leather shoes were getting wet. Lots of the children were in the same situation and the school mistress quickly recognised this. Miss Bell, the teacher, made the children remove their shoes; paper was handed to each child and they were told to stuff their shoes with paper and place them under the hot pipes which ran at low level around the classroom. An hour or so later, just before the 'milk break' all the students emptied their shoes, removing the damp paper, and re-stuffing with dry paper. Eventually the shoes were okay to wear. Both inside and out had dried out.

The teacher had given the young students a lesson on why and how they had dried out, because the children had witnessed it happening with their own shoes. A valuable lesson had been learned.

At playtime the children all went into the gymnasium and played on the stilts and climbing frames. "Pop Powell" The gym teacher gave them tennis balls to play with and they could climb the frames in the supervised area.

The 'nit' nurse had arrived and all the children were lined up in the gymnasium. Two nurses had a line each and a teacher called out their names. One by one they came through the door. The teacher ticked their names on the class register and the nurse fumbled through the children's hair. The nurse wore a pair of rubber gloves and several bottles of lotion stood on the table.

Occasionally the nurse would dab a drop of liquid on a child's head and his or her name would be recorded. Sometimes some gentian violet would be put on an impetigo sore. This was bright purple. Several children in any one classroom would have it. Amazingly children got used to seeing it and accepted the purple dye as normal.

The children the nit nurse had identified had letters sent to their parents. This was supposedly so the children didn't get embarrassed, children being very cruel to each other and constantly name-calling. The parents were advised to get hold of a bottle of named medication to wash the children's hair in. If they could not afford it, the doctor would give them an NHS prescription on receipt of a letter from school.

By the time as the children had come out of school at three-thirty, most of the snow had turned into wet slush. The snowmen had melted and only a few wet patches remained. Snow still managed to drip from the roofs of the houses, dark grey tiles had snow, which occasionally slipped from the sloping sides of the pitched roofs. People always warned each other to walk in the middle of the pavement in case the snow dragged loose tiles with it when it slipped.

Malc's Snake goes Missing

On arriving home, the children took off their shoes and placed them by the metal hob to dry. Mum always made the children pack them with paper, just as the teacher had done, to absorb a lot of the moisture and prevent the leather from cracking.

Andrew put on his 'bumpers' – a shoe with a canvas side – and wandered over to the Croft to find his friends unfortunately he only had one pair of leather shoes and he thought himself well-off because several of his contemporaries were still wearing leather clogs.. He came across Malcolm and together they wandered past the shop Andrew had a halfpenny in his pocket. Malc had a penny. As they entered the little emporium the smell of paraffin mixed with ale permeated the air.

'Can I have four bubble gums for a penny?' chimed Malc.

The man in his old brown overall reached for a box and counted our four brightly covered round bubble gums. 'And what can I get you, young man?' he looked at Andrew and said.

'I'll have a halfpenny worth of liquorice wood.'

The man reached into another box and came out with a thin twig of wood. 'Cor that's no good – it's too thin. I've got to have a thick bit mister.'

'You don't get thick bits for a halfpenny, sonny, you know that,' he retorted.

'But the thin bits go too quick, mister.'

'Hang on a minute,' he reached for the box underneath and took out a thick bit.

'I hope this isn't too old,' said Andrew, 'the flavour changes if it's too old you know.'

'I won't sell it to you in a minute' stuttered the old shopkeeper, 'you don't get much for a halfpenny.'

The boys handed over the money and walked back through the bundles of sticks for firewood, mop heads hanging with teacloth, dangling washing lines and the old kerosene pump, which always smelt. Andrew stuck the piece of liquorice wood in his mouth. Malc passed Andrew a bubble gum and put one in his mouth and the other two in his pocket.

The boys wandered up the back entry kicking a tin can until they reached the high street. Large lorries used to trundle up and down Great Cheetham Street; this was a major vehicle route into Manchester. Vehicles of all shapes and sizes drove down to the traffic lights and only there could you cross the road with any degree of safety.

The boys ran over the road looking both ways as they went. They headed for the post office which had a good collection of Dinky and Matchbox toys in its windows. The two lads pushed their noses against the glass and silently played with the boxed effigies in their minds. Andrew had fallen in love with a group of Dinky aeroplanes. There was a Vulcan Bomber, a Star Fighter, a Comet, a Vickers Viking, an Avro York, a Hawker Hunter, a Gloucester Javelin and a Sikorsky Helicopter. Andrew imagined the dogfights he could have with these, even though some of them were passenger planes.

The drizzle started and soon the boys had rain running into their eyes. 'I think it's time to go,' said Andrew, and the two boys turned away from the brightly lit windows making their way down two flights of steps and stood beside the road. The looked both ways allowing the traffic to rumble past en route to the traffic lights. Eventually a gap in the traffic came and the boys dashed across the road looking both ways as they went.

The rain was coming down harder now. Malcolm suggested they went back to his place to play with the snake. He needed a bit of help to get it inside up to his bedroom, where it would be warmer for the winter period.

The boys dried their hair when they entered the house. Mrs Thompson was sitting there in her smock, tied in the middle, a Woodbine burned in the ashtray beside her.

'What are you two young monkeys up to?' she asked suspiciously; she obviously hadn't heard the back door open.

'Just taking my tank up to my bedroom Gran,' called Malc. 'Andy's giving me a hand to carry it. It's too heavy for me.'

Gran grunted and heaved herself slowly from the chair.

'Want a cuppa?' she asked as she made directly to the kettle, which spent most of its lifetime on the hob bubbling away.

The boys heaved and panted with the tank until they reached the bedroom. A white painted chest of drawers awaited the tank which was hastily placed on the top. 'I reckon you'll have to leave the window open Malc, that thing really stinks.'

'Do you think she'll notice, Andy?'

'Cor I would and I don't mind smelly snakes,' replied Andy. 'I tell you what, why don't we take it out, put it in the bath and wash it. Clean out its tank and get rid of all the mess down the toilet. The newspaper we can take downstairs and then it will be nice and clean.'

'Great idea,' Malc agreed. So the boys set about the task at hand. The snake was washed in the bath, then placed on Malc's bed. It seemed sleepy enough and stayed put. The boys took out the paper and washed the rocks. Andy took the dirty paper bed downstairs and placed it in the dustbin. Gran gave him two mugs of tea to take back with him.

Malcolm washed the tank and cleaned the sides. The boys were really pleased with themselves. Malcolm and Andy took the tank back into the bedroom and placed it on the white painted chest of drawers. Andy handed Malc a mug of tea and both boys looked at the bed.

'Where's the snake gone?' They both spoke at the same time. No longer was it coiled up on the bed covers, it had vanished!

'It can't be far away,' said Malc, as Andy dived under the bed.

'I can't see it Malc. Maybe it's under the pillow or the clothes.'

The boys took the sheets and blankets off one by one. They looked under the pillow again. The lads got either end of the bed and lifted the bed out of the way. They checked the two leather suitcases and moved them around. Unfortunately and to no avail, the snake wasn't anywhere to be found.

'Oh my God, Gran will kill me,' cried out Malc.

'But on the good side, Malc, at least it won't smell, 'cos it's been washed,' said Andy.

'Promise you won't tell her, Andy?'

'I promise. Why should I tell her?'

The two boys had another look around and headed downstairs. They took the empty tea mugs with them and placed them in the sink.

Andy pulled his collar up as he slipped out of the door into the night air. Not only was it raining now, but it had gone dark. The cobblestones shone and glistened as the gas street light at the end of the entry shone and mirrored its glittering light of the squared granite cobbled road surface. The Croft looked muddy. Andy decided to walk around to his house. Five minutes later he was entering his back door.

'Where have you been, you young rascal?' Dad asked grumpily from his chair.

'Your dinner is ready in a minute,' Mum called from the kitchen. 'Go and wash your hands now and tell your sister to come down too.'

They all sat around the table. Andrew told the family about Malc's snake going missing. Dad roared with laughter, he thought it was quite a hoot. Mum took the tale differently, 'just think when she finds that slithering snake, it could give her quite a shock. She could have a heart attack. She's not a young woman, you know.'

Susan didn't say much, 'shouldn't be keeping a snake in the house,' was her contribution.

Mum Gets a Job

A delighted Mum waved a letter above her head. 'I've got a little job,' she said. I'll be working at Boots on Saturday from now until Christmas.'

She was delighted. Although this was not a lot of money, it would pay for the Christmas gifts without having to use any of the 'Australia Money'.

Dad was also pleased with this. 'Every little helps,' he said.

The two of them turned to the children. 'You'll have to be good now on Saturday.'

'We will,' cried the children, 'we can stay in bed a bit longer now on Saturday mornings.'

'Alright then, but on your honour now, to look after each other and not do anything naughty.' Mum had spoken.

'When do you start Mum?' asked Andrew.

'This Saturday,' came the reply.

The children looked at the calendar. It was only four weeks to Christmas. This was the last week in November. The children looked at each other; a real sense of anticipation was setting in. Not only was Christmas coming, but exams had to be done in two weeks' time. Christmas presents had to be bought for each other and their parents. Susan and Andrew loved going into Manchester to check out all the Christmas goodies on offer and see the decorations in the streets.

Bob and Celia Baker always permitted the children to choose one present. Anything else the parents chose and gave them, and then of course, there were the gifts from Santa Claus. The children toddled off to bed with plenty on their minds. Dad as usual chased them upstairs and Mum tucked them in and kissed them goodnight.

The next day, at school, the teachers had everyone in the class reading in general preparation for the exams due to take place in the near future.

Saturday Morning

The children rose from their beds and went down to have breakfast with their Mum. Dad had already gone. He always rose early and was out of the door by 6.00 am. Mother placed a pot of tea onto the table and put two cereal bowls in front of the children. Hot porridge was placed in a dish, the contents steaming in the big metal pot. Both children dived in with their spoons. Mum poured the tea into the mugs and the children sprinkled a little sugar over the steaming oats.

Mum took off her pinnie and hung it up in the kitchen, gulping a cup of tea as she did this. She slipped into her navy coat and placed the red beret on her head. 'Bye, bye children, wish me luck.'

The children grabbed her and kissed her on the cheek all in a single movement. Seconds later she was out of the door and walking up the darkened gas lit street to the main road. Typical of the weather, the drizzle started and Celia dashed for the bus stop.

The children washed the dishes and listened to the music on the radio for an hour or so while.

Knock! Knock! The noise resounded along the hallway.

Andrew and Susan both dashed to the front door; a scuffle broke out as to who would open it. Susan got her hand on the brass knob first and opened the door. Andrew poked his head around, 'Can we help you?'

A man stood before them a horse and cart in the background. 'Sarsaparilla, little lady? Your Mum always has some. Or maybe you'd prefer the dandelion and burdock?' he asked in an enquiring tone.

Susan said, 'Sarsaparilla please.'

Andrew said, 'Dandelion and burdock mister.'

'I guess that will be one of each then,' retorted the horse and cart man.

'We've only got enough money for one bottle mister.'

'Well the price is one shilling per bottle, so that will be two shillings.'

Susan ran back up the hallway and took the two-shilling piece from the mantelshelf. She gave it to the man and he placed is in his leather waistcoat. 'Tell you what, my dears, if you've got a couple of old wool jumpers I would give you three pence each. Mind, they've got to be good ones.'

Andrew shouted, 'just wait a minute mister,' and ran inside. He thought for a moment and decided it was going to be hot in Australia and therefore we won't want all the old jumpers.

Vanishing into his parent's room, he found a jumper from Dad's cupboard and one from Mum's. Dashing downstairs he gave these to the man and took two three-penny bits. He said to the man, 'meet me round the back in two minutes. I know where there are two more jumpers.'

The old boy trundled his horse and cart up the side entry. Meanwhile, Andrew had climbed over the wall and got into Mrs Gibson's next door, quick as a flash he'd removed two jumpers from the washing line and climbed over the back door.

He dashed to the side entry where the horse and cart was waiting. The old pony grazed on the Croft grass. The jumpers were still wet because they had just been washed. The old man smiled and gave Andrew a shining sixpence for his efforts.

'Thanks, mate!' he smiled as he put the sixpence in his pocket. Then he remembered, he'd better give Susan her three-penny bit or she might tell Dad. Retracing his steps, he climbed onto the back-door and slipped over the top into his backyard.

'Promise you won't tell Dad now?' he made his sister promise not to mention the jumpers and he slipped her the three-penny bit. Susan was a little hesitant, but as Andrew pointed out, there is a drawer full of jumpers and they will be giving some of them away soon before they go to Australia. Tentatively she agreed.

Just then Malc arrived at the front door.

'You'll never guess. Gran opened her knickers draw and the snake was fast asleep, all curled up. She screamed the place down. I thought she was being murdered or something. Just shows you, don't it, snakes cannot have much sense to sleep in a place like that. I wouldn't!'

The boys laughed. 'I've got to find Eddie and tell him, I'll see you later at the Croft.' With that, Malc ran off.

The children collected their pocket money from the mantelshelf where it had been left. Andrew had the front door key on a piece of string around his neck. He counted his one shilling and three-pence added his jumper money of three-pence and the sixpence from next door then promptly pocketed the cash in his pocket.

Feeling pretty important in a satisfied sort of way he closed the door behind him and headed towards the Croft to find his mates and decide just what Saturday was going to bring.

Susan did something similar; she headed up the street to catch a bus to her friend Christine Egan.

Andrew found Eddie and Malc on the Croft. 'Coming to the shops?' he called out as he approached the lads dabbing in the mud.

'Yeah, why not?' said Eddie looking at Malc.

'I've just got money for the cinema,' said Andrew.

'So have I,' said the other boys.

'That's great! Let's go.' Eddie pulled out a Craven A.

'Where did you get that?'

'My Dad left it lying around and then couldn't remember where he had left it.'

The three lads went to the air raid shelter on their way to the shops. Quickly they lit up the cigarette and passed it round; all of them took a few puffs and passed it on. Eddie delighted his mates by blowing rings and then blowing smoke through them. Malcolm and Andrew did not particularly like smoking and simply puffed the cigarette out of bravado.

Soon the three boys were walking back up the back entry towards the greengrocer 'Radigans',where the owner and his wife seemed to be forever having a "barney" , providing entertainment for the locals passing by, it was the tobacconist next door that the lads were heading for. This shop had many little toys that used caps, little guns and banging bombs, pea-shooters and rubber balls; all of these for sale for just a few pence. Most of them came from China. The boys, for just a few pence, could buy a plastic banger that you fitted caps into and threw on the concrete to make a loud report, a Mars bar and a trip to the cinema on Saturday morning. Such was the spending power of one and three-pence pocket money.

The three boys waited in the queue for the matinee to open; one of the lads had purchased a peashooter, but decided to hold onto it until they got inside, in case the concierge saw it and took it off them. Soon they were filing past the kiosk.

'Six-pence or nine-pence?' asked the young lady behind the glass who had mastered the art of talking as she masticated her chewing her gum.

'Six-pence please,' Andrew spoke to the glass hole, with the bespectacled gum-chewing young woman behind, she pressed the metal tab and a ticket flew up landing on the stainless steel in front of her. One by one the boys filed past; a repetition of the original performance.

They pushed through the dark maroon curtain hanging on polished brass rings and entered the cinema. An usherette stood by the curtained entrance.

She shone the torch at the boys' tickets and then indicated to the lads, 'sit anywhere on the ground floor; don't go up the stairs,' she said this in a mechanised voice, as if she had said it a thousand times before.

The lads trooped in, located the seats not too far from the front but close to where the ice cream lady stood with her tray and always in the centre section so they had a good view.

All the lights in the cinema were on dimmer switches and they were set about halfway, so although it was light enough to see it still wasn't dark. This didn't happen until the adverts came on. The boys sat there watching, waiting as young people filed into the theatre, the place had been a music hall at one point in its career and an old organ was in the music pit at the front just below the screen.

Eddie decided to blow a pea through the peashooter, just to see how far he could get it to go. He chose a place where a group of boys and girls were sitting, about five rows in front. When one of them jumped up clutching his ear, the boys knew they had found a target. They tried hard not to laugh; just then the lights started to go down.

Malc said, 'Fire another pea, now.'

Eddie was quick to oblige and heard the satisfactory yell as another little missile struck home. The lady with the torch walked up and down the steps trying to find the culprit; when she turned her back to walk down the steps, Eddie fired another pea at her. She jumped with shock, the torch spun round and the beam of light flashed backwards and forwards, but to no avail. Darkness had engulfed the cinema.

A large cockerel was fluffing its feathers in a triangle of cinematography, the music bellowed out and Pathé News started talking as soon as the bird had stopped crowing. The newsreel took a few minutes and then came the colourful capers of *Tom and Jerry*, the cartoon enemies. Everyone cheered;

this was always popular.

Next followed *Godzilla,* then *Superman episode 94.* Then a cowboy film. The lights went up at this point and the ice cream lady came round.

Eddie thought she was a girl from his school in her last year, just earning a few bob as a Saturday job. A line of children was in front of her by now and she sold Sun Pat raisins, choc-ices, wafers or Orange Maid lollies. All of these were being advertised on the screen at the same time as she sold them from her wooden tray, slung around her neck. This had a little light shining on the little money tray where she placed the change.

A few moments later another film came on; sometimes it was a cowboy or knights in armour, but the second film was always in colour whereas the first film was in black and white. A couple more peas were fired but the boys didn't want to get thrown out, so they decided not to draw attention to themselves.

The cinema blacked out and the film started. Everybody cheered when the goodies chased the baddies and loads of people shouted when the Indians came on the scene if it was a cowboy film. The film went on for about three-quarters of an hour; this was quickly followed by an episode of the *Z men*, a group who had invaded from outer space and had a proper space ship. This was always an episode which ended up with a major catastrophe, which the week before was impossible to get out of. But on the new episode something always happened to prevent the hero being harmed or maybe he just escaped in time.

The audience filed out fairly orderly, a large crowd of Mums and Dads were waiting at the entrance. This is when the little cap gun etcetera came out and the mini team created their own children's version of the cinema chaos they had just watched. Slowly they moved toward their homes, banging and shooting, firing the little pistols and letting off caps.

The Shoplifter

Half an hour later, they were sitting in their own homes enjoying the fire in the grate, which was building up and starting to throw a little heat into the room. Susan was setting the table for tea. Dad had just come in and placed a kettle on the range next to the grate. The teapot was infusing. Dad sat in his big wooden chair, he pulled out *'The Pink'* and opened it up to see what his football team had done. Then he turned the radio on and got his football coupon out. This was attached to a wooden board and, with a red biro, he marked with a tick the score draws on his coupon. The ritual was the same every Saturday.

Mrs Baker closed the front door behind her. She placed her wet umbrella in the stand, so that it didn't drip on the Lincrusta floor. Slowly she proceeded down the multi-coloured carpet in the centre of the hallway, removing her wet grey coat as she walked towards the open grate.

'Get me a cup of tea, Bob,' she spoke in a matter of fact way while placing her coat over a chair near the fire, she automatically headed for the kitchen.

It wasn't long before the family was sitting down around the wooden table. Susan deposited poached eggs on toast, in front of everyone. She managed to get the family eating more or less at the same time. Mum placed two vanilla slices and some pink fancies on the table for later, when the eggs were finished.

'Listen to this,' she said, 'today we had some real excitement at the shop. At about eleven o'clock this lady, with an old coat and looking really dishevelled, was at my counter. She picked up some Christmas decorations, then a minute or so later, she put them down again. Another lady and gentleman were also standing by the counter.

A moment went by and a middle aged woman came up and spoke to me, "Don't do anything unusual now," she said, "I'm the store detective."'She bent down and pressed a button under the counter. A green light lit up a few yards away, quite high upon the ceiling. It was only minutes later, when two other people approached the counter, I thought poor devil, she looks as if she needs a good meal, never mind about being arrested for shoplifting a few decorations for her family. The little group meandered casually towards the door; loads of people were milling around, you can imagine,' Mum paused and took a gulp of tea.

'Well, as soon as everyone went out of the door, there was this almighty scuffle and moments later the well-dressed couple were frog-marched back into the store. The dishevelled old lady, it turned out, was another store detective and the couple dressed up to the nines, were the shoplifters. I was asked to identify them as the couple that came to the counter. A few moments later, the police came in and I was asked to say what I had seen. Moments later they sent me back to my counter and thanked me for being honest, even though I hadn't seen anything.

'When the lady opened her coat, there were two jumpers and a skirt as well as decorations down the arms. Well,' said Mum, 'you could have knocked me down with a feather

All around the table, Andrew and Susan were aghast. Dad reached for a cake. 'It sounds like you've had quite a day of it then, Celia?'

'I certainly have, Bob,' she replied.

Saturday Night Entertainment

Dad headed downstairs to the cellar to do a bit more stencilling on the boxes and packing cases. Susan and Andrew sat by the fire; Andrew perched on a stool. They all listened to *Journey into Space*.

Before long the familiar rap on the wall came; this was 'Aunty Mina's' signal for Andrew and Susan to go next door and watch the television for an hour. Firstly *Muffin the Mule* came on, then *The Flowerpot Men* and finally the family programme called *In Town Tonight at the London Palladium*.

Aunty Mina opened a glass jar and they could choose three *Quality Street* sweets – this was a real treat for them. When it was finished, Andrew was always shooed of next-door first; Aunty Mina let Susan stay for half an hour longer because she was older. This routine never varied and Andrew always felt hard done by, even though he was grateful to watch some television. When he was inside, he wrapped on the wall to let Mina know he was safe.

Andrew had a cup of tea with his parents while looking at a book on Australia. It wasn't long before he was packed off to bed. Susan came through the door about this time and half an hour later she was heading upstairs.

The Sunday Outing

As usual the early morning routine followed by the procession; breakfast, then Mass, but today was different. Instead of Dad having his snooze after Sunday lunch, he told us he was taking us to Peel Park.

'Can we take a ball?' asked Andrew.

'Of course son, but make it a tennis ball, that will be easy to carry.'

It wasn't long before the family were down at the bus stop and heading for Piccadilly, where they changed buses for one to take them them to Peel Park.

The large metal gateway beckoned and the place heaved with Sunday afternoon trippers, even though the weather was cool and not particularly inviting. Large areas of grass were laid out with many flowerbeds, prepared and awaiting the riot of colour which would ensue in the Spring. Rose beds still had blooms bravely displaying their beauty in the cool climate. Trees lined the way down the tarmac paths.

The family meandered along; Susan and Andrew threw the ball to each other. Dad occasionally joined in.

Celia turned to Bob, 'This has always been one of my favourite parks. I expect they'll have similar places in Australia.'

'I don't know Bob,' said Celia, 'but this will always be my home.'

The family arrived at the bottom of the staircase heading up to the terrace. Gleefully the children strode up the long flights, stopping occasionally to goad their parents. 'Come on, you slowcoaches,' Andrew shouted from the top of the steps.

The Salford City Art Gallery stood proudly, it was like standing on an elevated platform looking out across the parkland with its lawns and tree-lined roads. A bandstand could be partially seen amongst the trees, the strains of a brass band creating a cacophony of sound melting into the green manicured gardens creating serene and relaxing surroundings.

From this lofty place, the city of Salford with its industrial vista stretched out encapsulating the perimeter view with its factories, chimneys belching smoke, waste gases and red brick terraced housing.

The family walked on, they passed the site of the Royal Technical College and wound their way back though the shrubs and trees eventually ending up by the bandstand. The dulcet tones of the instruments drifted on the light winds, the weathercock on the top of the pitched roof indicated North. People huddled together for a short time listening to and enjoying, but nobody stayed long; it was simply too cold.

'At least we'll get some fine weather in Oz,' mumbled Dad.

'Yeah, in a couple of months we'll be surfing at the beach,' chipped in Andrew.

The Bakers headed out of the park, Mum with her feeling of reticence; Dad totally ebullient and enthusiastic. Susan and Andrew simply looking forward to a new adventure before them.

Exam week

Andrew started the week knowing it was full of examinations prior to the break of school for the Christmas holidays. Monday, Tuesday and Wednesday were spent revising and going over reading, writing and arithmetic subjects.

Each child had to read a passage from a book of their choice that had been approved. This was no problem for Andrew as he really enjoyed reading books and treated it with enthusiasm.

Writing was simply a matter of imitating the letters they had been taught; this too went well. Maths was acceptable as long as it was straightforward and consisted of the basic adding, subtraction, multiplying and dividing. But this year, they had started on algebra and that truly was a mystery to him. As it happened it didn't have any consequential effect, as he was heading for a new school on a new continent. Exams at the end of the week came; stressful but uneventful.

Saturday morning found the group of boys playing as usual on the Croft. 'Excuse me boys,' a voice broke the contented air. The lads turned around, all of them caught by surprise. 'Can I have a word please?' A policeman in his uniform loomed over them. 'Can you boys tell me where you were on the night of the fourth of November?' he asked.

'Of course we can,' Eddie was quick with his reply. 'We were all gathering rubbish to burn on the bonfire on the fifth.'

The boys all joined in together now. 'Yes, we got some from up the alley and boxes from Radigan's, cardboard from the tobacconist,' they each contributed something in turn. The policemen asked them if they knew who started the fire at the furniture warehouse.

'We haven't heard anything, Constable. We'd tell you if we had. It was too far away for us to hear. You'll have to check around the flats area; that's closer, but this is too far away.' Malcolm added his contribution.

The policeman looked at them severely. 'It's a good job no one was hurt,' he said as he adjusted his helmet and started to walk away from the Croft, carefully dodging the mud and the little piles left by the visiting dogs.

The boys breathed a sigh of relief. 'Cor that was close,' Stephen said.

'No, not really, they always ask questions, especially when they aren't making much progress. You mark my words, they'll be checking all over the place. The most important thing is, no one must tell anybody what we know.' Malc had spoken. He was used to getting visits from the police; they always asked him where his Dad was. The little group looked on him as the expert in such matters.

Preparing for Australia.

The following day the whole family took a bus into Manchester. Firstly they went to the main line railway station where they had to sit in a large waiting room. Around the walls posters of different parts of England were situated. Andrew and Susan looked at the castles and harbours; some of them had strange sounding names underneath them. Eventually a man came to the hole in the glass.

'Can I help you, Sir?' he smiled cordially.

'Yes,' replied Dad, then promptly called Celia. 'Celia, can you come here a minute?' Mum handled many of the matters associated with talking to people.

She told the man in his railway uniform of their impending trip to Australia and that they needed to see relatives in East Anglia first. She then went through the itinerary. They wanted to go from Manchester to Peterborough and then to Holbeach, near Spalding. It was agreed upon that the second of January 1959 would be the right day and so it was that the arrangements were made.

Andrew and Susan, by this time, had wandered outside, a few yards across the pedestrian walkway on the station. Various sets of large metal concertina gates were pulled backwards and forwards depending on the arrival or departure of the trains. The station sounded like a badly tuned orchestra; all around noise accompanied blasts from whistles and fierce belching steam from the engine. Occasionally an engine would break steam and shriek. Bursts of noisy evaporated water would belch towards the domed ceiling.

As the children watched, the guard on the gate collected tickets and then slammed it closed. On the platform, the uniformed official had placed a whistle in his mouth and blew a blast, the other guard raced up the carriages and turned to the whistle-blower with a wave to signal 'all's well'. The uniformed guard blew his whistle again. The engine driver leaning out of his cab while standing his metal and brass-stepped footplate, waved cheerily at the guard with his oily rag, he watched the signal move from red to green and released the steam valve. Immediately a blast of steam covered the engine in a cloud. The three giant metal wheels raced and skidded for a second before gripping the metal rails and forming the traction to pull the engine and carriages. By this time, the engine fireman was stoking the fire as fast as he could.

The children's parents caught up with them. 'Cor, it's exciting isn't it, Dad?' Andrew's eyes were bright. Susan was covering her ears. They all watched the engine slowly gather speed with billows of smoke and steam puffing from the engine in several different places.

'Only a few more days now and we will all be on a similar train, starting our journey,' said Dad, 'but right now, we have to go and have our inoculations.'

The children's hearts fell. 'I don't like needles and jabs, Dad,' said Andrew. Susan was only just a few steps behind and echoed the same words.

'Tough!' said Dad, 'if you don't have these jabs, you may catch diseases, don't forget, we will be passing through countries where viruses are still present.'

Up until now, Andrew and Susan had enjoyed having a day off school, but now apprehension was setting in.

The drizzle had started as the little group stepped outside the station. In the background the trains could be heard screeching and blowing steam and smoke, but now the sound had mixed with bus diesel engines and cars as they pulled up into the bus stops one after another.

Eventually the little group alighted onto a double-decker bus with an open platform. The conductor rang the bell and slowly the vehicle chugged mechanically into the traffic. The family sat down on the seats, which appeared to have carpet on them, when the 'clippie' came round. Mr Baker asked for two and two halves to the medical centre.

The ticket collector said, 'Right oh, lad, I'll give you a shout in about six stops,' and then swung himself round the curved stairs, vanishing to the upper deck.

Sure enough, it wasn't too long before he tapped Mr Baker on the shoulder, 'second on the left, boss, and its twenty yards on the right.'

Dad thanked him as the little group jumped off the bus and made their way, at a brisk pace, down the road. The uniformed lady on reception welcomed them, 'Good morning, Sir, how can we help you?'

'We've come for inoculations for the migrant passage scheme to Australia.' The form was in Mum's hand and she pressed it forward.

'Is that four of you?' she asked and in the same voice said, 'please take a seat,' and pointed to the row of canvas backed chairs in the cream painted waiting room.

The nurse took the file from the reception lady and vanished behind a door. Susan and Andrew didn't say a lot; somehow this was one of those places where people don't talk and everything is said in whispers. A few minutes passed, the door opened and the nurse came out. 'Mr Baker please.'

Bob Baker vanished behind the door emerging just a few minutes later, a wry smile on his face. 'Nothing to it, just a quick jab and it's over.'

'Mrs Baker,' the nurse called. Once again it was all over in a moment of time. The nurse called the children in and this time Mrs Baker stayed with them.

'Who's first?' asked the doctor. 'It will just feel like a scratch.' Both the doctor and the nurse had little swabs which they rubbed on both arms of Andrew. 'Look at the top of the door,' said the doctor just to distract him. Then both the doctor on one side and the nurse on the other carried out the inoculation and wiped the little pinprick with the swab. True enough, it was over in the blink of an eye.

Susan had her jabs. 'Scratch now,' said the doctor. 'There that wasn't too bad was it children? Are you looking forward to going to Australia?'

The children chorused a loud 'Yes,' and soon they were ushered out into the Manchester drizzle.

Dad herded us a little further down the road and into another office. We all sat in a row and waited. A large Australian flag was hung on the wall and the current Prime Minister was staring out from his official photograph.

'Good day, Mr Baker,' a cheery voice said, the large jovial character bounded forward with his hand out-stretched to shake hands with Bob Baker. He looked at the children and said, 'You do realise that in a few weeks' time you'll be "little cobbers", that's the Australian term for children.'

The children laughed, they'd never heard the word before. Andrew asked, 'does this mean you speak a foreign language?'

The big man laughed, 'Some may say that son, but it's not really true.' He turned his attention to Mr and Mrs Baker, 'And what can we do for you today Bob?'

'We're just here to confirm the sailing date hasn't changed and to confirm the boxes will be collected this week.'

'Follow me folks. We'll just pop into my office and look at the sheets.'

The family followed the jovial migration officer, passed two uniformed men and into an office. He picked up a clipboard and read our names.

'That's right,' he said. 'Tilbury Docks, London, January sixth 1959. Sailing on the S.S. Orion. People will be embarking all day but the queues usually start at eleven o'clock. By two o'clock all the passengers will be on board but as you can imagine, there will always be a few stragglers.'

They all looked at each other, real excitement was building up with the children, but Mum looked at Dad with trepidation and just a hint of a tear forming in her eye. Dad said, 'Thanks for everything. We really do appreciate what you've done.' He pumped the officer's hand up and down asking as he backed away, and the boxes will be collected this week?'

Once again the officer looked at the clipboard, 'Thursday Bob, this week; can't tell you exactly when.' He waved and wished them luck and ushered them out of the door. As he did so, he made one final comment. 'Don't forget Bob, to confirm with Australia House, London, no more than twenty-four hours before your sailing date. The boarding passes will be sent by registered mail with the tickets, itinerary and destination hostel details, or you can collect them by arrangement from this office if you prefer. Okay mate?'

With that he closed the door and the Bakers stepped out once again into the busy street and drizzled atmosphere of Manchester.

'Where to next?' Dad asked the children. 'I know where we are going ... Lyon's Corner House for an iced vanilla slice and a cup of tea.'

The next few days were a pool of activity in the Baker household. It was amazing just how quickly the time flew by from the initial discussions about migrating to Australia.

The piano was crated by a professional company and this was ready to be moved, but not before much discussion between Bob and Celia. Dad had argued that the money could be put to better use than shipping a big old piano all that way. Mum had argued that the piano was the last link with her now deceased family and that a piano in the house where no entertainment was would be a good thing. 'Anyway,' she puffed, 'if the piano doesn't go then I don't go.' Well, that was the end of that conversation. The instrument sat in the hallway awaiting a label to say just where it was going.

The lounge suite was, as Mum was always telling us 'a Berger Suite'. She was very proud of this and very reluctant to get rid of it. She had contacted a house clearance man who had paid her fifty pounds for the contents of the house. He had agreed not to collect the furniture until the day we moved out. Apart from a beautiful carved sideboard with ornate spindles and clawed feet, their items she had given to the St Vincent de Paul Organisation and a pile of old clothes had been given to the orphanage. Dad and I lifted the silver painted boxes into the front parlour where a space had been cleared.

Mum had a list of items going into each box. Susan was wrapping items up and Mum started the packing. Dad and I trundled the mighty packing cases from the cellar, up the stairs, through the dining room and eventually to the parlour.

'Phew this is heavy work and to think at the moment they're still empty!' Andrew had complained as he collapsed on the lid of the box.

Dad said, 'Celia, can you pass that envelope love? The one with the address for the piano to go to. I'll fix it on while we think about it.'

In due course the Scotch tape and the address label was passed over. Labels were affixed, painted and stapled to the piano. No one was taking any chances with the end result of this instrument.

The next few days were a bit sorrowful for the children as they gave away the remainder of their toys and other personal belongings. The large sideboard was collected from the house and the suitcases were packed. Both Susan and Andrew had a case of their own and in it contained whatever we needed for the next six weeks. Each child had been told that they were responsible for their own luggage and no matter what, there were no more clothes until after the boxes arrived in Australia.

The one exception to this was one packing case which had to be marked with a big red cross and a stencilled message 'WANTED ON VOYAGE'. They had been informed that three evenly spaced visits to this box would be permitted while on voyage and had to be arranged with the purser's office.

Thursday came and eventually a lorry turned up. The boxes were pushed and shoved onto the lorry, the driver making sure he had them where he wanted them. Local children, Malc and Eddie, had turned up. Mrs Gorton from next door stood with her hand against the central pillar at the entrance to the houses, now but a memory of the days gone by when the houses each had a metal gate. The collection of locals had gathered to wish the Bakers good luck, many of them not realising that this was only the boxes going away at that moment.

'Well, got to go matey, I've got two more lots to pick up in Salford going on the same ship as you. Best of luck me old' mate,' he waved, passing his courtesies onto whoever was listening.

Everyone gave a cheery wave back; Andrew, Eddie and Malc followed the truck running alongside it until they could no longer keep up as it bounced over the cobblestones. Back in the house, Mum had started to cry. The realisation of what was happening finally dawned on her as she saw the boxes and some of her furniture leaving the house. The place was looking decidedly empty. Dad was placating her and telling all would be alright, not to worry. It was a whole new better life ahead of them.

'I'll just put the kettle on, Bob.' Somehow a cup of tea was often the answer to all the little problems.

Christmas

Christmas Eve was spent wrapping presents and placing them around the artificial tree, which had been retrieved from the loft cubby hole. For as long as we could remember, some decorations were hanging around but with only half of the furniture left in the dining room and lounge, it all looked a little bleak.

Susan and Andrew were chased up the stairs by their father. They cleaned their teeth, said goodnight and waited for their Mum to come and tuck them in.'

'Goodnight Andrew,' she whispered as she lovingly kissed him on the head. 'When you wake it will be Christmas morning. I wonder if Santa will bring anything?'

'Doubt it,' said Andrew, 'he probably thinks that we've gone to Australia.'

The following day, the children woke to find Santa had visited and placed a stocking at the bottom of Andrew's bed. It didn't take him long to start emptying it. First of all there was a hard blue rubber ball. It was followed by a set of jacks and a ball. Next came a metal badge and then a flying bat made out of thin paper on a frame and wound by an elastic band. Andrew tipped the remainder out of the sack and looked at a book of *Treasure Island* with illustrations, six nuts, an orange, an apple and a handful of Quality Street and Roses chocolates. He was delighted and dashed downstairs to see his sister to tell her what he had in his stocking.

Susan sat up in bed. She too had a similar array of goodies and a book *What Katy Did Next*.

The children dashed into their parent's bedroom and jumped on the bed. 'Merry Christmas, Mum! Merry Christmas, Dad!' they chorused. 'When can we go downstairs to see what's around the tree?'

'Now, now, you two. It's only seven o'clock in the morning. Come into bed for a few minutes then we'll all go down together.'

The children snuggled down with their parents and told them of the presents in the stockings that Santa had left. Andrew described his wind up bat and Susan spoke of her new book. After a while, they fell asleep snuggling with their parents. Time drifted by in a peaceful period when everyone was happy and content. The warmth and comfort had comatosed the family.

'Quick everybody! Wake up! We'll be late for church.'

There was a mad scurry for the bathroom and quickly they were all dressed and without even a cup of coffee, rushed up the road towards the church. Long before they got there, the peal of the bells could be heard welcoming them to visit the house of God.

The Christmas sermon was special; the priest told the Nativity story. Later people milled around outside, kissing each other on the cheek and shaking hands. The children told each other what they had had for Christmas. Unfortunately Susan and Andrew still did not know, but they were aware of many gift-wrapped presents under the tree.

The Bakers said goodbye and walked briskly through the dank fog that was forming. Soon a frying pan was on the stove, the bacon was cooking. Coffee was sending a beautiful aroma wafting through the house. Breakfast was simply delightful, even though the Christmas decorations were sparse and the familiarities were substantially absent.

The Christmas tree sat in the corner, presents all around its base. The children begged their parents to allow them to open their presents, 'Only when you have excused yourself from the table,' came Mum's reply.

'Please excuse me,' they said in unison and Mother said with a smile,

'Oh, go on then!'

Quickly they got off their chairs, pushing them back under the table and making a beeline for the presents. With some trepidation, they looked and fingered the presents with their names on trying to work out just what had been purchased for them by their parents. Andrew's gifts were square or oblong, fairly heavy but not bulky. These consisted of several boxed gifts and all individually wrapped.

Susan's gifts were more obvious because of the shape. She got a porcelain figurine lamp for the bedside. Sue like reading at night time, she also got a doll and some new puzzle toys.

When Andrew unwrapped his boxes he found he had the collection of aircraft, Dinky Toys he had seen in the local Post Office window. There was an Avro York and three passenger planes, the twin engine Vickers Viking, the Victor 800 aircraft, a Comet, two military aircraft and a Sikorsky helicopter. Andrew was delighted. Dad had said they would find a way of putting them in the luggage and as they were good quality, he could play with them for many years.

The climax of the day was Christmas Dinner which consisted of roast chicken. This had been sent from Aunt Ettie in Lincolnshire. She sent a bird every Christmas and surrounded it with carefully wrapped Christmas presents. These were always saved until after the Christmas pudding was lit and served with the blue flames spluttering. Andrew and Susan enjoyed this dinner, it was always a fine meal and they were allowed a glass of sherry.

Mum and Dad tried hard, but somehow with half the furniture missing and most of the children's toys missing too, this was turning into a sad occasion. Mum was certainly forlorn and towards the end of the meal she had a little weep.

'I hope you know what you're doing Bob,' she said quietly.

'Don't worry, old girl, you'll be glad of the move when we get there,' he replied affectionately.

Over the next few days, the children played with their friends. They visited several parks in and around Manchester and Salford. Mum took Susan shopping for clothes to wear on the ship. She had discretely kept some of the money from her Christmas job, just so she could take Susan to the January sales in Manchester. Susan was over the moon and chose two dresses and a swimming costume.

Over the next two or three days she visited her friend Christine and another Jean Battersby whose parents ran a corner shop in Salford.

On New Year's Eve the family drank a toast to their life in Australia as yet to come. Dad raised his glass to the Queen and absent friends, a little glistening in the eye was noticed. Dad was thinking of his shipmates who had died during The War in which he served.

That night both the children hid their pocket money under a stone only to find that it had been doubled by 'the fairies; overnight. Mum was full of old customs; she always said 'it's the Irish in me that makes me do it.'

That morning it poured with rain and the children got soaked coming back from Manchester. The evening was spent listening to the radio and drying clothes. They went to bed early; tomorrow they were leaving the house. Sue was a bit upset. Dad had told her he couldn't get her lamp in the bag because it was too big, but luckily when Mum told Mrs Smith this the lady who lived across the road, she bought it off Sue for twelve shillings and six-pence, so Susan was really pleased.

Dad breathed a sigh of relief.

Chapter 3   Friday January 2nd 1959 – Leaving Bradshaw Street

Daybreak came, although the light was having difficulty struggling through the clouds. Rain was pouring out of the heavens, as Mum looked through the back kitchen window.

Next door's ginger tom balanced along the top of the back gate. Dad opened the kitchen door 'Just going to the lav, Celia.'

She didn't really want to know that but anyway it had been said. Dad rushed through the back yard and pushed open the green door of the outside toilet. The walls were white washed and the paper was on a nail hammered into the bricks.

Mum had the tea ready when he got back and by now the family had gathered in the dining room. A pot of tea, four boiled eggs sat in eggcups and a pile of Hovis freshly buttered overflowed the plate. Mum said it felt like the 'Last Supper'.

Dad chided her, 'Don't be silly, love, why must you always think the worst of the situation?'

'It's my home, Bob, and in an hour's time I shall be leaving it forever. Don't you think I'm entitled to feel a bit miserable?'

Mum was upset again, but Dad chipped in, 'In a few days we will be setting sail for a whole new life, that's something to look forward to.'

The children agreed then proceeded to bash the crown of their eggs and pile into the brown bread and butter.

All the suitcases were sitting on the lino floor. The next-door neighbour had the key and was chatting to Mum, getting her final instructions on letting the house clearance man in and where to send the cheque for the remainder of the furniture contents money.

Eventually the taxi arrived. Several of the neighbours had arrived to wish the family a safe journey. Mrs Smith from the house opposite brought out a little brandy to toast the family. Susan and Christine were cuddled in each other's arms saying their farewells. Andrew's mates were each receiving the latest piles of comics and the remaining toys from Andrew.

'Well, come on now, it's time to make a move or we'll be missing the train to Peterborough,' Dad said. The bags safely stacked beside the cab driver, securely encased by a large, wide leather strap.

Andrew with his satchel containing fishing gear from The Shambles' and clutching his fishing rod, sat on the 'dickie' seat in the cab. Mum, Dad and Susan were on the bench seat facing the direction of travel. Everyone waved and just as Mum was about to burst into tears, the heavens opened, the rain poured out of the sky and danced on the glittering cobblestones, with a flurry of waving and people shouting 'goodbye' the little crowd was already dispersing. Within moments the well-known faces were a blur as the taxi gathered speed.

By the time Mum had turned for one last look, she was already out of sight of the door of the house. The wipers of the taxi struggled to move the water beating on the windscreen.

'So you're all off to Australia, are you?' chirped the taxi driver.

'That's about the size of it,' replied Bob. 'It'll be better weather than this, that's for sure.' he quipped.

The cab pulled into the main stream of the traffic and proceeded down Great Cheetham Street. It was hard to believe it was only a few days after Christmas, but true to form, it was cold and wet. The cobblestones sparkled as the rain bounced off them.

All around the cab, shops and businesses were lit up with Christmas lights. It was obvious they were getting closer to the city centre; the main street illuminations could be seen blowing in the wind. The children had seen them several times before when their parents had taken them into Manchester but this year they were trying to make the festive season as low key as possible, because they knew they could not take many presents with them to Australia. Besides, there was no place to pack them and Mr and Mrs Baker were saving all the money for Australia.

The taxi drove through the main street into Piccadilly. The large Christmas tree was covered with lights. The area all around adorned with festive lamps and illuminated figures of fun, even though many of the lights were not switched on. There was still plenty of Christmas paraphernalia blowing on the breeze. The children looked out of the window of the cab as it slowly made its way through the city, carefully avoiding the trams and trolley buses which careered around the Piccadilly area. Soon they were driving up the long ramp to London Road Station.

'Here we are sir,' the cheerful cabbie announced 'and the best of luck Down Under. Wish I was doing the same sometimes, especially when the weather is like this.' He shrugged his shoulders and cast a gaze at the heavens undoing the thick leather belt at the same time.

Carefully the suitcases were placed on the pavement; fortunately this was under the cover of a large overhanging canopy held up with ornate old cast metal piers as part of a much larger framework which vanished into the station. 'Five shillings and six-pence on the clock, guv.'

Dad reluctantly passed over the cab fare and gave him another shilling, this all happened a bit begrudgingly. Dad muttered 'robbing devil' under his cap, which he then doffed in courtesy to the cab driver. No matter how correct the fare was, Bob Baker begrudged paying money for anything. All his life he had worked hard and his interpretation of value for money was not associated with service trades—especially taxi drivers.

In front of the Baker family was a large old fashioned railway station with a high metal domed ceiling, cast iron pillars or a similar metal formed fabrications, with ornate sections supporting massive spans of metal, all permitting the giant dome shaped roof to sprawl in splendour over this vast expanse.

'When was it built, mister?' Andrew looked at the porter with his shiny cap badge. He just looked as if he should know about such things.

'I'm not sure son; Victorian times I think, but I'll tell you what, I'll just ask that Inspector for you – he'll know.'

The porter wandered across and vanished into the Inspector's office; within a moment he was walking back to the young lad and his father.

'Didn't mean to make a fuss sir,' said Bob Baker.

'Not a problem, always pleased to help.' The Inspector leaned forward and engaged Andrew's eye, 'all this building was constructed from the original railway station which was at the end of the line, known as the Manchester and Birmingham Railway Line. This was the terminus and it dated from 1842. Later this fine building was constructed using many of the old features and renamed London Road Station which was in 1880.

'I suppose an interesting way to look at all this, is to think of the alternative prior to the station, which was the horse-drawn carriage and that young fellow, took many hours to go to London, a few days of continuous driving overall.' The Inspector touched his cap, 'will you remember that now?' he asked.

'I'll remember it sir. I'll remember it for a long time and thanks,' said Andrew. 'We're going to Australia now,' and he smiled.

The Inspector wished them well and cheerily waved as he returned to his office. But not before he had offered his assistance in case the Bakers needed any other guidance.

'We're okay thanks, I bought the tickets the other day.'

He indicated which platform to go to and quietly vanished. The porter helped with the bags and showed the way to the waiting carriage. Because of the chat with the inspector, the local spectrum of excitement had gone almost unnoticed; people were to-ing and fro-ing. The group and individuals marching, some walking but all were heading purposefully along the platform.

The platform filled with steam and oil smells, the shrieks of noise pierced the air the rendition of steam screams hit the different pitches of sound as trains either steamed in or engines plied their loads out of the station. All around was tension and excitement in the air; movement, people, spirits, bodies and engines, all with a purpose, some working harder than others.

The Bakers got into their seats and closed the compartment door. Luggage was stowed in the rope slings above the seats. Somehow the family felt protected from the outside hustle and bustle. They relaxed a little, making small talk until they were jolted into the realism that the train had started to move.

Andrew rushed to the centre window and lowered the glass with a large leather strap, provided for the purpose; he stuck his head out, only to have it dragged back in by his father. 'If you don't keep in, you'll get it knocked off!' he said gruffly.

The engine had started to blow huge clouds of steam; very slowly it was gathering speed. Shrill noises pierced the already noisy station. Other trains could be seen how, as the engine moved further along the platform. Puffs of smoke, belches of steam poured out of the massive black engine as steadily it pulled itself over the rails. Still the rain came down.

Glimpses of Christmas festivities could be seen, but the dominant view was the rear of the buildings all around; shiny rail tracks encompassed on all sides by dark, dirty brickwork. Occasionally groups of buddlia devoid of leaves would be growing too close to the track, defying the moving bulks of tonnage not to tear them out of the ground.

The engine gathered speed now, click-clacking over the rails and dragging its load, heading south. The Bakers settled back in their seats and Dad told them, 'We'll get off at Peterborough, then we change trains and go to Spalding where we are going to spend the rest of the holidays and a few days with your cousins, Aunties and Uncles so this ends in a real family Christmas before we go to Australia.'

The statement was met with much approval. Andrew and Susan let out a small, gleeful cheer. They both enjoyed their cousins who were all great to play with.

The children pressed their noses against the glass, their parents chatted about everything and nothing. Rain continued to form rivulets of water dragged along by the speed of the train. Somehow vision became blurred but clear as your eyes looked though the running water, to focus on the outside elements along the track.

Stations came and quickly vanished; many of them just a blur of buildings and large gates. Occasionally the train would pull into local stations to allow passengers to depart from the carriages and then, just as before, the large jolt as the connecting chains took up the slack and then the steady pull as the engine cautiously pulled out of the station, leaving the hustle and bustle of passengers. The busy porters with their trolleys and luggage and always the constant smell of burnt coal, oil and steam, which belched from every orifice of the great engine, filling the station with cumulus type clouds and then dispersing.

Children waved from the bridges. Even though the rain kept coming, it was still exciting to see the engine with its clouds of steam engulfing the cheerful faces and joyful whoops of glee as the engine chuffed under the bridge and headed down the track.

After about an hour, a lady with a trolley packed with sandwiches, biscuits, crisps and two big urns – one containing coffee and one tea. Celia and Bob engaged the tea lady in conversation, while she poured the tea into cardboard-type cups and pointed to the sandwiches.

'Cheese and tomato alright for you luv, or do you prefer ham and cress, or maybe I've got an egg and lettuce, if you prefer?' The tea lady looked directly at the children and waited for an answer.

'I'll have the cheese,' said Andrew.

'Egg for me please,' said Susan.

'Any other two sandwiches my dear, but we would prefer them on brown bread if you've got them,' said Dad.

The lady obliged, bade her farewells and pushed the trolley to the next compartment.

Crewe was the next major station and once again, this proved to be a giant Victorian monolith. Dad told us that this station was the centre of most of the main lines throughout Great Britain like a hub with all the other lines branching out like a wheel.

After the usual to-ing and fro-ing of passengers and their luggage, the Baker family slipped into a stage of dozing; the children watching out of the window while their parents enjoyed forty winks. The train raced down the tracks, passing farms and villages, occasionally the click-clack of the wheels as they raced over the metal points, but always the musical beat of the rails, click-clacking in rhythm as it sped down the line.

It wasn't too long before the mighty engine was pulling into the main station of Peterborough. This was the place where most North to South train passengers changed for their transit to the East of England. With billows of smoke and steam the mighty engine came to a halt at the end of the platform; steam spat out from the release valves near the engine wheels. The driver climbed down from his cab, wiping his brow with a neckerchief of red and white spots. The coal man leaned on the guard rail on the engine door, peering up and down the platform.

Meanwhile Celia, Bob, Susan and Andrew handled their luggage out of the train doors and onto the platform. Andrew was careful to check his satchel around his shoulder and the fishing rod bought for him by his Mother.

'Excuse me,' said Dad to the passing porter, 'can you tell me which platform does the train to Spalding leave from?'

'Yes mate, you go over the bridge and onto the next platform over there,' he pointed through the gap in the carriages of the train they had just alighted from.

'Thank you,' said Dad, doffing his hat. Meanwhile Mum had checked the large moving sign which told everyone that the Spalding train wasn't due for at least half an hour.

Dad started to gather the luggage, when a little voice piped up, 'Can't we go and see the engine pull out of the station?'

'What in heaven's name do you want to do that for? You'd only get covered in soot.' Dad was often grumpy for no good reason.

Mother piped up, 'oh go on Bob, you've got plenty of time.'

Reluctantly Dad held the hands of Andrew and Susan; the children pulled their father down the platform towards the engine. Mrs Baker waited with the luggage and sat on a wooden bench on the platform. Several other people were gathered around the engine; some of them in rain macs with note pads. They had engaged the driver in conversation. Andrew overheard them talking about the configuration of the wheels and the use of the bogeys.

The minutes ticked away. Steam escaped on occasion out of the engine, even when the driver wasn't touching anything. Dad explained that was a release valve when the engine was developing pressure it was not using for its intended purpose.

A shriek of the whistle was heard from down the platform. 'All aboard!' shouted the Guard; he was at the rear carriage holding on to the door. The Stationmaster blew his whistle in acknowledgement to the man in control. The Guard waved his green flag; during these brief moments several doors slammed shut as the porters made sure everything was safe and ready for departure.

The engine driver put up his hand in recognition of the flag waving Stationmaster and the signal at the front of the platform moved to the 'safe to continue' position.

The engineer went to the controls of this mighty steam-snorting machine, a loud screech of high-pitched steam screamed forth in a mighty outburst of power. 'Chuff! Chuff!' then a series of smaller 'chuffs'; the engine erupted like a volcano – steam and smoke billowed from the stack, the wheels skidded, doing wheelies on the track yet the engine stayed in the same place. Then very slowly they gripped and the engine lurched forward, moving slowly but gathering speed.

Susan and Andrew gripped their father; suddenly pleased at his presence and the safety of his touch as he held them both close to him. The train had moved a few feet and the coal tender was now passing. The whole platform was covered in warm steam.

A cheery wave came from the engine driver as the carriages rolled slowly by, leaving the platform behind in a cloud. The click-clack of the steel wheels methodically made their way out of the station and finally the Guard In his van pulled up his window as it passed by the end of the platform, leaving the station onlookers behind.

In the distance the steam engine passed under the large brick constructed bridge, plummeting all and sundry into a massive cumulus-type cloud of steam.

The Bakers looked at each other, gleeful smiles on the children's faces then they burst out laughing. Just as Dad had predicted, they had soot on their faces and once again Dad started to grumble as they all made their way back to the suitcases and Mum sitting on the bench.

'I expect you'll be off to the toilets now to wash your faces,' she was smiling as she said it and chided Dad for being so grumpy. When Dad was out of earshot she turned to the children and said, 'Don't worry about Dad, I expect he's just a bit anxious, after all this is a very big step we're taking.'

Mum pulled out a handkerchief and wet it at the station tap. Quickly she wiped the soot off the children's faces. 'There now, that's better. We'll wait for your father and then carry these bags to the next platform.'

A few moments passed and Dad returned. Together they carried the suitcases and fishing rod to the next platform. Andrew peered between the steel fabrication of the bridge; as they crossed over a small tender was shunting the carriages up and down the line changing tracks en route. It wasn't long before his father called to him to come down.

The family sat and chatted on the bench while waiting for the train to arrive. After a few minutes Mum or Dad would get up and walk down to the large moving sign and look for the latest information.

Before long the engine approached the platform; it was just as smoky and full of steam as the one that had just brought them down from Manchester, but this engine was smaller, with not as many wheels. The carriages were a different layout; people sat opposite one another and appeared to mentally assess each other. Some smoked, some ate and a few made small talk.

The train raced along at a steady speed, click-clacking over the rails, occasionally stopping at stations and on one occasion pulled up beside a large water tank set high up on four steel legs. A large hose was pulled above the boiler and water was dispatched along the water trunk into the engine. Whenever any surplus water hit the engine, large puffs of steam burst into the air. Eventually Dad came to the doorway where the children had been leaning out and watching and told them to come inside.

'Come on now, you two scallywags, you're making the whole carriage cold. Don't forget we're in the middle of Winter. Come on now and close up the window.' Dad had spoken and the children knew he meant it.

A few moments later, the freshly watered steam engine pulled out of the siding and clattered over the tracks to the main line again. Within moments they were on their way heading towards Lincoln station. They passed many other small stations and occasionally stopped to allow a few people to dismount from the carriages; this was very much a rural area and apart from fields and fences, a few animals grazing and small cottages surrounded by a copse of trees, there wasn't a lot of activity. The children spotted a Ferguson tractor pulling a plough; it stood out because of its distinctive grey colour. Dad pointed out that their uncle had a 'Fergie' as they were known.

The seagulls whirled and twisted, dived and coveted any worms being dug up by the plough working hard behind the tractor. The ground turned over and spilt in to the furrow next to it as the machine dragged the blades through the ground.

Many fields were ploughed and furrowed being prepared for the crops to follow. Dad explained that this area was the food basket of England, and provided most of the vegetables for the country. The soil was fertile enough over to provide double the quantity of crops and bulbs which made it expensive agricultural land.

Soon the houses with large gardens came into view. Then the smaller houses lined up in streets, but not the same as Manchester, all these houses had gardens and many of them had chicken sheds and home-grown produce in the dug over areas. Some large silos came into view and a small town was quickly enveloping the passenger train as it steamily cruised into Spalding station.

Once again the Bakers gathered their belongings. They bundled out onto the platform to be met by their two cousins, Valerie and Janice who rushed up to greet the family.

'Hello my duck there, you made it then?' Valerie was the first to speak.

'Gosh it's a long time since we've seen you,' Mum answered, 'is Irene here?' she asked.

Janice replied, 'Yes, she's coming down the platform now, pushing a bike.'

Meanwhile Dad was loading the luggage onto a little porter's trolley he'd acquired from somewhere.

Dad threw his arms around his sister. He hadn't seen her for a long time and now their time together was going to be short.

'Oh Bob, it's lovely to see you, my duck,' she said with affection, she quickly jibed 'that old moustache still tickles!'

She quickly moved on to Celia, How are you, my duck?' she asked. 'Are you keeping well?' The singsong accent was different to anything Andrew and Susan were used to.

Susan, Andrew, Valerie and Janice quickly started talking amongst themselves. Dad had gathered the luggage which was loaded on the trolley.

'Have you got your rod?' Bob quipped to his son. Without waiting for an answer, he moved towards the exit of the station. They all passed through the ticket barrier. The clerk acknowledged Dad who in return doffed his cap.

'Taxi!' Dad hailed the black cab by the kerb. Soon they had loaded up the luggage. Aunty Irene came with them in the cab and the two girls cycled their bicycles behind the cab following as the speed of the vehicle permitted.

It wasn't too far to Holbeach where Dad's sister lived, but en route they passed some really flat cultivated land. The children had never seen fields as flat as the ones they passed through. Occasionally one would be full of glasshouses. Aunt Irene told them these were for early tulips. Later they would be used for lettuce.

The little village came into view, its church spire standing proud and surrounded by trees. Christmas decorations still sparkled in the shop windows, with all the excitement of the trip Susan and Andrew hadn't given much thought to the festive season and now it was over.

The taxi soon pulled up outside Hallgate where the Overson family lived. Uncle Albert had just arrived at the same time. He pushed his bike up the pathway, placed it in the store shed and came back to greet us. He shook hands with Dad and gave Mum a kiss on the cheek.

We all went inside and Aunty Irene put the kettle on. The children were shown to their respective sleeping arrangements, meanwhile the parents chatted surrounded by tea and cakes.

The Christmas tree looked festive and the lights twinkled on and off. Paper chains hung from the ceiling and tinsel dangled from wherever it could be hung. Auntie and Uncle were determined they were going to make this a Christmas we wouldn't forget, even though it was now eight o'clock on the second of January 1959.

The following day, up early, hair brushed and teeth cleaned, Auntie Nellie and Frank her butcher husband picked us up along with Aunt Ettie and we travelled to see their aunt, known as Grandma Tiffin, and Uncle Jack at White House Farm, Stow Bridge. It was quite a long journey as they had to travel to Downham Market, Norfolk

The land en route was very flat, much of it ploughed over awaiting the furrowing and planting in the next few weeks. When we all arrived at the farm, Uncle Jack let Susan and Andrew play on the haystack. The children had a great time jumping from the top of the stack into a pile of hay, climbing back to the top and jumping again.

They went looking for eggs in the barns and were shown how to collect them in a trug, a wooden basket that you place some straw in to prevent the eggs from breaking.

Next Uncle Jack said he had a real treat for the children. He took them over a little brook, then over a stile into a field. There, under a big old oak tree, was the biggest horse Andrew and Susan had ever seen. At first they were frightened to approach it, but then when they saw how friendly it was with their uncle, they got braver. Jack slipped a halter over her neck and in one swift movement he had lifted Susan up onto the Suffolk Punch's back; it stood motionless, then shook its head a little. Andrew was next and landed behind Susan.

'Now just hang on to its mane and grip with your legs, but don't kick it or it may go faster than you want.'

Uncle Jack continued to parade the giant horse around the field. Its back was so broad the children sat on top of it rather than with their legs on the side and it appeared to be a really long way to the ground. Andrew commented on Uncle Jack's bald spot, which he could clearly see from above as he was in such an elevated position. The horse plodded on around the field.

Uncle Jack tossed the reins up to Susan who squealed in terror at the thought of being in charge of such a giant animal. Uncle Jack carried on walking towards the stable and the horse followed. The giant Suffolk plodded into the stable and stood still. Uncle Jack raised his big arms and Susan slid into them, he placed her gently on the ground.

He said to Andrew, 'now young un, slide down its side, I'm here to catch you if you can't make it.' But Andrew, in one fluid movement, slipped off the horse's back more by luck and momentum than by judgement.

Inside the old farmhouse was a massive inglenook fireplace with a kettle set in amongst the burning embers. Their auntie poured them a cup of tea and gave them cakes. Susan and Andrew told of the haystack and chickens and the ride around the field on the horse.

Andrew noticed the piano at the back of the room they were sitting in.

'I bet you've never seen one like that young Andrew,' and Ettie slid onto the stool. She pressed her feet on the pedals and moved them about. The lid was lifted and the keys were moving, music started coming out of it but she was holding onto the stool; only her feet were moving. 'See its magic!' she laughed. Andrew and Susan had never seen anything like it.

'I think it's even more magic than that.'

'Why's that, young un?' Jack asked.

'Well it looks as if it's holding up the house.'

Sure enough, as he pointed to the various piles of books on the top of the piano they were all tucked up tight to the beams of the roof. Everyone laughed.

'It's not really called a piano, Andrew' Ettie said, 'it's a pianola and can be used mechanically with rollers or manually like a piano.'

It soon came time for the family to say goodbye and once again there was a little weeping and kissing. Susan and Andrew didn't mind because they were given half a crown each to spend on the boat. They were delighted and what a fantastic day it had been at the little house on the bank of the River Ouse.

On the way home the children fell asleep. The adults spend the hour or so talking. When they arrived home, they told Valerie and Janice of the great day out they had enjoyed. After tea they played snakes and ladders, then later vanished to bed.

On Sunday the 4 January after breakfast, once again, Uncle Albert collected the Baker family in his Austin Somerset. He took them to see Grandma and Granddad at their little cottage. On arriving the children tripped down the stone staircase and brick entrance through the garden and into the door. Grandma was standing there to greet them. She gave the children a big hug and a kiss, then greeted her son and held on to him tightly for a minute or two. Mum just got a little hug. 'Hello Celia, are you keeping well, my duck?' The ladies chatted for a few moments.

Meanwhile the children went exploring around the gardens. Granddad was at the bottom of the field in the apple orchard and all around his feet were a scattering of hens and a big old rooster.

'This fellow's a Rhode Island Red,' he said pointing at the strutting cockerel, 'and these ladies are White Leghorns. Would you like to help me collect the eggs, my ducks?' It seemed everyone was using this term of endearment.

He showed Andrew and Susan how to slide their hand under the sitting chicken and take the egg off the nest. They had never felt warm eggs before. 'Is it half cooked, Grandpa?' asked Andrew.

'No boy, that's because she's sitting on it,' referring to the chicken, rising in indignation after being disturbed. Soon the trug was full of eggs and Grandpa indicated the trio should go to the cottage. They all walked along the edge of the orchard. 'Mind you don't fall in now, it's very cold this time of year.' He looked and pointed at the dyke running alongside the perimeter of the orchard.

'These drains get quite full in the Winter and at certain time the council open the sluice gates and let the water run out. Get plenty of eels in there if you like fishing,' he said to Andrew, whose interest was suddenly aroused. The little group reached the cottage and went inside.

The floor was made of slabs of slate which was cold to the touch, but Grandma had rugs covering large sections of it. A fire of coal with a big log on it was burning in an old cast iron grate, this was the focal point. Mum and Dad, Grandma and a big old tabby cat sat around the hearth drinking tea or milk. 'Any tea in the pot, me old duck?' he said jovially.

Grandma was already rising, 'Come in and warm yourselves by the fire,' she indicated to the children. 'If you wander round the field with this old devil, you'll catch your death.' Grandma reached out and took the trug from the children. 'Same every day, regular as clockwork, only need a drop of milk and some bread. Got cabbage and kale, neaps and carrots, always plenty of spuds round here and the occasional rooster sits on the plate,' she smiled at the children not wanting to mention how Grandad dispatched them.

They stayed for an hour or so, chatting of the past and the future. Bob had explained that they had to go to see Johnnie, his other brother and his family. Sorrowful goodbyes were said; Granddad and Grandma promised they'd see them at the station on the day they were going to London.

Albert bought the Austin around to the front door and the Bakers filed in. Soon they were motoring along the wintry lanes admiring the flat countryside and commenting on how different all this was to the built-up city they had just come from. It took them about an hour to reach The Wash. Johnnie's house was down a lane bounded on both sides by a spit of land and two 'drains' as they were called in this area. These were quite wide, maybe ten metres, and in the winter when frozen people used to skate up and down them; in the Spring and Summer they were fished for eels.

Locals would catch the fish by tying worms in a knotted hairy string and when the fish swallowed the worms, they were lifted into the boat or the bank and the string was shaken. No hooks were needed or used. When Andrew heard this he was suitably amused and listened intently to his uncle.

Aunty Grace and Uncle Johnnie stood at the cottage entrance and greeted them all with the usual 'Hello my duck, how are you? Are you well then?' They exchanged the usual courtesies and greetings, then Aunty Grace said, 'I've got a roast beef dinner cooking for lunch. Will that be alright?'

Andrew, Susan, and Stephen and Anthony their cousins were already making their way into the back garden. The boys showed their visitors the bank of the dyke where they played. They also had allotments where they grew cabbages, cauliflowers and potatoes. Stephen showed Andrew a radio he had made which fitted into a little cigarette box. Then Anthony produced an air pistol and the children took turns at shooting Airfix models on a washing line and watching them jump every time they were hit.

Soon they were called in for lunch and once again the family enjoyed a dinner cooked with many country grown vegetables, later a dessert of bread and butter pudding was served.

Uncle Albert and Johnnie both smoked cigarettes, and together with Bob, the three brothers went into the garden to discuss their parents. While they were 'chewing the fat' and talking of times gone by, Andrew joined them.

'Uncle Johnnie,' he said, 'Who owns that cottage just up the lane on the dyke?'

'Why?' asked Johnnie, 'do you want to buy it,' he laughed, it's up for sale actually for £100.

Andrew turned to his father, 'Why don't you buy it Dad, then if things don't work out we have a house to return to—in the meantime you can rent it?' The nine year-old boy asked his father.

'Don't be silly boy, we need every penny we've got for Australia,' Dad replied. Somehow the little lad thought what he had said was okay, but then, he was just a little boy.

The wind was starting to blow across the Fen; seagulls whirled in the sky above. A Ferguson tractor could be heard toiling as it pulled its plough through the rich fertile soil. The seagulls dived and landed in the furrows, accepting any nutritious morsel the land was offering to these continuously ravenous, food-devouring birds. One could see for miles across these flatlands, occasionally the skyline would be punctuated by an odd windmill or cottage.

'Go and play for a while,' Dad broke the silence. 'We'll have to be going soon, Albert needs to get us all back and we need to see Aunt Ettie this evening in Holbeach.

Sometime later, the usual round of hugging and kisses took place; everyone promised to write to each other. Stephen gave Andrew a well-used Dinky toy. The family squeezed into the Austin and raced off up the lane with much waving from the windows.

On the way back they called to see their Aunt Ettie and Uncle Reg; he used to drive an old Steamroller for the roads department of the Holbeach Council. He proudly told Andrew of the Invicta emblem on the front of his machine.

They all enjoyed little sandwiches with potted paste and some with home made strawberry jam, these were really delicious. This was followed by cups of tea for the adults and Tizer for the children.

By the time the children eventually went to bed that night they really felt stuffed. Everywhere they had been, their relatives bestowed hospitality on them wishing them well and giving them little amounts of money to spend on the ship.

They went to sleep excited; the following day they were off to London, the start of the last phase before their epic voyage.

Monday 5th January 1959   London

Once again the Baker family got into the taxi. Drizzle slowly turning to sleet. It was cold and very uninviting. Several comments were made regarding the weather. This time Auntie Irene and the family said their goodbyes from Holbeach by the gate of the Overson's house. By the time the taxi left all the ladies were crying. The children waved to each other and Dad making a comment, 'You've not left anything behind, now?' as he brushed his moustache from side to side.

At Spalding station the situation repeated itself; many relatives had turned up to wish Celia, Bob and the children good luck and a happy voyage.

Soon the family were making their way, driven by the mighty engine pulling the carriages towards London Kings Cross station. En route they had some breakfast from the trolley lady and drank cups of tea from a flask which had been given to them. Small talk bounced between the family, each one in turn remembering a poignant moment and needed to resurrect its relevance.

The giant locomotive pulled slowly into Kings Cross. Steam filled the huge enclosed area and the smell of oils and coal lingered in the air, causing your nostrils to twitch like a rabbit. Many other engines were in the station, the carriages that sat neatly behind them were all dressed in different liveries, indicating the counties or areas they predominantly came from or worked in. Even some of these engines were different; one had a pointed front and the funnel was disguised in a sleeker body. This engine, painted blue, had a different wheel arrangement. The more Andrew looked at the different trains, the more he realised there were several different configurations of wheels.

Dad shouted 'come on son, don't gawp at everything. We've got things to do and don't forget your fishing rod.'

He was already loading up the porter's trolley. The Baker family trooped off down the platform, carrying, pulling or pushing items of luggage, everyone heading for the black taxi rank where a snake of people waited with their bags until the allocated taxi pulled up in front of them. During this period Andrew and Susan simply 'people watched' queuing between them where each one was going for their taxi trip. A large shiny black cab pulled up; Dad started to load the luggage.

'Where to, guv?' the cabbie called out of the window. Dad handed him an address; it turned out to be fairly close by. The cabbie was almost reluctant to take them but took pity because of the cases they were carrying. Once seated, the taxi pulled away; getting stuck in traffic almost immediately. Andrew looked round to see great billows of steam puffing out of the railway station roof vents the little clouds dispersing as they gained height and vanished.

The taxi turned at the traffic lights and moved slowly into a formal square with black railings all around it, a few seats were evident and large plane trees grew spread their branches.

'You were right,' said Dad, 'It wasn't far, but at least you knew where you were going.' Dad handed over the two shillings and six-pence, adding another six-pence for the tip.

'I suppose that's for taking you to the right place,' said the sarcastic cabbie.

Dad as usual doffed his cap and said 'Thank you.'

Mum was already knocking at the blue painted door. 'I like the brass knocker,' she said, 'it reminds me of Manchester.' Why she said that we'll never know. Susan and Andrew looked blankly at each other.

A lady appeared at the door. 'Good morning, I presume you are Mr and Mrs Baker and family,' she twiddled her fingers in the direction of the children. Mum acknowledged her. 'Come on in now, I believe you're going to the migrant boat, is that right? spect you know what you're doing; it wouldn't do for me though.'

The landlady was asking and answering her own questions, in fact, almost having a conversation with herself. 'spect you'd like a cup of tea dear?' she pushed open the door of the room on the first floor. 'That'll be a shilling extra for the tea and if you want a bath that will be two bob, that okay luv? Everything costs money these days as you rightly know.'

'Thanks for the tea, I'll pay you when you bring it,' Celia answered in her 'telephone' voice. Dad moaned the second she was out of earshot. 'I'll be glad to get out of here, everything is getting more and more expensive.'

Mum unpacked the essentials for the night's stay. Andrew and Susan shared a bed and that left the double bed. It was only a small room and Dad certainly wasn't giving away money to the likes of this landlady.

The afternoon of Monday 5th January 1959, The Bakers trailed down to the bus stop and caught a bus to Pall Mall where they walked down the Mall to Buckingham Palace. Andrew commented on the pink tarmac; he'd never seen this before. 'I think it's pink because Her Majesty is a queen,' said Susan.

'Don't be daft,' replied Andrew, 'Girls always want things in pink!' This was the little lad's logic; they never did find out the real reason but everyone strolled down the Mall looking at the grand residences, the other Royal dwelling where the Queen mother lived and the house where Princess Margaret spent much of her time.

The children darted in and out of the trees along the Mall and once they were lucky enough to see a detachment of soldiers marching down the Mall to change guards.

Andrew and Susan pressed their noses up against the black metal railings with their ornate designs, the space was large and they could look clearly through into the courtyard. Neither the children or their parents had ever seen anything as large and grand as Buckingham Palace; not only was the parade ground vast, but the property behind stretched as far as you could see through the black railings.

Soldiers marched backwards and forwards stamping their feet and shouting orders, then turning around and marching away. 'Is that the sort of soldier you were?' Andrew asked his dad.

'No son, I was a Royal Marine, we were soldiers on the ships and hit the beaches when the fighting was necessary. These men are guardsmen; they protect the Queen and royal family in peacetime and have fighting duties during the wartime.' Dad thought the explanation was good enough to keep Andrew happy.

Soon the family walked on down by the side of Buckingham Palace and passed 'Petite France' then the ornate front of The Rubens Hotel, crossing roads and into the bus station at Victoria.

The weather had deteriorated and a light snow had started to fall. Andrew was wearing a multi-coloured Fair Isle sweater and his bomber jacket, which he wore just about everywhere. Mr and Mrs Baker had raincoats on and Susan wore her school uniform which had a brown coat. She was probably the warmest. Hence, the Baker family picked up their walking pace and quickly headed for Westminster Cathedral.

Dad popped into a phone booth and called Australia House to confirm they were en route. This done they carried on walking.

The traffic was starting to build up, cars, buses and pedestrians had converged on the corner and everyone seemed determined to dominate the flow. The Bakers crossed the busy road towards a towering red brick building with cream courses intermittently breaking up the brickwork façade. As the family absorbed the magnificent construction they were left in no doubt about the importance which exuded from the structure. They had arrived at

Westminster Cathedral.

The rain continued to pour. Hundreds of people were making their way through the doorways, umbrellas and raincoats were being slipped off as the congregation attempted to make themselves more comfortable. The initial moments consisted of being herded along with the rest of the damp fraternity; slowly and systematically people progressed to their desired point of worship. Mr Baker genuflected and moved into the aisle, followed by Susan, mother and Andrew.

The Bakers took off their macs and raincoats settling in and making themselves more comfortable. The seats they were sitting on were all individual with woven lattice covers. Andrew thought this was unusual and made a comment to his mother, 'I've never seen seats like this in a church it's always been pews made of wood,' he whispered.

'Maybe it's because it's a cathedral and the services are often longer,' she replied to her son.

Andrew seemed satisfied with the answer and continued to peer around. The place of worship was filling up rapidly. It was surprising how many people went to Mass on their way to work or coming home in the evening. The whole place felt a little damp and was quite cool even though there were large radiators around the walls.

The cathedral was huge. The main area, full of seats, broken only by the magnificent structure uniquely carved where the choirboys sat. Slowly the clergy started to filter from a side door. Men and boys some dressed in black and white, some in red and white, filtered their way along the benches all of them carrying hymn books and music sheets. The choir arranged the paperwork in front of them; this was new to Susan and Andrew, who were mesmerized by the activity going on around them.

Suddenly a noise sufficient to wake the dead rang out. The whole cathedral reverberated. The organ had bust into life and the sound dominated every sense in the body. Immediately the whole congregation stood as one. The soggy mass of people reached for their hymn books and after a few opening bars from the organ, the voices of the congregation filled the air with a mist of musical reverence.

The priest emerged with an entourage of religious clothed disciples all dressed in matching chasubles and surplices. Slowly they made their way towards the altar; two brightly clothed men, one carrying a huge brass cross the other swinging an incense burner; little puffs of fragrant smoke escaped from the ornate swinging brass container. Occasionally the priest would reach for this receptacle and hold it upwards swinging it towards the congregation, encouraging it to emit the incense smoke ignited within.

On reaching the altar, the priest took his position, the altar boys fanned out and very slowly and meaningfully he turned to bless the congregation gathered within the cathedral. All this time the congregation was singing their hearts out, even though everyone was soaking wet. It was a moving performance and one this little boy would not forget.

The Mass progressed, following the recognised format. The acknowledged pomp and circumstance the formal prayers, occasionally a member of the congregation would step forward and read from the bible, one of the selected epistles.

Meanwhile not only was Andrew partially absorbing the clerical atmosphere but also having a look around him. He noticed that the first twenty feet of the supporting pillars, or thereabouts, was quite ornate and followed the extension pattern of colours, but above this was course after course of yellow Stock bricks. The more he looked around the massive cathedral, the more he absorbed its construction. The first area of visual impact was colourful and beautifully adorned, the remainder of this massive structure was simple but reverent and basically, honestly constructed.

The blessing of the host followed and soon the congregation filed up to the altar for communion. Hundreds of simply dressed, damp and bedraggled-looking people from all walks of life and all shapes and sizes including the Baker family took their turn and knelt reverently to receive communion from the priest.

Slowly with heads bowed, they walked back to their seats and knelt with dignity, remembering the reason why they were there. The priest returned to the altar and washed then locked away the chalice and its accoutrements. Turning to the congregation he said in Latin, 'The Mass is over go in peace,' he gave his blessing and filed with his entourage and incense burner back to the vestry.

The organ music and choir sang gloriously to God, the cathedral vibrated with majesty and power as the congregation humbly made their way through the main entrance onto the misty damp square at the front of the cathedral.

Humbled but enlightened, the Bakers returned to the Victoria railway station. Somehow each of them appeared quiet; it had been a moving service and flippancy would not have been appropriate.

They returned to the boarding house, had a meal, a walk around the square as the rain had stopped then went to bed, knowing that in the morning they were leaving England forever.

Chapter 4   The voyage

Tuesday 6th January 1959

The Bakers rose early, had their breakfast at the hotel, paid the bill and made their way to the end of the road; suitcases, fishing rod and all their current worldly goods in hand. Eventually a black cab came along; the family filled its interior compartment and suitcases were well and truly strapped to the outside luggage area. They were glad to get inside out of the crisp air.

'Where to boss?' asked the cabbie.

'Victoria station,' replied Dad.

'Going anywhere nice mate? You've got plenty of luggage.' Enquired the inquisitive cabbie.

Dad smiled, 'we are now on our way to get the boat train, which will take us to Tilbury and from there to Australia.' Mr Baker spoke proudly and wanted to be positive.

''Strewth!' said the cabbie, 'so this will be your last trip in a London Cab?' The driver was a little taken aback, but very chatty and the two men talked all the way to Victoria station. Once there, Mr Baker took out the money to pay off the cabbie and gave him a tip. To everyone's surprise the cabbie said, 'You keep it mate, just to wish you good luck. I've never met anyone going to Australia before and you've probably never met a London taxi driver who gave a tip back.' With a cheery wave he was gone.

The Bakers struggled with their luggage until they found a porter to help them with the big suitcases. The large signs which kept tumbling over with a clickety-clack noise, informed them of the platform numbers to various destinations; many were heading for the Kent coast and Sussex, but one stood out in bold letters, 'Boat Train – Tilbury'. The porter with the luggage was already pacing along pushing his leather-filled trolley. Bob Baker showed the tickets to the gate inspector as the little convoy of people passed through.

All the doors of the train were wide open. Little groups of people were standing in huddles but many appeared quite silent. Groups of men stood with a couple of bottles of ale, women kissed and hugged, kids ran around and suitcases, dozens of suitcases, scattered in random chaos, but grouped as if ready for the start of a race. Three-quarters of the way up the platform a small church band was playing music. Andrew could see a fat lady with heaving bosoms pushing air into a euphonium which appeared to be part of her ample countenance.

'Come on then, we'll get on board and get a seat while we can.' Celia boarded the steps of the train. Dad's statement had been an automatic logical gesture; the suitcases were handed up the stairs and for a moment blocked the passage.

'This will do,' Mum spoke to the family and started to lift the suitcases onto the seat. Mr Baker took them and swung them up into the netted luggage rack. The bags all sat like ducks in a row.

'Can we go and explore the train?' asked Andrew.

Susan said, 'Can I come too?'

'Okay, but stay together and the golden rule is don't leave the train,' Dad said sternly.

Mr and Mrs Baker sat down and breathed a sigh of relief. The last few days had been hectic, ensuring that everyone had been seen and the paperwork, bank transfers, tickets and medical documents were all intact. Now they knew they were almost completing the last leg of the step to get on board the ship to Australia.

Fifteen minutes went by, Mr Baker began to wonder where the children were. They hadn't seen them since they left their parents. All of a sudden a loud whistle blew and panic set in, at the station. Frantic relatives started kissing each other, some people leaped on board, grabbing their suitcases as they boarded. Couples hugged and lovers kissed while gushing deluges of tears. Others acted more sedately and quietly but with purpose, and moved from the platform to the carriages.

Mr Baker started to look up the interior corridor for his children. Mrs Baker was leaning out of the window looking up the platform even though she had clearly heard her husband tell the children not to get off the train.

The whistle blew again and this time the remaining passengers acted with a degree of urgency, the platform started to empty as the passengers mounted the steps of the carriage and squeezed along the passageway in the carriages. Doors were pulled open and the Bakers few seats were invaded by leather luggage-carrying people. A couple threw their bags into the netting and two young men squeezed into the remaining seats. Mr Baker was hanging out of the door looking for his children. Mrs Baker was tugging at his jacket in panic.

'Where are the little devils. It's all your fault letting them go by themselves,' she squawked, like a chicken.

The conductor appeared on the platform. Mr Baker caught sight of Andrew at the other end of the carriage. The children were having trouble getting past the people and suitcases. Bob gave a wave to show the children where they were. Susan waved back; she was taller than Andrew.

'Oh, stop moaning Celia, the kids are al right. There are just a lot of people in the corridor, that's all. They'll be here in a moment.' The parents relaxed a little. Soon the guard blew his whistle again and this time a green flag was waved.

Many people stood on the platform waving handkerchiefs, both ladies and gents with floods of tears wept openly. A Scotsman played the bagpipes. The guard waved his flag and blew the whistle. At the end of the platform the little brass band played It's A *Long Way to Tipperary.* The mighty steam blowing engine juddered and a cloud of steam engulfed the platform, a whistle cut the air and slowly the engine pulled the nostalgic, tearful adventurous group of migrants slowly up the line. A few people held onto toilet rolls until the paper was strained and severed; others had coloured paper chains, hundred wept and watched. Others were silent. The powerful locomotive hissed its way slowly along the track and as we passed the little band it was playing *We'll Meet Again* which prompted a chorus in the carriages as people sang the familiar words.

Celia and Susan were crying their eyes out together with the other lady in the compartment. The engine gathered speed. One of the men in the carriage comforted Andrew's mum.

Dad said, 'she'll be al right in a minute mate, thank you,' and he took over the husbandly duty.

The engine rattled over the tracks, occasionally letting off a long blast of steam, combined with an elongated shriek on its whistle proclaiming its dominance on the track.

Soon everyone were chatting to each other. The two main questions were always the same; 'Where do you come from?' and 'What part of Australia are you going to?' Before long even the people in the passageway were taking part amongst the general chatter. The proclamations of 'Where's my passport?' or 'Have you got the tickets?' could be heard.

It wasn't any real length of time before the engine was slowing down, approximately an hour had gone by. The steamy locomotive slowly hissed its way into a large timber shed with platforms and dozens of porters all lined up clutching their trolleys and waiting to pounce on the battered or shiny new suitcases. The trick was to select the size that looked big so that you could get the maximum tip, but ensure it balanced well so as not to release too much exertion.

Andrew had studied a few of these porters and had calculated his own theory on the subject. He also noticed no one seemed to like suitcases stacked together one on top of each other, unless they had secured the verbal contract of one shilling per case. Only then did this become viable.

The Bakers, like every other family and group, had a series of numbers and letters on their labels. These had to be matched with the large numbers and letters hanging from the shed ceiling and this is where the porter earned his few shillings because he knew where in the shed people had to go.

'Me name's Tom, Guv, can I help you with your suitcases?' The question was posed.

Mr Baker, quick as a light bulb; 'How much will that cost then?'

'Well if you don't want me to help Guv, I'll go to the next customer.'

Dad still didn't know the price but decided that if he wasn't to carry the suitcases himself then he had to succumb to the tactic. 'No that's okay Tom, but you must have some idea of the cost.'

'Well it's like this Guv, if your name begins with 'A' then you're right at the far end of the shed. So depending on where you got off the train in relation to your name and number, depends on the distance the porter has to push the trolley. You see, Guv, it's all fairly worked out.'

Bob Baker told him his name and number and let the porter work it out. He didn't really relish trying to find the number and drag the luggage around. It turned out the porter was a bit of a dab hand at this business and soon had all the Baker's luggage stacked neatly fairly close to the front of the queue.

'Five shillings, sir,' said Tom, the porter.

Dad paid up muttering under his breath; he wasn't used to this method of people getting money for next to no work.

'And the best of luck to you in Australia, guv!' Tom vanished into the sea of people moving like a ballet dancer on wheels and searching out his new prey, trying to match numbers to distance in order to extract the best value for the distance and work equation.

The Customs and Excise officers took over at this stage randomly checking luggage and or people as and when they desired, then placing a large "x" in chalk on each case

The day was cold; many people had partially dried off in the train but drizzle still persisted and could be clearly seen through the large doors which lay halfway open. People carried their luggage as they were called and quickly climbed the sloping gangplank walkway, entering into the corn coloured ship at a low level, via the large metal folding doors.

The Bakers saw many families called by the loading staff and soon it was their turn to step out into daylight through the giant doors of the embarkation marshalling shed. Andrew gasped, he'd never seen a ship as big as the RMS Orion.

She sat at the berth like a queen in all her majesty. Her livery was light corn colour for the main body and above the deck her superstructure painted white. The ship had a buff funnel with the foghorn facing forward and high above the deck fluttered the 'Blue Peter' from the top of the masthead. Both Andrew and Susan stood in awe taking in the sight of the gigantic vessel.

'Come on you two, move along now. I want you up the gangplank first and don't drop your fishing rod. You next Celia, hold on to the rail with one hand.' Dad was an old matelot and had climbed many a gangplank.

Susan and Andrew were very excited; things were really starting to happen now. Up until this point, they had heard about the ship and the voyage, but now they were actually climbing the timber walkway to board the vessel.

A steward greeted them at the entrance. Heavy piled carpet led the way to the desk. The steward pointed to a large board with numbers and names and helped us locate the cabin numbers with the appropriate deck. He pointed to the desk and asked us to register our names and cabin numbers so that the ship's company knew we were on board. A steward then helped us to our cabins, carrying two of the heavy suitcases. Everybody was really polite and helpful. The purser and his assistants made sure the desk operation ran smoothly.

Soon we were outside our cabins and Dad gave the steward a tip for carrying the bags. Mum and Susan had one cabin and Andrew and Dad had the other, although the arrangement only lasted for half an hour, when Mum and Dad decided they would take one cabin and Susan and Andrew would take the other.

All the cabins were small with a thin passage running down to a porthole which could be opened, although a sign asked you not to while the vessel was in motion. Once in the cabin Dad had asked in his usual instructive manner, 'Now whatever happens, don't get off the ship. Yes you can go and explore, but make sure you come back down here half an hour before we are due to sail, then we can all go up on deck together and say goodbye to England.'

The prominent statement had not registered with Susan and Andrew; the children spend the next two hours wandering around the ship's passageways and decks. They climbed staircases in the outside wandering from deck to deck. They examined the strange markings on the decks and had a look at the swimming pool, although it was empty. Every now and then the children looked over the railings at the hustle and bustle below; people still continued to come and go, but it was evident that more and more people were walking around the deck, even though it was cold and drizzling. Stacks of green canvas chairs were tied in bundles along the promenade decks. The ship's metal structure now dripped with cold water.

A band played at the end of the pier. People were starting to gather on the decks, leaning over the railings. Andrew and Susan chatted and decided they would go and seek out their parents.

By this time they were familiar with their route back to their allocated cabins; en route they passed many people of all different sizes and shapes, young and old, all struggling and wrestling with luggage.

As they arrived at the cabins, Dad was talking to their steward. 'I want you to look after us now,' he handed the white uniformed young man a five-pound note. 'There'll be another one for you at the end of the voyage if everything is satisfactory.'

The children had never seen Dad hand out money before, especially for 'doing nothing'. They pushed past the pair blocking the doorway and crossed the little cabin to their mother.

'Thought we'd better come back. It must be close to leaving now, people are putting banners and long tapes down to their friends on the quayside.'

Dad came in, 'is it half an hour before sailing already?' The steward is just going to bring us a nice cup of tea, then we'll all go on deck.'

Andrew mused to himself, 'why is it that 'old people' always call it a 'nice cup of tea' and not just a 'cup of tea'?'

Ten minutes later the family pushed open the large double doors; groups of people were huddled over the railings and people hustled and bustled along the decks.

The Bakers made their way aft to the rear of the ship. Many other families had the same idea. Crowds stood, some noisy and shouting to their friends and relatives, others quietly conscious of the voyage ahead and the decision they had made. Celia and Bob, Susan and Andrew huddled together close to the stern rope position, which was on the deck below them. Crew members were gathering at their stations. An officer stood with a walkie-talkie awaiting instructions from senior members of staff. Little teams of sailors scurried around unlocking winches and checking mechanisms. Meanwhile the throngs of people, groups and families, all huddled along the railings. On the quayside people cheered and shouted last minute messages.

From nowhere, came the almighty blast of the foghorn and again and again black smoke was billowing out of the funnel. The loudspeaker called out, 'Would all visitors going ashore make their way to the gangway? This is the final call for all visitors going ashore.'

All the passengers watched as the last stragglers and visitors disembarked. A couple of trades' people ran up the gangway and handed something over. All of a sudden a degree of urgency had motivated the crew. This infectious attitude ran through the passengers. People started waving, more paper tapes, entwined with toilet rolls some folks had thrown to their relatives. The sailors started to untie the gangway and a small derrick assisted in bringing the gangway back into its permanent position. The large metal door was partially closed.

The front bow ropes were slackened off and the one farthest from the bow had already splashed into the water. The order 'cast off forward' was given and other ropes were steadily being winched in. The stern rope was slackened. People cheered and drove themselves into a frenzy. The band played *A Life on the Ocean Waves*. The foghorn blasted out again and suddenly everyone was aware that the ship, although moving slowly, was already ten feet from the quayside.

People shouted and waved, women children, young men and old, all wiped tears from their eyes. The moment had come when we were all leaving England. I looked at Mum and tears were rolling down her cheeks. Somehow

Dad had managed to keep his composure.

It was hardly noticeable, but the stern propellers were churning up the bottom of the dock. The crew were winching in the massive hemp ropes that up until a moment or two ago had tethered this twenty-four thousand tons of steel to the quayside; now the umbilical line was stretching to the point of defiance. The massive hawsers suddenly crashed and splashed into the sea.

The strains of *Auld Lang Syne* were heard the length and breadth of the dock, people cried openly visibly affected by the finality of the ship dragging itself away from the quayside. Eventually the last of the toilet rolls snapped, the paper chains drifted into the sea and already people at the rear of the quayside were starting to drift away. The strains of the band played on, but slowly and steadily the massive transporter of human flesh forced the water apart and throbbed itself through the damp drizzle towards the main body of the Thames.

Ever since the vessel had slipped its moorings the inevitability of the decision to migrate had registered with everyone on the railings. Now the journey had begun.

The cranes all the way along the Thames waved their derricks appearing to acknowledge the large passenger liner, but in reality they were simply unloading visiting cargo vessels. Although most of the wharves were further upstream, the Orion passed a few tankers at anchor as she slowly proceeded downstream under the watchful supervision of the pilot and the guidance of the tugs.

A light mist was rising from the Thames as the air temperature changed and now the vessel was starting to cut a ghostly countenance as the light faded and the mist rolled in. The roads, factories, and wharves on the banks of the Thames were still clearly defined in the twilight. People were retreating from the decks to their cabins; a place of refuge and security for the next few weeks. The Bakers did the same.

They had only been in the cabin about an hour and thirty minutes when the foghorn bellowed out the emergency signal. The cabin staff dashed up and down the aisle banging on the cabin doors instructing everyone to take their life-jackets and go to the muster stations.

Mrs Baker yelled at the children, 'Put your life belts on.'

The children had already taken their life-jackets. Mr Baker had his in his hand and only Mrs Baker was going in circles. Dad raised his voice, grabbed his wife and her life-jacket, looked at the children and said,

'Right altogether, we shall go on deck and get instructions from the officer. Celia, lock the door and give me the key when we are on deck.'

He countered Mum's instruction and told the children to carry their life-jackets upstairs.

With that the Baker family made their way to the Muster Station, ably pointed out by the personnel on deck, who in an attempt to stop the panic, quickly pointed out that this was a drill to show everyone what they must do in the event of a real emergency.

Amazingly enough, the crew had told everyone this would happen after they set sail, but still a large majority of people were panicking and running around like headless chickens. Eventually when they saw others standing in neat orderly lines, they came to their senses. The Bosun in charge quickly told all under his care to relax and await the announcement from the Captain.

Meanwhile people chatted to each other, but the Bosun still kept everyone in line and within the confines of the allocated Muster Station. All of these were numbered and displayed in prominent positions the full length of the deck. Soon the ship's tannoy announced 'This is the Captain speaking,' he went on to tell the assembled passengers that in the event of an emergency this was the type of procedure which would take place. He then welcomed everyone on board and wished them a pleasant voyage.

The daylight had departed; lights were shining up and down the deck and a mist had engulfed the vessel. As the passengers returned to their cabins everyone was quite chirpy. Dad unlocked the cabin door and we all went in and stowed the life jackets back in their respective positions.

'That's the last time we use them,' said Dad and touched wood as he said it.

'How do you know that, Dad?' asked Sue.

'Well, on a voyage like this you are never very far from land. Probably at the worst case maybe three days.'

'Cor, that seems like a long way to me. The Titanic was only a few minutes from the iceberg but people didn't climb onto them,' interjected Andrew.

'Well, it's not going to happen,' said Dad, 'this ship has been carrying passengers for years and we're not going anywhere near icebergs!'

Just then the ships music system started playing *Roast Beef of Old England*. Dad recalled that the steward had told him this was the sign for everyone to head towards the dining room for the evening meal. Without more ado, the Bakers found their allocated dining area. In the hallway large board indicated the table layout. The children found their table number and showed their parents to the seating arrangement.

A chirpy little Cockney, small with black hair greeted them with a big smile and witty remark. 'I look after all the beautiful ladies,' he said, winking at Mum and ushering her to her chair which he held out for her. He winked at Susan, 'and young ones too.'

He told us his name was Mel and we all introduced ourselves. Soon we were joined by other couples, and another group of four too, everyone began chatting and discussing where they had come from and the destination port of their choice.

Mel quickly told us all that although the menu was for our choice of food, the best and fastest food service that evening was the soup, followed by the roast turkey, potatoes and veg. He also told us that because all the tables were being served at the same time, it was advisable to be prompt.

Most at the table took notice of what he said, after all it was his job and he knew the system. Consequently the majority had soup, followed by turkey, but a couple from Wales decided to order something different and it turned out that when we were eating our dessert, they were still on their starters. It was evident that a routine and a system had to be learned and indulged in, depending upon how critical and conscientiously the menu was to be addressed. We all agreed that the food we had all eaten was very good and it was probably true to say that many of the folks who sat down in that dining room had not eaten as well for many a long period.

That evening, after getting changed, Celia and Bob Baker made their way to the lounge for drinks, with some new-found friends, and a dance to the eight piece band. Susan and Andrew went to the cinema on the ship and watched the film *High Noon*. Later that evening they found their parents and sat with an orange squash made by the barman with real soda from a syphon.

As they made their way back to the cabin, they paused for a turn around the deck. The wind was freshening now and the ship was starting to pitch and toss through the foaming sea. A definite movement had set into the vessel as it ploughed through the agitated waves and a fog was slowly enveloping the ship.

'Come on everyone, let's get an early night, then you'll be fine for the morning.' Dad was enjoying this, he was never happier than when he was at sea or in the countryside.

That night at the vessel hurried along, most of the passengers slept soundly, but the constant motion eventually caused Mrs Baker to awaken. She announced to her husband how sick she was feeling. She wasn't to know, but in the cabin next door her daughter Susan was also suffering the nausea known as seasickness.

Wednesday 7<u>th</u> January 1959 – The Bay of Biscay

Both Mrs Baker and Susan were going 'green' and throwing up their last night's meal. They didn't even accept the cup of tea presented by the hospitable steward who gleefully wished them a good morning and informed them that the ship was enjoying a steady swell as it navigated the English Channel.

It wasn't long before the breakfast tune was played and Mr Baker and his son presented themselves at the table. The majority of the passengers had decided to miss breakfast, but not Andrew and Dad.

'Good morning sirs,' greeted the waiter, a little peeved because he was one of the few having to work.

As they sat down they realised that more than half of the tables were empty; a substantial number of passengers were suffering from 'mal du mer'.

They had a hearty bacon and egg breakfast and then returned to see how Mum and Susan were faring. Alas they were both suffering and declined Andrew's offer to explore the ship, which he quickly applied himself to do.

Andrew started on 'D' Deck and one by one he climbed the staircases, pulling himself up the stairs by the beautifully polished wood and brass stair rails, admiring the fixtures and fittings, the huge mirror with a picture of the constellation of Orion etched into the glass. Steadily he absorbed the layout of the steamship that was to be his home for the next four weeks.

On arriving at a new floor, Andrew pushed open the large heavy doors on either the port or starboard side, venturing out to be hit by the battering wind and the salt spray as the ship ploughed its way steadily through the waves.

Sometimes he would walk to the most forward point of the ship's deck and look through the spray watching it crash on the forward deck, far below where he stood. The ship pitched and tossed and simultaneously rocked and rolled, only a few people remained on deck. Several of them hugged the railings and cried 'Huey' releasing the contents of their stomachs to the ever crying, wheeling and diving seagulls, who appeared to be forever following the billowing smokestack as she belched the residue of her giant boilers. The men, women and children to whom this floating embodiment of wood and steel which is now their home clung onto the railings for protection.

The ship ploughed on, the waves crashed and sprayed as she dived up and down, churning as they headed towards the very soul of the Bay of Biscay.

At eleven o'clock, the jingle we all learned to be aware of, signalled the ice cream steward who stopped on each deck in several places. Hordes of children, sick or not, miraculously recovered in time to claim their ice cream. The came in two different colours, white or pink and was made on the ship; it was delicious.

An hour later, *Roast Beef of Old England* signalled the first sitting in the dining halls and those that dared to dine, did so, some with more trepidation than others.

Sometime later Dad appeared with Mum and Susan in tow. They had taken a turn around the deck and although the ship continued her movement, as she headed South, the rhythm was more consistent and people started to get a little more used to the motion. Despite this, only Dad and Andrew ate the lunchtime meal.

'What's tote Dad?' Andrew's enquiring mind had heard people on board discussing the new word, as far as he was concerned.

'Well,' he said, 'it's a form of gambling but in this instance, quite interesting. You see, between a certain given time the ship travels a certain distance and this takes into account the time it spends in port. So the ship's Captain, for a fixed fee of six-pence, is inviting anyone who wants to pay the six-pence to guess the distance the ship has travelled over the given time. The person who gets closets wins the total collection of money.'

'Cor! That's terrific! Can we play tomorrow, Dad?' asked Andrew.

'We'll see, but don't forget we pass through the Bay of Biscay tomorrow,' he said with a question mark in his voice, but he didn't want to dampen the lad's spirits. He knew this was a rough sea and the passage would be slow.

The children explored the library and chose books to read. Andrew selected the *Sea of Adventure* by Enid Blyton. During the course of the day, the children found many new and exciting things to do. Andrew liked playing table tennis and quickly made friends with other boys and girls. Susan attended a fashion show, for clothes to wear in the sun.

The surprising thing was that many more people were settling down to the steady rock and roll of the ship's passage. That evening Mum joined us all for a light meal in the dining room and later went up to the promenade deck and had a dance with Dad, then listened to the band in the bar. Later Dad noticed that the wind was freshening and once again he ushered his family below decks, suggesting an early night.

Dad knew that by the middle of the night the ship would be ploughing through the Bay of Biscay with waves thirty to forty feet depending on the wind. During that night, many folk were sick and a lot spent time up on deck retching over the railings; still the ship ploughed on, diving headlong then defiantly rising and crashing forward.

As dawn broke, Andrew was up on deck. He was sick twice but did not feel that bad. The strange thing was that the excitement of seeing the ship pitching and tossing through the waves made him feel excited. He had never known a feeling like this before. On the horizon he saw the smoke of another vessel and this in itself gave him something to focus on. After a while he saw the cargo ship reaching for the sky, then plunging and crashing through the waves. Somehow he forgot how sick he had felt, mentally absorbed y the ship passing in the opposite direction

'Well here you are young 'un, I've been looking for you everywhere.'

It was Dad. He was always up early, no matter how rough it was. I suppose it was no surprise to find out that both Susan and Mum had decided to miss breakfast again.

After a couple of turns round the deck with Andrew telling his Dad about the cargo ship burying itself through the pounding waves and pushing itself out through the foaming tons of crashing water, they headed off to breakfast together. Once again to be met by the sarcastically humorous remarks from Mel the waiter.

Only a few people turned up for breakfast. In fact, for most of the day the ship looked deserted. Eleven o'clock came and went, which was the cake and coffee time for anyone who felt peckish, known affectionately as 'elevenses'. Shortly afterwards ice cream was available for anyone who wanted it. The tote was announced for anyone who had a desire to gamble.

Andrew and his new friends played deck quoits on the upper deck, venturing onto deck tennis whereby a hoop was thrown across a net to be caught and returned to the opposite party. Table tennis was also a firm favourite and most days saw a frog racing competition on 'D' Deck, near the stage. Here the adults would all gamble on the outcome of the wooden frogs, who hopped along and slid on a string as they were jolted by their 'riders' at the other end of the deck.

Activities such as these were broken only by lunch. Some then took a stroll or run around the deck, others went to the afternoon cinema or to bingo. At teatime some cakes and tea were served and an hour later the evening meal was served. Activities such as singing or dancing in the theatre took place in the evening and later a pianist played in the bar.

This was the basic routine of a day at sea on the RMS Orion. There was no doubt that the ship's personnel put a lot of time and effort into making the time pass as actively and pleasantly as possible for the duration of the voyage.

Meanwhile, the ship pitched and tossed its way through the waves and only a limited number of voyagers took part in any of the activities on offer. Surprisingly that evening the weather calmed down and the ship progressed through a heavy swell which it coped with, without problem.

That night everyone slept well to awaken the next day to a relatively calm sea. All of a sudden hundreds of people came on deck, the dining rooms were buzzing; seats were occupied and no one complained of seasickness, although there were a few claiming they would get off at the next stop and go home. But most people laughed at them and told them not to be so daft.

By eleven o'clock the sun was shining through. The sea was just a little choppy but deck activities were taking place. Deckchairs were laid out and ladies put on swimsuits. The ice cream man was inundated with children and adults. All the deck games were being tried out. The visit to the bridge was very popular when the officers showed the ladies and gentlemen how the vessel was manoeuvred and the complexities of the radar system and so forth.

Today was undoubtedly the first day of relaxation for most of the migrants. That evening the dance floor was full. All the ladies wore long dresses and everyone looked glamorous. Some of the ladies made comments like, 'She's wearing a dress that looked like my curtains.'

'Probably is,' came the reply and they giggled together.

However, everyone enjoyed themselves. Andrew and Susan caught up with their parents about eight o'clock and had an orange juice and Dad enjoyed a gin and tonic. Mum sat chatting to other ladies, a small sherry delicately poised between her fingers. The conversation soon came round to tomorrow's arrival at Gibraltar. Everyone seemed to think it was a good idea to disembark and have a tour around 'The Rock' as it was affectionately known. The Purser had given a little talk after dinner about the history of Gibraltar and many people had signed up to go on the guided tour. However Mum and Dad had said this was not in their budget and we would have a look around ourselves.

Andrew and Susan went to bed really excited. Susan had enjoyed the day without the ship rocking and rolling and she looked forward to tomorrow.

The children went to bed with real smiles on their faces.

Saturday 10th January – Gibraltar

Andrew awoke to the sound of the machinery—clanking, whining, whizzing, and grinding. He rose cautiously from the top bunk, feeling for the ladder at the side of his wooden bed and stealthily slipped down the narrow passageway adjacent to his bunk to peep out of the porthole, he had pushed open.

His eyes opened in awe, hardly daring to take in the miscellaneous wonders that presented themselves. It was as if a kaleidoscope of completely different aspects were all happening at once and directly in front of him.

The ship had dropped anchor half a mile from the quayside. The backdrop of the giant rock rose in all its glory out of the water and seemed to go on forever, climbing higher and higher into the night sky. The myriad of multi-coloured lights ran in strips up the rock, blending and intertwining until they ran into the blackness. Occasionally the lights could be seen marking out the route to the summit, clearly defined by a mast with a bright red light.

The cacophony of sound dictated the sleep pattern of most of the residents of this giant floating hotel. Andrew woke Susan and together they went upstairs to gaze at the comings and goings of the barges and tenders unloading cargo and passengers alike. Occasionally a small boat would push against the gangway and only then would the swell be evident as the boat rose and fell in sequence with the waves. Passengers disembarking would launch themselves forward to be caught by sailors dressed in their whites. The change to white uniforms indicated the change of the climate and where better to do it than the entrance to the Mediterranean.

An hour or so passed by with the children leaning over the railings absorbing the new Mediterranean scenery. Eventually their mother and father caught up with them and in an excited verbal transmittal, informed their Mum and Dad of what they had witnessed that morning.

The breakfast time beckoned them to the morning repast and this was one of the few times to date that the Bakers had breakfast together. At the table Dad informed the family that at ten o'clock they were all to be at the departure station because they were going ashore on the tender for a trip round *'The Rock'*.

The Baker family gathered with hundreds of other excited little groups. The Purser, in his crisp white uniform, and many staff gave advice and instructions; steadily the passengers made their way down the swaying gangway and onto the little ferries lining up to collect them. A sailor reached out and held Mum's shoulder and arm, helping to steady her as she crossed to the bobbing vessel. One by one the family embarked and sat down; the motion of the little boat was more obvious now, but not unpleasant, more like a fairground ride. Eventually the skipper had his group and shouted to his crew. 'Cast off forward,' and looking behind him, 'cast off aft.'

The sailors flicked their painter. Andrew had learned this was the name for the short rope wrapped around the bollard which tethered it to the ship. The engine chugged louder and black diesel smoke belched out of the little funnel. The vessel pitched and tossed its way towards the huge rock magnificently rising out of the busy harbour. All around various marine craft jostled for position while carrying out their lawful business. The little ferry pushed its way through the choppy waters to the harbour steps. Andrew could see another ferry making its way adjacently alongside simultaneously from the mighty passenger ship from which they had just disembarked.

As the steamer moved away, chugging its way towards land, the Orion appeared to be incredibly big. It was a hub of activity. The derricks were swinging large rope cargo nets full of luggage; containers were vanishing down into the open holds; sections of the starboard side had opened up and barges were loading goods into the awaiting entrance. The whole combined scene was one of high activity and enterprise.

Soon the ferry master was tying up and folks all clambered for the concrete steps leading to the quayside. Mum and Dad quickly gathered their charges and ushered them along the massive concrete and granite sets, which had stood solidly for hundreds of years, supporting the unceremonious walkway they were all ambling along.

'Want a tour of the Rock, governor?' a cockney sounding man had accosted Dad's arm.

'No thanks,' Dad muttered.

Seconds later a Spanish guide had accosted Mum 'You want me to show you round, beautiful lady?'

'Oh Bob, we do need someone to show us the place.'

'No thanks, mate,' Dad had bluntly shunned the Spaniard.

He turned to Mum, 'The place is only a few square miles. By the time you walk up the hill to the marine barracks that's as far as you're allowed to go. We can catch a bus up to the top of The Rock and see the monkeys and that's all they are going to take you to see.' Dad had put his foot down.

The Bakers ambled off up the high street leaving the buses, taxis and guides plying their wares, looking for fresh customers. Tobacconists selling many English, Spanish and French cigarettes in packets, cartons of 200 or larger, a hundred and one types of lighters, glittering Spanish dolls in Flamenco dresses, bull fighter dolls dressed in Picador or Matador tunics were hanging from the doorways. Hundreds of bottles of alcohol in all shapes and sizes adorned the windows and promised to be cheaper than England or practically anywhere in the world, were being offered enticingly.

In a corner of the dockyard a seedy bar door was open and two ladies with bright dresses and plunging necklines asked the passing sailors 'If they saw anything they might fancy, come inside boys'. Dad quickly pulled

Andrew a little faster up the street to show them the shops with watches and electronic devices.

Restaurants, bodegas and café bars adorned the pavements and all around Spaniards, Arabs and tourists mingled or sat down in the shaded areas to enjoy the ambiance created by the many colourful characters bustling up and down the small thoroughfare.

The Bakers enjoyed the busy street but soon the shops became very repetitious. An hour later Dad proudly stood in front of the barrack gateway. A Marine on duty proudly stood to attention by his sentry box; a few old local built houses stood whitewashed and in sympathy with the local barrack details. Dad almost bristled at the sight of the Royal Marine in full uniform.

Mum asked, 'Can we go and see the apes on the top of the Rock now.'

Reluctantly Dad pulled himself away from the rigid stance of the military man; it was only a few years beforehand that he had been a Royal Marine.

'I think we can get a bus from the square,' he said and the family moved towards the bus stop which had been pointed out to them.

They didn't have long to wait; dozens of tourists, many of them they recognised from the ship, were all doing the same thing. The old bus chugged its way up the hill, groaning at every gear change. The driver almost reluctantly coaxing the vintage machine round the bends to the elevated destination near to the peak of the rock.

All around people were gathered around the baboons who anxiously snatched any morsel recognisable as food. Vendors sold bags of nuts and bananas to feed to the animals and sleazy professional photographers took photos at extortionate prices and promised to have them developed in time for the ship's departure later that day.

The Bakers stayed for a while taking in the beautiful view and peering in turn through the telescope at the mountains of Morocco in the distance. From this height they could see the beautiful panorama of the coastlines stretching out in front of them, ships sailing into the Mediterranean and ferries going between Gibraltar and the African ports. Susan took photos with her Box Brownie.

The bus gave a couple of honks of its horn. Dad said, 'Come on, we'll catch this one back to town and have a bite to eat.' They all scrambled back onto the bus, together with another fifty people doing the same thing.

A baboon sat on the bonnet of the bus, much to the annoyance of the driver. It made a grab at the windscreen wipers; the driver revved his engine and the baboon leaped on another bus parked next to the one we all sat on. Half of the people laughed, but the driver shook his fist in anger at the monkey. A few moments later, the old bus was trundling its way back down the hillside road, gears churning and dust rising behind us. The passengers were all taken by the view from The Rock. The shores and hillside of the African coastline cut a contour between the dark blue sea and the sky above.

Soon the bus entered the town area and the built up dwellings which clung to The Rock as we crashed from one gear change to the next. The rickety old bus pulled into the square and quickly discharged its passengers.

'How about a sandwich and a drink?' suggested Dad. The little group meandered through the side street with its colour awnings, eventually being enticed by the smell of coffee floating on the light air and drifting in the direction of their nostrils.

'That coffee smells like yours, Mum,' said Susan. As she peered into the shop window a large brown machine was turning beans and flames could be seen under the metal plate. Every so often a hand would appear and push the beans onto another rack, then scoop them onto a grinder.

The family found a place to sit and promptly asked the waiter for some coffee and a plate of meatballs; Mr Baker had seen them on another table and fancied they would make a good snack. He suddenly bellowed at the inoffensive waiter, 'and forks please, with a jug of water and glasses.'

The waiter suddenly woke up; previously it almost appeared that he was operating on a semi-conscious automatic mode. The repast quickly appeared on a large copper tray. The meatballs had been placed on a bed of couscous surrounded by tomatoes and piled in the middle like a group of cannon balls. Plates were handed to each person, with a fork. The waiter duly came with the water and explained that the coffee would be served in five minutes. The little group simultaneously said, 'Thank you' and Mother at once set about dividing the spoils of the tray.

The sun beat down on the street in front of them, the Bakers delighted that they had chosen a place in the shade. Many passers-by were walking up and down the street carrying out their daily chores.

'It's an interesting hobby,' said Celia to her husband.

'What is?' he replied.

'People-watching, Bob. Just looking at the way people dress and carry on their business on a day-to-day way. Everyone is dressed differently. Some are shopping. Some are arguing. Others are obviously in love.

'And 'we',' said Andrew, 'are on our way to Australia.'

'That's right son, and now all we have to do is pay the bill and we'll make our way slowly back to the ship.'

And so without much more fuss, the family meandered slowly looking at shops and eventually buying a small set of castanets as a souvenir. The party made its way back to the massive stone quayside, with its steps leading down to the tender bobbing about at the mooring.

Eventually enough passengers arrived and signed the register to say they were returning and the little craft rocked and bounced its way through the waves towards the giant ocean liner moored dominantly out in the bay. The family scrambled its way up the gangway into the large hold door and onto the welcome area. A customs man beckoned them through. This appeared to be a formality more than a duty but it certainly didn't concern the Baker family.

Dad gave the children a stern warning, 'Now whatever happens, don't be tempted to get off the ship again. Don't forget we'll meet for dinner. Come down and wash your hands, okay?'

The children full of excitement vanished up the corridors and onto the decks to find their friends. People were lying around sun bathing, some looking over the rails checking the coastline with binoculars, others hovered with a drink, but a real holiday atmosphere had overtaken the boat and its crowd of migrants. Andrew thought philosophically, it must be something to do with the sun.

The children found their friends and everyone chatted and expounded the day's comings and goings. Several hours passed by and as the sun started to go down, a large blast from the foghorn bellowed out followed by a further three blasts. The ship's flags were changed and smoke started coming from the funnel.

Suddenly, what at first had been a lazy drift of smoke turned into a mighty blow, poured through some hidden pipework and thrust itself into the atmosphere. The flags beckoned and unfurled telling the naval fraternity of the new intentions; several blasts from the giant ship's foghorn dominated the crying seagulls' calls and the general cacophony of sounds. The noise was so poignant, that for no apparent reason a tear started to form in Andrew's eye; a feeling so deep it defied the logic of normality.

The clang of the links of the anchor chain could be heard. The sailors scurried back and forth on the lower fore deck and the stern. The uniformed officer stood on the bridge deck quietly speaking into the communications system, occasionally he could be seen turning to the left and then behind him to check that all was as directed.

The engines had started to vibrate and quickly we were all to learn that this was the propeller slowly engaging in motion against the momentum of the sea. Slowly, but very slowly, the giant ship was slipping through the dark blue liquid of the Mediterranean Sea. During the excitement of the ship's departure we had failed to notice that the sun had slipped away and the vessel was now moving through the twilight, leaving behind the giant rock with its myriad of twinkling lights.

It wasn't long before the dining signature tune *Roast Beef of Old England* came, beckoning its hungry guests to the dining halls. Remembering their father's wishes to make sure they washed their hands, the children duly called into the ablutions to perform this task.

On arrival at their table the waiter was already engaging his gastronomic wards with the latest culinary delights available on the menu. Because the ship had been moored near Spain, the main dish—Chef's special, was paella, but as was the custom several other more British dishes were always available. The talk around the table was, as one would expect, the recently completed trip to The Rock and who did what and how much did it cost.

The Baker family later went on deck. The ship was by now steaming along, a large fluorescent wake broke the low wave as she plied her way to the next destination. The plan of the voyage informed us that we would pass by Sardinia around mid-morning the following day.

We all ended up in the main lounge. Mum and Dad had joined new friends the Williams family; they all got drinks then settled down to play a game of bingo. A little later, the families moved along to the dance floor and waltzed the evening away to the five-man combo.

As we all drifted down to our cabins it was noticeable that the weather was once again freshening, that night we fell asleep with a little trepidation as to how the weather was going to develop.

Sunday 11th January 1959 – Naples

The Bakers went to breakfast although it has to be said Celia was not too keen. During the night the weather had worsened and although it was not too rough, the vessel was definitely lurching.

After breakfast, the family attended the service on board, during this Susan suddenly felt ill due to the motion of the ship. She headed as rapidly as she could to feed the seagulls a warm meal from the railings of the ship. On this occasion she wasn't the only one, and to top it all it started to rain.

The tote was announced and the position of the ship was disclosed on the big chart outside the Purser's office. Lunchtime saw only a small number of passengers tucking into the Sunday roast, but true to form, two of them were Robert and his son Andrew.

Shortly after lunch the ship steamed past Sardinia, which sat like a giant rock in the middle of the ocean shrouded in rain.

During the night we steamed on to Naples, arriving there very early in the morning of 12th January. By seven o'clock, passengers were disembarking.

We all ate a healthy breakfast, then made our way to the disembarkation lounge having first called at the Purser's office to exchange some sterling currency for Italian lire. As this was the first currency Andrew and Susan had experienced they were very surprised to see million lire notes and laughingly enjoyed being millionaires for a while.

The ship was berthed at a quayside with a large warehouse adjacent. All the disembarking passengers went into the warehouse where they were met by customs officials behind desks; all of them asking 'if they had anything to declare'. After this theatrical performance where everyone said 'no', the passengers all meandered out into a large piazza with hundreds of taxi cabs around the perimeter and horse-drawn carriages awaiting to whisk people away.

The place was very crowded and already it was starting to get warm. The sun was rising and throwing long shadows between the buildings on the outside of the square. Men wearing armbands were pestering many of the visitors coming from the customs building. 'We are official guides from Naples, only we are permitted to escort you round our beautiful town and we do this as a service,' the guide offered.

Celia, Bob and the children listened to this. However, they were still very cautious and decided to walk on a little further. The moment came when one of these 'official guides' eventually hung onto mother's arm. 'Beautiful lady, would you not like to be shown the wonderful sights of Naples?'

Dad a pace or two in front spun round to see his wife being accosted by the Italian with the armband, 'Oi, take your hand off my wife!'

'Do not be alarmed, señora, I only want to show you the place where my people say "see Naples and die". You remember it was in a film? I can show you a private angora factory and a place where the finest cameos in the world are made.' This rather seedy fellow reeked of garlic and somehow came over as slightly offensive to Bob Baker, who decided to verbally dispatch him.

It wasn't long though before Celia and Bob decided that if they were to make the most of their time in Naples, then a guide would be a useful entity. They were soon approached by another arm-banded guide offering his services and apart from insisting on showing us his photographs of his wife and three children, he appeared fairly inoffensive. As we all walked over the cobbled piazza, the heavens opened and rain fell from the sky.

Mario's first suggestion was to go to the angora factory. This turned out to be two back rooms down a street of ancient sandstone coloured buildings. Some of them had coloured shutters which brightened the initial façade, but most had washing strung between them on about the third floor. Occasionally a red or pink geranium broke the sand coloured block work and brightened the scene.

We entered the doorway. 'Buongiorno señor, señora. Come in – welcome.' The lady was huge with voluptuous breasts encaptured within a large colourful apron, when she moved it appeared as if everything was struggling to get out. She asked in broken English if we have just got off the giant liner in the harbour and proceeded to tell us that her bother had migrated to Australia two years beforehand and he had taken several sweaters with him, as it got cold in the Winter in Australia. The advice was thrown in, more as a sales pitch rather than as a genuine piece of information.

The ample señorita displayed several lady's angora cardigans and while doing this, Mario the guide opened the large adjoining wooden doors and proudly displayed a collection of female relatives; five of them in number all sewing or knitting on long machines with balls of wool hanging from their metal appendages, appropriately linked to the knitting machine.

After a period of talking, trying on knitwear and haggling or bargaining, a jumper was purchase and wrapped. The Bakers, with Mario, embraced and thanked the large Italian woman, then headed with the guide towards the funicular railway; a feature of Naples which appears to split the town in half.

Leaving the old harbour area and heading upwards, this amazing travelling carriage perched at an angle on the side of a large hillside with buildings and roads growing out of it of all shapes, sizes and angles, the majority of which appear to be hanging on like limpets, occasionally surrounded by tiny gardens. The ancient carriage slowly, steadily rumbled its way up the old ladder system of sliding mechanics, scaring and exciting the patrons foolish enough to travel up in this mechanical crate. It arrived at the top with Mario enthusing the virtues of their marvellous system of transport.

The ten or twelve passengers scurried away into the jostling crowd, while Mario shepherded his human flock towards the next Italian marvel. The

Bakers meandered in and out of several piazzas eventually arriving at a small open terraced area adjacent to the edge of the cliff top. This had a stone parapet and several trees growing out of the surrounding gardens and walled areas.

Mario suddenly decided that this was the most beautiful place in Naples and continued to press home his advantage by telling us the quotation "See Naples and die" was coined at this very spot and came from a famous play in which Christopher Lee took part.

We all peered through the rain and gloom of the day and although it was in a beautiful position with its view over the Bay of Naples, only a few plants struggled to escape from the dilapidating masonry, we really couldn't see what all the fuss was about. Surprisingly enough, other assembled guides were gathering to show their respective clients the same spot inevitably to be caught by the Box Brownies and recorded forever.

We moved on, shuffling rather damply, stopping on occasion to be photographed by the tomb of someone or other and the statue of another ancient hero, long vanished into the memory bank.

A break came in the weather just as we arrived at his brother's famous marcasite factory. The family were ushered through the painted front door by the enthusiastic guide; the hallway smelt of garlic and acetone. An enthusiastic brother, another fat, black-clothed lady bustled in pumping Dad's hand like a manual water pump. 'Welcome, welcome. Come into our little factory.'

The Bakers stepped forward; six or eight benches were laid out covered with half-finished or just started, filigree-type artefacts various cameo brooches were in the process of being crafted on another bench. Two little boys were welding butterfly brooches, some larger than others; both were using very delicate blowtorches to form the basic shapes required. A large black-garbed woman, with over-developed breasts, was accepting the basic shapes from the young boys and very delicately installing wings and stamens with coloured metal strands. For a large lady she performed with the lightness of a fairy wielding her magic wand and enticing the coloured metal strands to lock together.

A gent, who was introduced as 'grandpa', was teasing the oyster shell from the cameo. He demonstrated years of practice, dexterity and skill, eventually to produce the beautiful cameo brooches. Indeed a treasure to be seen. Mum and Dad were impressed and promptly made a purchase. Mother enthused at the beauty of the craftsmanship. Dad moaned about the cost every step of the way back to the ship.

But the fun wasn't completely over because Mario who had said his services were free when they first met, and that he was paid by the government State Tourism department, suddenly had more debt than the Treasury of Italy; with a family to support, another baby on the way and a child that needed an operation, he was sure that Mr Baker would understand and contribute to his plight. What he hadn't bargained for, when he initially met Mr Baker, was that Bob believed that every penny had to be physically worked for and was tighter than a dam when it came to money matters. The two men argued for a few moments until Bob eventually gave him a small donation for his time, which left Mario muttering something under his breath with every step, as he reluctantly said 'Arriverderci' as he walked away.

The Bakers scurried along the bustling quayside making their way past uniformed officials and dockside workmen, taking in the wet musky smells of the dockside, through the aromas of the waterside café as the coffee permeated the air. They eventually came to the entrance to the Orion's gangway with the now familiar blue and white canvas awning. Pursers and other ship's officials stood beside the table, signing the passengers back on board.

The family entourage clambered up the temporary gangway and into the belly of the giant vessel, quickly making their way down to the dining room, aware that they were quite late for their usual dining time, but determined not to miss the meal

'Now wash your hands children, before you enter the dining room,' Dad called as the family hurried down the passage.

The waiter stood erect in his starched uniform 'I thought you'd make it for dinner,' he said sarcastically.

No one else had managed to get back to our table; the small cheeky waiter greeted the Bakers as they made their dash between the dining tables. Only a scattering of passengers had bothered to return to the ship.

'I thought you were going on the Pompeii trip,' the waiter engaged Dad in conversation as he politely helped Mum to her seat.

'Yes, we are, but that's not until fourteen-hundred hours, so we thought we'd have a spot of lunch first.'

'Very wise, sir,' replied the water.

'Would everyone like minestrone for starters?' He glanced round the little group sitting in their respective chairs. 'Possibly followed by the spaghetti?' he continued, attempting to be helpful; but Dad wanted the steak and Mum had the tagliatelli. He vanished along with a string of other starchily dressed waiters through the large swinging double doors.

Only a few moments passed by because there were not many people to take care of, and the waiter returned bringing the soup in bowls; one in each hand and two balancing on his forearms. He quickly dispatched them to the table and carefully placed them in front of his respective charges, wiping a drop which had spilled onto the rim, before returning to the kitchen for the main course.

Mrs Anderson and family joined the table and everyone quickly engaged in conversation.

When lunch was over, they all left to once again join the bus waiting on the quayside. This was all carried out very efficiently; passengers were checked in and given a leaflet telling the story of Pompeii. Soon the bus moved off with its passengers and guide.

The microphone burst into life. 'Good afternoon, ladies and gentlemen. I trust you are all well fed and ready to enjoy this memorable trip you are about to embark upon?'

The beautiful señorita had caught everyone's attention; her perfect pitch and pronunciation had surprised the many passengers of the chattering bus-load. She tossed her shoulder-length hair, which ensured every male decided to listen; the ladies became equally attentive as she introduced herself.

'I am Maria. I was born in Naples but migrated with my parents to Cambridge where they had a little Italian Restaurant. I am a student of history at Cambridge University, specialising in Italian history and ancient fashion. I will be your guide throughout the Pompeii trip, but first I would like to tell you of the history of Ancient Pompeii.

The beautiful young woman had captured the attention of her audience. After a brief respite she took a breath. The old jalopy moved us through Naples, she quietly informed us that the site of Pompeii was located on the western region, called Campania. It had a coast in the west and the Apennines Mountains on the east. She spoke quietly but distinctly and everyone strained to listen to her words.

Campania is a fertile plain traversed by the major rivers and blessed with rich alluvial soil rich in potash. The region's crops would yield higher than average, and certainly more than the rest of the peninsula. The main olive groves of Italy are in this region and the local slopes of the mountainside provided nourishment for thousands of sheep.

She continued, 'Little was known about the early settlers, they were probably prehistoric hunters and fishermen. By the eighth century BC, a group of Italic people, known as the Oscars, occupied the region. It is thought that these were the first people to establish Pompeii. Slightly later Ionians also settled in Campania.'

Maria flicked her hair again, once again capturing everyone's attention. 'Later the Greeks established a merchant trading port, which eventually dominated this locality. For a few centuries the two main cities of Pompeii and Herculaneum grew under Hellenic control.'

She paused for a moment. About this time some of the passengers were getting a bit lethargic and started to lose their original interest. They looked out of the bus window and talked between themselves. Maria still pressed home her advantage of having a captive audience and told us of the invasion of the Sammites in the fifth century and the fact that Rome's control was distant. Pompeii had its own language and culture and that Rome reluctantly accepted the situation.

'Tell us about the volcano.' A voice from the back of the bus broke the continuity and brought everyone back to attention.

'I'm sorry,' she said, 'I didn't mean to turn this into a lecture. The volcano, okay! As you know, it's called Vesuvius. On August twentieth 79 AD the earth began to rumble and crack. The waves in the sea became agitated, the animals and birds restless and alarmed. Four days later, on the twenty-fourth, the volcano blasted open with a huge crack and an ear-splitting noise; smoke, mud, flames and burning debris burst forth from the summit of the mountain. Smoke and burning lava spewed from the gaping cracks appearing all around the top of the volcano. Mud and a rain of flaming ash ran down the rock. A river of uncontrollable molten streams gouged out a pathway for themselves spreading all over the surrounding countryside.

'Mud seeped down the side of Vesuvius swallowing nearby olive groves, farmsteads, orchards and villas. The mephitic vapours, which accompanied the falling debris, caused deliriousness in the local community before suffocating them.'

Now once again she had everyone's attention. It seems that everyone liked a good horror story.

She continued, 'Some people took their horses and cattle attempting to escape. Others chose to wait until the streets were clear of the panicking crowds, while others sealed themselves in their villas and rooms; the falling buildings, or the gases killed many people instantly; the falling ashes buried many people also. The volcano mineral deposit was later found to be over thirty feet deep in places.'

Maria rambled on for a while but just before they arrived at the Pompeii site, she explained that the site of the ancient city was discovered by an old man digging a well and that the excavation of Pompeii commenced on March twenty-third, 1748. From that day to this, people are still discovering the secrets buried in the surrounding area.

With that the bus rumbled into a massive, but rather unkempt parking area. One by one everyone alighted from the bus, while Maria went to sort out our entrance tickets. Eventually the bus load of migrants moved forward and entered this macabre city of ruins.

Like a giant crocodile, everyone followed the guide and it wasn't long before they were standing along the cobbled Roman road. The various villas came into sight and one by one the tourists entered and examined the frescoes and mosaics. They went to the *Garden of Fugitives* where the plaster casts, set in macabre fashion, of victims—including the children who had been caught by the molten ash and preserved as they played in the garden. Maria took them into the spas and the baths and through the massive gates of the *Villa of Mysteries*. She explained this was one of the greatest houses to come down to us from the ancient world.

'I hope you children are taking this in,' chipped in Dad.

One of the archaeologists working on them told them that only fifty per cent of the ruins had been exposed, and even this figure wasn't confirmed. The party spent at least four hours walking round and by the conclusion of the tour, everyone was happy to get back on the bus and rest their feet.

Once Maria started talking again, Susan and Andrew fell asleep and it wasn't long before their Mum and Dad were waking them to get off and go through the customs shed and back onto the ship. Wearily, they climbed the gangway and made their way to their cabin to wash their hands in readiness for dinner.

Just as they were finishing dinner, the Orion gave a sound shattering blast of its horn.

'Please may we be excused,' pleaded the children. They both knew it would take thirty minutes or so to leave the dock, but the passengers who had embarked would be saying goodbye to their families.

As the two children pushed their way through the heavy doors, which opened onto the dock, they could hear the band playing *All Over Italy*. Andrew and Susan pushed their way through the new Italian passengers and everyone else who had come to say their farewells. Streamers had been thrown, and a man on the dock was playing a piano accordion. Streamers and flags adorned the side of the ship. Three blasts from the horn made everyone jump, the gap widening as the Orion slackened its berth while the passengers watched as the dissipating streamers were breaking and vanishing into the darkening sky. The band continued and ladies and gentlemen wept openly as they waved goodbye to their loved ones.

Lights all over Naples were glowing in a myriad of colours. A tug was already attached to the small forward capstan patiently awaiting instruction. The Captain could be seen high up on the bridge. He spoke into a walkie-talkie and the deck officer gave instructions to the crew. Slowly the capstan slackened off. Dockers on the shore released the last of the great hawsers and the splash could be heard. As the last of the lines slipped away, a team of sailors operated the winch and hauled the ropes aboard; simultaneously a similar operation was taking place on the aft deck. The vibration from the engine quivered through the deck and the little tug belched black smoke as it took the strain of the bowline. Slowly, very slowly, the ocean-going liner inched its way from the harbour wall.

Meanwhile the remaining streamers held by the departing migrants, many of them wailing and crying, some of them singing but all of them filled with emotion, watched and tried to keep eye contact with their loved ones left behind. The streamers severed that last tenuous link with the families and friends was broken. Both men and women wept openly, waving hankies, the band played its melodies and the tug pulled the ship farther away from the dockside. The streamers vanished in the wind, like ribboned confetti.

Andrew and Susan ran round to the other side of the ship; a second tug could be seen pulling the giant liner away from the shore. The pilot was still on board and his boat hovered in the waves bobbing up and down and following the Orion as it slowly moved away. On both the aft and fore decks, crew scurried backwards and forwards, winding and laying ropes, lashing down pieces of equipment and generally tidying the ship.

Passengers had started to move away from the railings. The quayside, exposed now, presented the names of ships, graffiti, displaying the various craft that had lain alongside.

The children ran to the aft deck and watched the powerful engine of the

Orion churn the waters of the Bay of Naples. Slowly the massive oil-burning vessel agitated the sea, like a great washing machine. When the tugs had the vessel in the correct position and she was moving under her own steam, they relinquished their charge and pulled in their tow-lines.

Many people still milled around on the decks, even though it was dark. The lights of the Bay of Naples shone out. We could see the relatives disappearing from the quay and the strains of the Italian band dissipated on the breeze. Andrew and Susan watched the pilot climb down the wooden rope ladder, his own craft, deftly coming alongside. He grabbed the safety rail and swung onto the deck of the little pilot boat, which instantly sped into the night.

That evening, the festivities on board all took an Italian flavour. The music, the dancing, the food was all Italian and to our delight we watched the swimming pool being filled with water. They dashed off to find their parents and tell them what they had seen. Mum and Dad came up onto the deck and together watched the coastal lights of Italy as the ship made headway, fluorescence breaking on the surface as the vessel ploughed through the waves.

'Come and see the swimming pool, Dad.' Andrew urged his father down to the aft of the vessel. Together they looked at the water in the pool sloshing, brilliantly illuminated by the lights under the water. Andrew had never seen a pool lit up before and somehow this had a magical appearance.

'You'll be able to swim when you reach Australia,' Dad said, looking proudly down at his son.

Andrew smiled back, 'Can we go in tomorrow, Dad?' he asked.

'I expect they'll tell us tomorrow son.'

The two of them walked back to 'C' Deck to meet Mum and Susan. Together they made their way to the entertainments area. The coast of Italy seemed far away although they were only crawling along the coast en route for Palermo, which they would pass in the morning at breakfast time. In the lounge they settled down to listen to the band and watch the dancing, which most of the ladies and gentlemen took part in.

'Come on Andrew, I'll teach you to waltz.' Mum stood up quickly leaving her son no time to complain. She stood him in front of her and showed him how to hold her around the waist and, with effortless grace, moved him and manoeuvred him. 'One, two, three – one, two, three,' she demonstrated the box-type steps and soon they were both moving to the beat of the music.

The evening progressed and Mum explained the other dances and how the music allowed the couples to use other steps. It wasn't long before Susan wanted her turn, 'Can I have a go Mum?'

She quickly responded to her daughter's enthusiasm and soon they were manoeuvring their way around the dance floor, along with a hundred or so other couples of all ages and standards. The evening progressed, couples swished around the floor, young men and women introduced themselves and bought each other drinks. Everyone soon began chatting and getting to know each other and developed a conviviality and rapport.

Mr and Mrs Baker decided it was time for bed for the Baker family. They bid goodnight to the other couples around the table at which they were sitting, and they agreed to meet again the following day.

Once Bob and Celia had their children tucked into their berths, they slipped upstairs to one of the other bars for a nightcap and a stroll around the deck. Up until this point, they had not had much time to be by themselves and the quiet moment was undoubtedly welcome.

Cruising through The Mediterranean

Six am. and the children were scampering around the ship. They both loved being up bright and early. The sailors were scrubbing the decks and the early morning walkers were enjoying the exercise. Six turns around the deck was a mile and many couples paced quickly to get an appetite before breakfast at seven o'clock. The ship ploughed through the waves gently progressing in a steady rhythm, white foaming phosphorous breaking as the ship broke the waves.

On the horizon, land was clearly evident. Susan and Andrew had visited the 'C' Deck Foyer and read the ship's notices. They knew that at eight-fifteen they would see Messina in the distance and the toe of Italy on the other side of the ship. For them this was the place that the Orion sailed between the Straits of Sicily and Italy and headed for a tiny Greek island where she was due to stop in order to allow some clergymen and women to depart.

From the moment the ship entered the strait, and for the next eight hours, the vessel pitched and tossed, rocked and rolled, the weather was really foul. This was Tuesday thirteenth January, 1959. Most of the people had come to the rails to be sick. Hardly anyone attended meals that is of course, with the exception of Andrew and his Dad. Once again they and only a handful of other passengers managed not to have a kaleidoscope lunch as the vessel slowly manoeuvred between the Greek Islands.

The weather had abated and many more people were walking around the decks. It was still rocking, but not to the extent that it had been during the day. Night-time had closed in around the huge cream painted vessel, thousands of lights illuminated her as she crept slowly to the berthing point. It must have been close to midnight when she weighed anchor. The massive anchor dropped from the stem of the vessel followed immediately by the rumble and clanking of the moving chains. The ship slowly drifted to a position acceptable to the captain, the skipper then dropped another anchor from the stern to steady the vessel.

Meanwhile on deck, the ship was a hive of activity; sailors scurried back and forth, the derrick was prepared and a large cargo net was set out on the deck away from the public area. Sailors and pursers were arranging the luggage of the people about to depart; the passengers were waiting at the side entrance of the vessel. The two davits held the gangway in position; this was slowly lowered close to the water. The ship's store was opened to take aboard whatever fresh produce and fruit that was available. The quartermaster stood by the massive bulkhead door checking the vittles and produce as it came alongside.

From the decks high above the waterline, it was clear to see the slow swell that the little boats ferrying goods to the ship had to battle through. Because of their size they were rocking and rolling until they came close to the Orion, where her size stabilized the swell and assisted the tiny supply boats, permitting a more tranquil passage to the bulkhead door.

Susan and Andrew peered over the railings, the gentle rain dripped from the bulkhead above, but the two siblings didn't get wet. The ship was like a giant umbrella protecting them from the weather. As they peered out into the darkness, they saw a small boat manoeuvring towards the gangway. It wasn't long before the assistant purser was helping the departing nuns down the gangway which although securely tethered, still moved back and forth.

As the clergy stepped onto the stairway, two sailors held the boat steady and a pair of Greek sailors assisted them to alight onto the rocking work boat. The nuns turned and looked up, waving to the passengers on the decks above, many of them waving and shouting salutations. The little boat cast off its painter and the black smoke chugged from its diesel engine as it slowly puffed away from the corn coloured hull of the Orion. Within moments the little tender had vanished into the darkness.

As the children cast their eyes around the harbour, they became aware of another boat making its way to the side of the ship. The derrick with the cargo net, now full of trunks and suitcases had been swung out over the sea. The wooden tender grew closer and closer, it was obvious the skipper was aiming to position his craft beneath the cargo net, now dangling precariously from the boom, holding it away from the Orion's hold.

By now, the Orion had settled into a slow motion roll caused by the seas. The small vessel was affected considerably by the motions and was bobbing substantially. The skipper of the little boat misjudged the cargo net position and manoeuvred past it with the differential of the bobbing and rolling, caused by the two craft in the water.

Once again, the skipper sailed out in an arc, he gave himself plenty of room, lined the boat up and steadily made his way towards the pendulum of the luggage filled net. He approached with as much caution as he could muster; the phosphorous broke as each wave pounded against the tiny hull. The movement did not appear to synchronize, but the skipper with his knowledge and seamanship, just for a moment appeared to hover on the waves. The old diesel belched smoke and as he revved the engine, a machete cut the rope securing the net and just for a moment it looked as if the contents were going to unceremoniously end up on the floor of the little boat.

But at that moment, the hand of Neptune tossed the mobile bobbing tender, and the ensuing cascading luggage toppled, some caught in the squares of the rope cargo net and some dropped freely. But the little boat, still moving forward with the motion of the sea, even though the engine was now in reverse and at a point when the hawser from the boom was rolling in a forward motion caused by the swell.

Luggage toppled on both sides of the little tender, seamen with boathooks grabbed at the luggage as travelling bags slowly dissipated in several directions around the little wooden tender. By the time the skipper had realigned his craft, pieces of luggage had vanished beneath the waves into the watery blackness, only a percentage actually ended up on the little vessel, which slowly chugged away into the darkness of the night.

Many people on board, both passengers and crew, had witnessed the demise of the baggage, but apart from the amusement created by this sad affair, nothing more was heard of the situation.

Within an hour, the Orion was preparing to sail. The vibrations of the powerful engines came to life, all derricks were secured and gangways back in position. The capstan hauled in the anchors and the children clinging to the railings felt the rain on their faces as the giant passenger liner broke the swell and slowly ploughed forward.

Once again, the Orion was progressing to her next destination. Andrew and Susan went back to their cabin and slept soundly until the morning.

Each day the Bakers went through a similar routine; on awakening the children pressed their noses against the porthole to see what sort of day it was, they showered and cleaned their teeth, quickly dressed then as a unit they all made their way to breakfast.

Their waiter greeted them heartily; 'Good morning Sir, Madam,' he touched his forelock with a saucy grin and held the back of the chair for Mrs Baker to make herself comfortable. 'I trust the noise didn't wake you last night?'

The children who had scrambled onto their chairs decided not to say anything, as they thought their parents may not approve of them being on deck to late at night.

'No, we slept well, thank you,' Dad politely replied.

'Poached eggs, sir? With halloumi cheese?' the waiter ventured the suggestion for breakfast. Nobody took him up on his suggestion.

'Rice Krispies please, followed by bacon and eggs,' Andrew chirped up.

'Cornflakes for me please,' said Susan, 'then I'll have poached eggs on toast.'

'And I'll have kippers please,' said Dad.

'And I'll have the same as Susan,' said Mum 'but we will have a pot of tea first. Thank you.'

The waiter scurried off towards the galley and almost as quickly as he had left, he was back again carrying a large tray at head height, with a large silver teapot and a pot of boiled water. Quickly he went about his business and made sure that one and all had a cup of tea before disappearing again into the galley. Other guests arrived at the table and good morning greetings took place as usual. Once again, the waiter tried to coax his breakfast guests into having Halloumi cheese, obviously picked up in Greece that morning and therefore fresh and in keeping with the region.

Breakfast over, the children made their way up to 'C' Deck, pushing open the heavy doors. They were greeted by a blast of warm air. The temperature was getting considerably hotter now, even though they were in January. Steadily the ship had been heading South; the passengers were now wearing shorts. Andrew and Susan made their way round to the swimming pool area. Young people were already lying round the swimming pool area soaking up the warm sun, occasionally jumping from the high sides and causing a splash.

The motion of the ship caused its contents to splash backwards and forwards – the emerald green salt water glistened like a jewel in an oasis. Laughter broke the background hum of conversation mixed with the mechanical throb of the engine vibration which by now had become commonplace.

Wooden green canvas chairs were tucked under the white painted metal deck supports, which provided an awning partially protecting the people from the sun. Ladies were already wearing swimming costumes and large colourful hats. A raised decking area, about six planks wide, surrounded three quarters of the pool. This provided a perch for anyone who wished to sit and enjoy the rays from the sun.

Susan and Andrew decided to go and find their friends. While doing this, they passed the open ballroom, which doubled as a recreation room during the day. A large billboard displayed the ship's activities for the day and next to this was a chart showing the position of the vessel on the ocean and where it had steamed from over the past twelve hours. Each day the position was reassessed and the passengers were invited to try and guess the distance the Orion had travelled during the previous twelve hours.

The tote was a regular, event promoted by the entertainments officer and many people took part.

The cost was six-pence a guess and the accumulated prize was allocated to the person who guessed closest in nautical miles.

Frog racing with large wooden cut out frogs was popular. Deck quoits competition, whist drives, table tennis, deck tennis and selected people were invited to talk on specialist subjects each day. Nearly every day the entertainment committee provided a varied selection of entertainments for the passengers.

Andrew caught up with one of his new friends. 'Hello, John, where are you off to?'

'I was looking for you actually. Fancy a game of table tennis?'

'Yes, that's a good idea, but let's get some ice cream first.'

Just then, Susan saw two of her friends and dashed off to greet them. The boys made their way to the lounge where the ice-cream lady always started from.

'Two pink ones please, one's for my sister,' chirped Andrew.

'I suppose you want two as well? Do you have a sister?' asked the waitress.

'No, actually I've got a brother,' said John, 'but yes I'd like two pink ones as well.'

She smiled at the boys and handed over the ice-cream. Andrew and John made their way to the table tennis area, several people were already there. This was indeed a popular venue. For a while the two lads peered over the railings watching the ship pitch and toss, suddenly the two boys simultaneously cried out, 'Look at that!'

At first they did not know what they had seen, by now other people were peering over the railings and pointing. 'Porpoise,' said one.

'No they're dolphins,' said another.

The two boys stared in amazement; they had never seen anything like this before. They didn't even know fish could grow as big as that. As they stared over the side, the fish leapt and dived into the wake caused by the ship. Suddenly there appeared to be dolphins in abundance. The two boys counted up to ten, then there were even more. Just a short way off, it seemed that the more they looked, the more they saw.

'Do you boys want this table now?' a voice from behind them called.

'Yes please,' echoed the lads and they scampered back to collect the two Ping-Pong balls being offered. The man smiled, 'Have a good one boys' and vanished with his lady along the deck.

The lads served the ball and batted it backwards and forwards for a while. Soon they felt warmed up enough. John called to Andrew, 'Okay now, best of three?'

For the next twenty minutes, the boys concentrated on playing the game to the best of their ability, the two of them evenly matched. The boys had been playing each other for about a week now, and both of them seemed to be getting better by the day. As time went by, the games became longer and soon the initial set of three games had turned into six—then twelve. Two hours later, the music *Roast Beef of Old England* piped out to announce the first serving of lunch.

'That's me,' cried Andrew, 'Time for dinner.'

Andrew and John were on different dinner sittings, so the two boys agreed to meet on the starboard deck at fourteen-hundred hours giving them both time to eat their lunch. Andrew raced away to wash his hands and get town to the dining room. Andrew, Susan, Mum and Dad sat and enjoyed lunch together. They told each other what they had done and how they had spent the morning. Bob Baker was especially pleased because he had won the tote and his share was eleven shillings and six-pence. This was enough to pay for their entertainment on the boat for the next few days.

After dinner the children went along to the library and then to the afternoon cinema. Later they ran up on deck and played quoits. Once again, the day had passed quickly, the ship's company made sure there was always plenty of activities to keep everyone happy and, of course, while all this was happening, the giant ship steamed even closed to her destination. The Bakers washed and changed for dinner that evening.

The talk all round the table was of the next destination. This seemed to have the assembled group full of excited anticipation. After dinner, the little party headed for the deck lounge where they were joined by a group of passengers who had become their friends. Together they sat listening to the quartet and enjoyed a few drinks and repeatedly the conversation kept returning to the next destination.

At nine o'clock most of the party walked around to the dance, which was a regular occurrence on 'B' Deck. The children went off to bed at ten o'clock and Celia and Bob stayed until eleven.

They had a stroll around the deck and checked that Susan and Andrew were tucked up in their bunks before turning in themselves.

Thursday 15ᵗʰ January 1959 – Approaching The Suez Canal

The ship had stopped, the motion everyone was used to by now had changed and the fact that the ship was silent in the water was even more noticeable than when it was moving. Andrew and Susan peeped out of their porthole.

'Cor, we're lying at anchor,' Andrew shouted to his sister. 'Just look at all the ships out there! There are dozens of them. C'mon Sue, let's get up on deck.'

The children told their parents. 'We're going on deck, Dad, there are ships everywhere you look.'

'I know son, you know where you are don't you? Do you remember last night we were all discussing the ship arriving at the Suez Canal? Some people are getting off here and going to see the Pyramids, so whatever you do, don't get off the ship, even if someone says you can go for free!'

Dad had already given us a lecture of people being kidnapped from ports like this, the truth is we didn't know whether to believe him or not.

'Why can't we go and see the Pyramids?'

'You know why son, we need to save all our money for when we get to Australia.'

'But Dad, you could put your tote winnings towards it. We will never get a chance like this again.'

'I know it's disappointing son, but we just don't have the spare cash to do these things. When you grow up you'll understand, but for now, you'll just have to believe us.'

The two children went off up the stairs to 'B' Deck which was the best promenade deck on the ship. They weren't too happy, but they knew money was always tight. When they arrived on deck they realised that the ship wasn't at anchor, but moving very slowly navigating between the vessels already riding at anchor. As they peered over the rail, they saw the pilot boat approach; the uniformed officer climbed the ladder which had been lowered for him.

The little pilot launch sped away and the Orion very slowly progressed to its anchor point where it dropped just one forward anchor and responded to the tidal action while it waited for its approach call to Port Said.

Port Said

Meanwhile, dozens of little vessels were approaching. The giant passenger vessel was only half a mile offshore. The town was clearly visible on the port side. Its mosque domes and minarets pointing to the sky. It wasn't long before the occupants of the little bobbing boats were tossing ropes with a round knot tied in a ball to enable it to be thrown onto the ship's deck.

The men in the boats called out, 'Tie on, tie on' to anyone who would catch the rope and tie it to a railing. Soon a small flat-decked platform was towed to the hull of the Orion and tied up against the giant cream ship. A dozen traders or more were on the deck trying to ply their wares of baskets and camel-skin bags, beaded purses, camel-skin wallets and shoes all stitched from sections of leather, wooden camels, and carved pieces were available for anyone who wished to trade. Local sweetmeats and boxes of Turkish Delight sat tantalising on the deck of the pontoon. Little bags of spices and nuts were amongst many items the local Egyptian traders were offering.

The natives milled around on the deck of the pontoon, all of them shouting up at the passengers. Dozens of people had gathered by now, clinging to the deck railings. The buying and selling process was in full swing.

People would point to an item the trader had on deck and after a series of 'left a bit, no not that one, the one next to the saddle' the identified item would be placed in a hessian bag or tied on to the rope, depending on the size or shape. The recipient would haul the rope or bag up to the deck and examine the goods. Then the now familiar call of 'how much' would start the bartering.

Now, fortunately the Purser had given a talk in one of the lounges the afternoon prior to arrival on how to barter and negotiate the prices in general. It was recommended that all prices should start by being cut in half from whatever was first requested by the trader. If after bartering done the figure was agreed upon, then the cash money was placed in the bag and the transaction concluded with satisfaction on both sides. The deal usually concluded with a third being knocked off the asking price, but some people got smarter and waited for a while and achieved even keener prices.

Bartering and selling carried on all day. At lunch the conversation around the dining room was all about what had been purchased and how much each individual has spent. Guffaws of laughter could be heard all around the dining room as the various passengers realised they had spent far too much on items that could be similarly purchased by other occupants around the table at a cheaper price. This was indeed a sharp learning period! By now, many realised that the smart negotiations or the canny businessmen had a lot more facts at their disposal than the folks who had waded in right at the beginning.

All at once, a loud blast on the ship's horn sounded out. This was quickly followed by the Tannoy voicing to one and all that the ship would be making steam in one hour precisely. This also gave a warning to everyone that all transactions should be wound up and the boats so neatly tied to the railings needed to be released in the very near future.

'Can we be excused, Dad, we must go and see the boats leaving and the barge being pulled away.'

Susan chipped in, 'And we haven't bought our camel yet either.' Susan had been promised a little leather camel by her Mum, but Dad was a bit reluctant as they had found out that some of them had been stuffed with used surgical dressings and the general consensus was that this was not very hygienic.

'Alright, alright,' said Dad, 'but I am coming with you.' Mum, Dad and Susan left the dining room along with a dozen or so other passengers, all anxious now to secure whatever goodies they had been waiting until the end of the trading period for.

Andrew had other plans. He raced up on deck to locate one of his new friends, Stephen, and Andrew had already hatched a plan to get their hands on a couple of items they has espied on the little trading craft.

Andrew dashed along the deck looking for his mate, who was nowhere to be found. He ran down to 'B' Deck, then down the companion way, onto 'C' Deck. All around people were bargaining, ropes and baskets were being pulled up and down, this last period was a real hectic shouting and bartering period. Suddenly he cast eyes on his friend.

'I've been searching for you everywhere,' he said in a raised voice.

'It's okay,' said Stephen, 'we still have half an hour before the ship goes.'

'I know, but all the ropes have to be released way before that,' said Andrew.

'Come on,' said Stephen, 'we'll go down to our cabin porthole where no one can see us.'

The two lads scarpered off, both of them agile and fleet of foot. In no time at all, they were in Stephen's cabin. This cabin was really good because they had two portholes. Quickly, they opened them and shouted to the men below on the boats.

Several of the boats had already untied their lines and were already making their way back to the shore, but a few who were either greedy or anxious to secure the last bit of trade, were hovering against the ship's hull. The crew on deck were already tossing the ropes back to the men below. Andrew and Stephen caught the eye of a boatman anxious to do a last minute trade. The rope was thrown and secured to the boys craning out of the porthole.

They called down 'send up some sweets,' and they pointed at the Turkish Delight in boxes. 'Two boxes, mate,' they shouted, 'and tell me how much.'

Quickly the boxes were placed in the hessian bag and the booty was hauled up by the enthusiastic pair. On deck the crew were shouting at the boatman to release the line, voices were getting seriously raised. The lads looked up at the crew members who were shouting at them to throw back the tethered ropes. Quick as a flash the lads took out the Turkish Delight and untied the ropes. The crew were happy. The boatman yelled up to the porthole as the bag splashed in the water.

'Quick, let's hide the sweets. We'll get them later.' Stephen pushed them behind his pillow and the two boys sealed the portholes and at that moment the might engines of the ship burst into life.

Black smoke was belching out of the funnel as the two boys burst through the double doors onto 'C' Deck. Quickly they raced round to see if the boatman was still there, as they peered over the railings they could see him peering into the bag to see what money was inside. The two boys smiled at each other.

'Must have fallen out,' Andrew said to Stephen.

'Yep, not our fault that crew fella told us to undo the rope.'

The boatman was pulling on the oars as quickly as he could, glancing at the ship trying to catch a glimpse of the boys, but anxious now to place some distance between him and the great ocean liner he knew was about to move off. If he didn't put a hundred yards between himself and the Orion, there was a chance he could be capsized by the wake of the ship or the propulsion caused by the turbulent water as the vessel moved away.

All around the ship small boats could be seen rowing as fast as they could, all of them wanting to create as much space as possible. Because the decks were fifty to one hundred feet from the waterline, the ship must have looked like a tower block from the little boats bobbing around. It was by now impossible to distinguish individual faces. Ten minutes later the rumble and clank of the anchor chain could be heard slowly section by section winding its way around the capstans.

The boys peered over the forward section of 'C' Deck, they could see the ship slowly pulling towards the chain, steadily instead of laying at an angle, this was now almost vertical. Suddenly mud started to cloud the clear blue water, large bubbles burst onto the surface. The chain continued to rumble and clank. More people were peering over the railings and bigger clouds of black smoke were now spewing out of the funnel.

'Look there it is,' Andrew shouted to his friend, just as the anchor broke the surface, mud still dripping from its fluke, steadily it clinked to its position where is nestled against the ship's hull.

'C'mon, let's go aft and see the props start.'

The two boys dashed along the deck dodging passengers standing and talking and saying 'Hi' or 'Hello' to people they knew as they made their way to the curved viewing area at the rear of the ship.

Already many people had gathered there to see the ship move forward. From the funnel, a mighty blast of steam spouted from the whistle and the air horns bellowed, signalling the ship was about to leave. The Blue Peter was lowered and other flags were run up the mast, signalling the intention of the vessel. With a mighty vibration from below deck, the water erupted like a cauldron boiling the surface.

The whole surface of the surrounding sea broke in an arc of bubbling water. This continued for a minute or so with the ship not appearing to move an inch. The water continued to pulse and tremble, the surface foamed and bubbled, a trembling and vibration far beneath the deck could be felt, slowly, very slowly, the giant ocean liner broke the friction of the surface. The ship paused no longer, the SS Orion was again moving, very slowly, but she was once again making headway.

By now, the passengers were already leaving the viewing area and making their way back to carry out their own business; some promenading, some taking a long look over the railings watching the little craft head for the shore. The young folks headed for the pool and recreation areas.

The Suez Canal

The following morning many of the migrants leaned against the railings watching the Orion progress along the narrow canal. A ship followed and behind that one a convoy vanished in a line, a similar pattern was visible from the forward deck.

Bored with the situation once the novelty wore off, passengers continued with their normal routine aboard, many played deck games, lounged in the sun or went to whist drives or bingo. Once the boys and friends met up they played Ping-Pong or headed for the pool.

On 'C' Deck a talk was being given about the history of the canal by the pursers mate. Susan, Andrew and friends decided to attend. The little team listened attentively to the speaker.

'The Suez Canal is a waterway in Egypt that joins the Red Sea and the Mediterranean Sea. This ship canal in Egypt is a major navigational route for world trade. It crosses the isthmus of Suez and links the Mediterranean Sea with the Gulf of Suez, an arm of the Red Sea, thus eliminating the long voyage around Africa or ships travelling between East and West. When everything is running correctly this is one of the busiest waterways in the world.

'In its course of slightly more than 100 miles, the Suez Canal crosses a sandy desert and passes through several natural bodies of water including Lake Timsah and the Bitter Lakes. The canal has no locks, there being virtually no difference in the levels of the Mediterranean and Red Seas.

'Throughout most of its length, the canal can handle only one way traffic. Bypasses in the Bitter Lakes and at Ballah permit ships sailing in opposite directions to pass. Widened and deepened over the years, the Suez Canal can accommodate all ships other than the largest crude oil super-tankers.

Constant dredging is required to maintain the channel. The canal is operated by the Egyptian government through the Suez Canal Authority, whose headquarters are at Ismailia. More than a dozen stations along the shore help regulate the traffic.

'Special pilots take ships in and out of port at Port Said and Suez and navigate the canal proper. The average transit time is about 15hrs. Crude and refined petroleum products bound mainly for Western Europe from the Persian Gulf area account for most of the tonnage carried on the canal. The revenues from the operations contribute heavily to the Egyptian economy.' The purser brought his lecture to a close for which he was applauded.

'Well that was interesting. Shall we go for a swim now or may be a game of quoits or deck tennis?' The boys had important decisions to make.

Port Suez was the next stop and this was a repetition of Port Said. Little boat and barges lined up against the side of the ship all selling their wares; people bargaining, everyone a little wiser now having learned their lessons from the previous port.

The folks who visited the pyramids re-joined the ship telling their stories. Meal times turned into a 'what did you buy this time' period. A few hours later the ship was on the move again, progressing into the Gulf of Suez and down the Red Sea.

Two more days followed with the Orion progressing steadily. The sun beat down; the fish were visible and the passengers lounged like lizards. Without a doubt the pool was the favourite spot for most people to congregate and those who weren't swimming or lounging were playing cards or drinking in the bar.

Monday 19 January – Djibouti

The Orion was diverted to Djibouti, due to a strike in Aden; the only advantage this had was a little diversity in the culture of the populous. Passengers were allowed off the ship but could not leave the quayside. All around were armed guards; at the time we couldn't make out if this was to keep out the general population, or keep us from going into town.

The temperature and the stench were most noticeable. This hung like a cloud over the general area. Arabs plied their wares on the quayside transformed itself into a foreign market; once again the skin camels and poofs were everywhere. Fishing rods in boxes were a popular purchase, rugs, carpets and prayer mats were also very popular. By the time we had walked from one end to the next, everything that was to be seen had been, so the majority of people got back on the ship and carried on with the regular ship activities.

The time passed as usual and it wasn't long before the ship was pulling out and leaving the desert state to its own endeavours. By nightfall the Orion was well out to sea, contentedly refuelled and on its way making progress.

One day merged into the next. The boys spent hours running around the decks, stopping many times to look out to sea for sharks but never managing to see them. Porpoises followed or ran before the wake; flying fish were in abundance and could be seen nearly every time the children peered over the railings.

On the 21st January the ship's bulletin advised them that they would glimpse the Maldives in the distance, and everyone knew that it would only be a relatively short time before they would reach Colombo.

Sunday 25th January, Colombo

Clank, clank, clank, clank. It was a familiar sound but why was it happening. The two children woke with a start.

'Did you hear that, Susan?' Andrew jumped out of the bunk and quickly made his way along the small passage to the porthole; Susan was right behind him hot on his heels.

'What can you see, Andrew?' she asked.

Andrew was too busy unlocking the brass mechanism to answer, he pulled open the porthole and by standing on the heating pipe protection, he could peer out of the window.

'Can't see much, but there are a few little boats around. I reckon it's all happening on the other side of the ship.'

The two children quickly showered, clean their teeth and were dressed quicker than a seagull can take off after a bag of fish.

They made their way along the passages and up the stairs to 'C' Deck. As they burst out through the heavy double doors, they became aware of how early it was. The ship's company were mustered on the deck. There were just about to disperse into the cleaning parties to swab the decks and polish the brass.

The sun was just breaking on the horizon and a kaleidoscope of colours, mostly yellows, orange and reds had started to emanate from the domes of light growing larger by the second, as the two children clung to the wooden railings. At this stage, only the anchor chain had been dropped and the ship was slowly swinging to the position dictated by the tide and acceptable to the Captain. The gentle blue sea became more evident as the sun slowly rose into the sky.

The usual smell of brass and soapsuds from the cleaning activities of the deck crew started to change as a smell of spices and cloves permeated and wafted over the ship. Although we were about a mile offshore, the Orion was slowly swinging round offering a new perspective to be viewed moment by moment. Small tugs and several vessels steadily gained momentum. Cargo doors were opened, more clanking and banging of metal hatch covers became offensive to the eardrums.

The port of Colombo bit by bit revealed itself as the ship continued to swing around. A green line of palm trees with intermittent white buildings displayed themselves on the perimeter and stretched to the sandy beach horizon. A closer visual inspection revealed a township and port with many buildings and masts. Funnels from other ships which must have been tucked away behind harbour walls permeated the skyline. Minarets and mosques were evident. Cockerels crowed in the background and more and more the smell of spices started to dominate the air surrounding the ship.

An hour or so had passed since the children had just slipped on to the deck. The crew had vanished from sight. All the deck loungers sat still on parade and passengers slowly meandered up and down the decks. As usual the keep fit brigade ran, dashed or power-walked around they freshly scrubbed planking.

Susan and Andrew decided it was time to tell their parents of all they had witnesses that morning. Quickly they manoeuvred the stairways and headed down the passage to the family cabin. 'You'll never believe what we've seen this morning!'

Bob was already standing at the porthole, binoculars in hand, perusing the shoreline and the city of Colombo. 'Don't forget now, at eight-thirty we are going on a tour of the city so I don't want you wandering off. Make sure that you're back here in the cabin by eight, then we'll all go down to the departure area together.'

Just as Dad had spoken the Tannoy called out the now familiar tune of *Roast Beef of All England,* signalling the start of breakfast. 'Come on you two, let's to and get a good breakfast before our little trip. He ushered the children and their mum out of the door before turning and locking it.

Along with the other dining companions, they discussed the tour of Colombo and the features they anticipated discovering. 'Have a nice day and don't eat too many spicy foods,' the waiter called out as they left the dining table.

The Bakers gathered with the other passengers at the Purser's desk by the large bulkhead door. Several people had already left the ship via the companionway steps and onto the small craft waiting in turn to take the passengers ashore.

The little boats bobbed their way towards the harbour area but once away from the protection of the ship's hull, the waves although comparatively small, still made the little boats bob up and down like corks. It was only a short journey to the shore, but many people were quite sick and complained bitterly but illogically about the swell.

Concrete steps loomed and the turbaned sailors leaped ashore with a rope, quickly tying off the boat and deftly catching the rear painter as it was thrown. Once secured the boat despatched its cargo of mildly traumatised passengers, helped by an assortment of uniformed and traditionally dressed personnel.

'Please Memsab, come this way,' a brightly coloured and uniformed local was beckoning everyone towards an old painted charabanc. The seating was like old carpets, moth-eaten and holed, tassels hung from the dashboard and any other place they could find to hang adornments.

Once on board and seated, the local leaped to the footplate signalling to the driver to start his engine.

'Welcome, Welcome everybody. Today I will show you the beautiful city of Colombo in this majestically country of Ceylon. Already the complaints were coming from the rear of the bus about it being too hot but Saed, as he had introduced himself, had already started his diatribe about the history of the harbour and where the trip was heading today.

Minutes later we were passing along the city roads of tinned roof shacks selling fruits and assortments of spices. Goats and sheep wandering around the roads, hundreds of bikes, old cars and pedestrians all trying to use the same thoroughfare. It seemed that just as fast as we had come from the more seedy part of town that we had turned into an up-market road with large mansions and gardens. Large trees adorned the edge of the roads, the fragrance of exotic flowers drifted on the air and the guide, in his best voice, proudly told us this was the diplomatic quarter where all the wealthy people lived. Guards stood in sentry boxes outside and adjacent to the metal-gated entrances, some of them armed, but mostly in brightly coloured uniforms. The bus passed slowly down the road. Saed was very pleased to show off this area.

At the end, the old 'chara' pulled around the corner and stopped at a Buddhist Shrine. He explained that many workers paid homage to Buddha on their way to work and advised us to do the same.

The bus moved on and soon came to a halt at the market area. The first and most obvious item to catch the attention was the array of colourful stalls. Soon we had all alighted and Saed paraded us as a group through the market. We started in the fruit and veg area with collections of fruit and vegetables we had never seen, or heard of, before. Quickly moving on to spices which sat on wooden compartments, piled up in many different colours; all the time we were surrounded by smells and fragrances which filled the air and were completely foreign to our senses. Saffron, curry powder, cinnamon and nutmegs, every way you turned a different spice tantalised and delighted the nostrils.

Then we hit the fish section and although it was interesting to view, the smell was a different aroma and definitely not one to be remembered favourably. We passed through other sections and material shops with tailors wanting to make you suits and shirts the same day. Saed was anxious that the bus would not wait, he was on a tight schedule which had to be met and his brother would make any clothes required at a later shopping mall of better quality, so he said. The snake of passengers eventually arrived back at the bus, but only by going via the camera stall, watch straps and electronic goods.

Soon we were all counted back on the bus and the old charabanc made its way along York Street, the most fashionable street in Colombo. The road was wider than most, and the buildings higher and more grandly constructed. It was plain to see that this street was for the wealthy. As the old bus jogged along, we passed a row of two-wheeled ox drawn vehicles. Saed informed us that these were called bullocks and a driver dressed in what appeared to be a white bed sheet, with floppy white trousers and the compulsory turban.

At the end of the famous street, the old bus took a turn or two and drew to a halt. 'I want to show you a famous Mosque in Ceylon, please be courteous and remove your shoes. Do not play any form of music in this reverent place.' He went on to say that prayers were said five times a day and that we were in between the prayer calls at the moment.

Susan and Andrew were amazed at the sights they had never been into a church or place of worship that was not the one they were brought up in and consequently knew nothing of other religions. 'I wonder how many different styles of religion there are. Do you know Daddy?'

'Sorry, Susan, I really haven't a clue but there must be hundreds of them.

The only thing I can tell is that this Mosque is part of the Muslim religion, which came approximately five-hundred years after Christianity was formed.

Susan was satisfied with that for the moment. She was learning new things every moment.

Andrew chipped in, 'Do they have big snakes here, Dad?'

'I don't know what that has to do with Mosques but yes they do have several very deadly snakes here. The main one is the cobra.'

Saed pointed out the place in the wall where the Imam stood when he was talking to the other Muslims, although he also pointed out that the Imam called the prayers from the front of the Mosque and always pointing towards Mecca, the place all Muslims believe to be the holiest place in the Islamic world.

Saed went on to say that all Muslims removed their shoes, washed their feet, hands, heads, eyes and faces before kneeling down in rows behind the leader and praying to Allah. The interior of the building was very plain reaching in height to the beautiful painted dome. Several niches were carved out or formed in the perimeter and an area partially disguised for the ladies, so that they caused no distraction during the prayers. Just beside the entrance was an area with running water and stone seats for the faithful to carry out their ablutions or ritual cleanliness.

'Why don't they wash at home?' asked Andrew.

'Because it's a ritual,' said Dad, 'they're not having a wash,' he explained to his son.

It seemed that almost as quickly as Saed had his charges inside the Mosque than he was whisking them out and onto the bus again. The little group headed out along the road past the palm tree grove but Saed briefly paused the bus and asked one and all to look out of the window. On both sides, various sort of transport were available in no particular order, a makeshift market was scattered on both sides of the dusty road. Camels loaded with packs of bananas, bullock vehicles with bananas, old trucks with piles of hands of bananas and all around groups of men haggling, buying and selling pile upon pile of bananas.

Saed turned to us and said. 'This is the b...' but before he could finish, the whole bus load of people said, 'banana market.' A little laugh ruffled throughout the bus, and the driver weaved his way thought the menagerie of animals and miscellaneous vehicles. He paused for a moment to collect a little boy waiting patiently on the dusty road.

All around us now was palm trees and dense undergrowth, tropical plants and hanging vines. Occasionally we would drive through a plantation or coconut grove but mostly it was a light jungle which flanked the road.

'You may have noticed,' shouted Saed through his microphone, 'we have just picked up my nephew. He will measure up anyone who wants any clothes made. We can make shirts, suits or dresses for the ladies. These will all be finished to the correct size by the time this trip delivers you back to the ship.'

All around the bus people were saying 'it's a fiddle. You can't do that. It's not possible. We can't make clothes that quick in Manchester.'

Dad turned to Andrew and said, 'they can do it son, and they'll make a good job of it.'

One or two people were measured for a pair of trousers and half a dozen shirts and a lady had her measurements taken for a shirtwaister dress. The bus rumbled into the little village of Pettah and the boy jumped out with a deposit from the two gentlemen and the lady. Immediately the driver asked 'did anyone want a cold drink?', Although it was still early the sun was starting to heat up and people were getting thirsty.

Half an hour later, another lady in a long sari got on with a young man and spoke of the many dresses they could make. She had swatches of colourful silk pieces to show the bus. The young man went straight to the gentlemen with a sample of the shirt material and made a note of the colours and any personal amendments they required. He was abruptly told he was too late. Within minutes of their unscheduled stop, the bus was pulling away, weaving through the animals in the shantytown and vanishing in a cloud of dust up the road.

'Why do the men have red stains on their teeth, Dad,' Andrew asked his father.

'It's a nut called beetle nut that the locals chew. It's a bit like you chewing gum, I suppose, it's habit forming. You will notice that a large number of the male population chew it,' he said.

'Seems a bit weird to me,' said Andrew. 'You always make us brush our teeth and all these fellows have red stained teeth. They obviously don't have any toothpaste here.'

Dad interjected, 'You'll also see them brushing their teeth with little twigs, with frayed ends.'

'Cor, they do some strange things over here, Dad.'

'Well not strange, but the habits are certainly different.

'How do you know about these people, Dad? You've never been here before, have you?'

'Well. As a matter of fact, I have. Several years before you were born I was on one of Her Majesty's battleships and we were in a place further up the coast called Trimcomallee. We called into the deep water harbour when we were preparing to fight the Japanese in World War II.'

'Blimey, Dad, you never told me that before. What did you do on the ship? I always thought you were a Royal Marine.'

'That's right, son. When Marines are at sea, they have naval duties and I was part of the Fourteen Inch Gun Team,' Bob answered his son. It was probably the longest conversation they had had on the trip. Andrew was learning many things, both about his Dad and the different countries they had passed by and visited.

Andrew and Susan looked out of the window at the lush vegetation. Mum sat patiently with her husband, she found it all interesting but she wasn't the adventurous type and would have settled for a good cup of tea and a plate of cucumber sandwiches.

The bus rumbled on past a tea plantation where Saed tried to explain how the leaves were picked, dried and selected. We all rambled and bounced along in the bus, the conversation continued with many points of view being expressed about the heat and the country, the dress code of the locals and the political situation, which no one seemed to know anything about.

Soon Saed started to fumble with the microphone again. He was anxious to draw our attention to the river we were going to see in a few moments.

'Very soon we will be arriving at the place where the elephant boys bring their elephants to bathe every day. This takes place every day of the year and when the elephants are selected to work, a boy is chosen to stay with them for the rest of their lives. They become companions for each other. Soon the bus pulled off the road they parked beside two other cars and another old bus. People quickly alighted. They were happy to stretch their legs and many lit up a cigarette or pipe, many of the regular smokers had been smoking on the bus and although the windows were open it still left smoke curling around the interior. At least with the doors open it gave the bus a chance to get some fresh air in.

The little group walked down to the river, most of them gave the elephants a wide berth. The elephants rolled in the river tossing their stumpy legs around, and rolled backwards and forwards. On a command from their companions they stopped and the boys scrubbed them with yard brooms on their heads and behind their ears. The river tumbled and curled soaking the animals. It was plain to see they really enjoyed this. Some of the boys led their charges onto the dusty bank where the massive beasts once again rolled in the sand and dust.

A boy on a bike appeared from nowhere with a crate of Pepsi Cola and did a roaring trade, with inflated prices but no one cared. It was hot and they were thirsty. The smokers were the last to get back on the bus, reluctant to leave water and anxious to enjoy the last drag of their cigarettes. The engine revved and the old charabanc pulled away.

'That was great, Sue, wasn't it? Did you see the big one blowing water everywhere with its trunk? And did you see 'How Much' getting wet when he got to close trying to take photographs.'

'How Much?' had been nicknamed because that's what he used to call out to the Arab boys when bargaining. The Scotsman was certainly stuck with the name for the trip.

Kandy

A few moments later the bus rumbled into Kandy. The driver was very keen and proud to announce that he was from Kandy and proceeded to tell us the finest street was Colombo Street and we were now driving up it. He said he would take us to the most beautiful park called Hew Park and there we could look over lake Kandy. No sooner was it said than we were rolling into the car park, where many locals were sweeping with palm brooms on a large square surrounded by palm trees. The place was indeed very beautiful with many plants in bloom and delightful fragrances all around. Within a few minutes of being there other buses were pulling up this was definitely a pre-arranged popular resting place.

A lady and gentleman in costume stepped forward and proceeded to tell us of the history of the Kandyan dancers. The dances derive from ancient history, about 543 BCE and there are three main styles of dance depending from where they originate. Some dances are performed just by males and depict purification, such as the Ves Dance. Another dance, Naiyandi, originated from a festival of lighting the lamps in preparation of foods for the demons. People believe that Uddekki dance was given to the people by the gods. Pantheru Dance originates from the time of Buddha. The last dance, Vannams, derives from a time when a king, Sri Weeraparakrama gave considerable importance to the dance, songs and poetry.

One by one the dances, as described by the orator, took place. The dancers in their brilliantly colours costumes took over the square and performed with a practised dexterity and the dancing continued for over an hour. Boys sold cans of Pepsi Colas as fast as they could supply them as the sun blazed down and the audience sweltered in the sun-drenched square, which had only a few wooden benches to sit on and a few swaying palms to give some respite from the heat.

'I'll be glad when this is over,' said mum to her husband. 'I really cannot take too much more of this heat.'

Most of the people around were muttering similar comments and then, as if on cue, the dancing came to an abrupt end and the drums stopped beating. Everyone clapped and quickly made a beeline back to the air-conditioned building close by, where they were invited to purchase souvenirs of dolls in costume or artefacts made from wood, brass Buddahs and Kandyan drums with skin tops and noisy beads.

Soon we could hear 'How much?' bargaining in the background, he was purchasing a pair of leather thong sandals.

A few moments later Saed bellowed out and waved his umbrella, for keeping off the sun, 'Follow me, please. We are going to visit the temple in the park next.'

At this stage most of the trippers would have gladly got back on the bus, but as it turned out the temple was only a short walk away. The crocodile of people walked alongside the lake to the temple which rose from the ground with majestic turrets and towers. A beautiful dome dominated the skyline and steps led up to a higher level. Vines and exotic plants surrounded and adorned the wondrous sculptures. Monkeys pranced and bounced around the trees gobbling food, especially fruit as it was offered; much being sold by the local boys at inflated prices to the tourists to feed the animals. The elephant boys had made their way back from the river and stood around with their giant charges, all of them proffering tins for any financial remuneration they could secure

Meanwhile the bus load of tourists made their way up the steps to the entrance of the Buddhist temple. A large entrance welcomed them and the brightly-clothed monks requested that people remove their shoes. Their saffron and orange garments stood out from the darker background, although much of the inner temple was adorned with gold and exotic flowers – the fragrance of the frangipani drifted heavily on the warm air. The monks beckoned us inwards.

'Wow!' cried out Andrew, 'Look at that!' The curious lad had been one of the first to step inside the temple. There, in front of him, was a giant gold statue of the Sitting Buddha; he guessed it must be about thirty to forty feet tall and sat in the centre of the giant dome. Monks in bright saffron robes knelt and prayed to their God and many times little bells could be heard. The monks encouraged the tourists to say a prayer and place a donation in a font. When complete they clanged the bell.

Slowly and steadily the tourists worked their way in and out of the beautiful temple. Inside the giant dome it was much cooler and the atmosphere was pious and serene.

Soon everyone was collecting their shoes and paying the 'monkey boy' some coins. This young man spent his time making sure the monkeys didn't run off with a pair of the shoes, which was quite a feat considering the agility of the troop.

Mount Lavinia

Once on board the bus, various folks discussed what they had purchased and gradually settled down to the long drive towards the city. Saed suggested a nap may be a good idea as they had a two-hour drive in front of them before their next stop.

Gradually the busload drifted off; some slept, some looked out of the windows, but most had a doze for about an hour anyway. The old charabanc rumbled on down the dusty pot-holed road. They passed villages, crossed rivers, drove through the plantations and several jungle areas, and soon the little group found themselves catching glimpses of the sea. The standard of the road appeared to be improving.

Saed decided that now was the time to enlighten the bus-load of passengers about the history of Mount Lavinia. He produced a document and in his Celanese dialect he read the history to us:

'Mount Lavinia is a major commercial suburb of Colombo. It is the largest suburb and a largely middle class area, escaping the ravages of industrialisation. It is famed for its famous Golden Beaches.

'The city built up around the original residence of Sir Thomas Maitland who was the founding Governor of Ceylon in the early 1800s. The area was named after the lead mestizo dancer of her father's troupe, Lovinia, at his welcoming party. Lovinia was half Portuguese and half Sinhalese; a ravishing beauty with jet-black hair. He was smitten by her charms and mesmerized by her beauty he fell in love with her and took every opportunity to see more of her. It was unconventional for a British officer to associate with a local girl and so he met her in secret. The legend says she was smuggled into his mansion through a secret tunnel.

'After six years as Governor of Ceylon Maitland was transferred to Malta where he lived and died as a bachelor. Successive Governors of Ceylon took up residence there; Sir Robert Brownrigg, Sir Edward Paget and Sir Edward Barners. The hotel was used as a military hospital in the Second World War and afterwards it was converted into a hotel and the tunnel was sealed. Some scenes of the film *The Bridge on the River Kwai* were filmed there.'

The old bus continued up the now beautifully tarmacked drive and although the surroundings were jungle-like, it was obvious there were well-tended gardens. Every now and then glimpses of the sun dazzled undergrowth and fleeting glimpses of the sea could be seen. Suddenly the bus broke from the dense greenery and an old, but beautiful palace constructed of white stone came into sight. All around the perimeter of this extravagant piece of architecture a tablecloth of beautifully sculptured lawns reached out and embraced the surrounding wall on the boundaries; beyond this was the azure blue of the sea.

'We suggest that you don't swim in the sea, sir,' said the Maître D' who had appeared from nowhere in his starched uniform. Although he spoke to one man, he was clearly addressing the whole group. He went on to say that the area was well known for its large shark population. The busload of tourists was invited to enter the beautifully marbled building. Opulent floors and sweeping staircases graced the initial welcome. Slowly the tourists made their way to the stately arched balcony.

The visitors were all requested to be seated and a sample teatime menu was offered by the uniformed staff. The waiters all highly attired with turbans, feathers adorning their headgear, and starched whites with gold braid embellishments. Various types of tea were available and cucumber sandwiches with the crusts cut off; fancy cakes and buttered crumpets arranged on the dishes placed before us. Lemon and orange squash was available for the children or those who preferred cooler refreshment.

Saed and the driver mingled with the party telling talks of interest and historical fact. For an hour the guests relaxed and perused the immediate environment, but when the time had passed, everyone was invited to return to the bus.

The experience of Mount Lavinia had been substantial; the exotic fragrances which adorned the balconies and the driveways lingered on the evening air.

Soon the old bus was making its way back along the road and heading for Colombo, which was only a forty-minute drive from the prominent headland. It seemed like only a few minutes before the shanty towns and the tin huts were crowding the gutters and the basic streets which adjoined the outskirts of Colombo. The wharves and derricks of the shipyards came into view and soon the old charabanc was turning to run along beside the giant hull of the SS Orion, now safely berthed in the shipyard.

Several buses had pulled up and passengers were once again in the hands of the pursers and the Orion's uniformed staff. Slowly but surely the passengers embarked, with whatever souvenirs they had purchased, onto the decks of the giant passenger liner.

Once on board, the strange but now familiar sounds of the music from Kandy could be heard coming from 'C' Deck aft lounge and bar. It was no surprise to find the Kandyan dancers performing their ritual dancing to the folks who had not endured it in the baking sun at Kandy.

Roast Beef of Old England rang out and all the passengers headed for the dining rooms. Everyone had plenty to talk about and every table buzzed with their localised adventures associated with the individual trips in Ceylon.

After dinner, Susan and Andrew headed up to the deck looking for their friends, so that they could swap stories of their day. By now the Kandyan dancers had left the ship and the crew were scurrying around obviously making ready to get the ship under way.

Suddenly the foghorn on the funnel blasted out its signal to prepare for departure. The mighty engine sprang into life, vibrating through the ship. The massive hawsers, both fore and aft, were removed from the fixed bollards on the quayside. The giant capstan started to turn and the Bosun and crew engaged the hawser around the moving capstans; the crew methodically guiding the rope into a neat configuration as it wound its way up the hull and onto the beautifully timbered deck, slowly and steadily forming an ever-increasing coil of rope.

Meanwhile vibrations rumbled through the deck and the funnel started to belch smoke. On completion of the first mooring line, the other four lines splashed into the water and were recovered and hauled onto the deck in a similar fashion. The Captain stood in a prominent position overseeing all that was going on and talking into a walkie-talkie. By now, the bow thruster was bubbling tumultuous gushes of water, together with dirt, debris and mud from the ocean bed at the side of the ship. Andrew had been too busy watching this to notice that a tug had been tethered to the forward bollard and the tightened line now taking the strain lead the ship away from the quayside.

The children dashed to the aft section in time to see the giant propellers engage and cause a cauldron of activity, only to settle into a slower but rhythmic pulse of propulsion. Another tug had engaged with Orion and slowly but very definitely the giant ship was edging away from the quayside. The ship's horn had created three mighty blasts which brought a shiver to Andrew's spine. Andrew always ended up with tears in his eyes, 'though he knew not why; the excitement was always nostalgic, emotional and real, the thought of visiting and seeing a place and then moving on.

It wasn't long before the distance was increasing between the quayside and the ship. Half an hour later the tug had relinquished its umbilical cord and the Orion was once again on its way.

That evening, the crew and many of the passengers dressed up in grass skirts for a Southern Ocean Festival of partying and dancing. The cocktails flowed freely and ladies performed in their hula-hula skirts. Dancing carried on well into the night and a barbecue was available late on into the evening. The music could still be heard even after the children had been ordered to bed.

Monday 26th January 1959 – The Merit Badge

Today, we were informed, is Foundation Day in Australia. Traditionally there was always a party the night before. The water was a lot choppier, so Mum and Susan decided not to go to breakfast, however that did not stop Dad and Andrew—as usual they ploughed through a solid breakfast. Surprisingly only about half the dining room was full although in hindsight this was to be expected, considering the events of the night before and the state of the choppy weather causing the ship to react to the motion of the waves.

Once breakfast was over, Andrew made his way to the decks in search of his mates. It wasn't long before he came across Richard and Steven.

'Hi Rich, hi Steve, are you going to scouts today?' asked Andrew.

'Think we should; we missed the last meeting,' replied Steve.

The boys made their way along the rolling decks hanging onto the rails and avoiding the spray being tossed up from the sea and carried on the wind. Only a few passengers were on the promenade deck, even though it was sunny and warm. The boys met up with Chunky and Akela. In a corner of the lounge several other boys were already there.

'Weather's taken a bit of a turn, hasn't it?' said one of the lads.

'Yes, but we'll still get a good swim a bit later; the water's really warm now.'

'Alright boys, let's be having you in a straight line now. Today your task is to find two people on the deck. Now I'm not going to tell you which deck, but they will be in a prominent position and I will give you their description. When you find these people, you are to identify yourselves with your name and troop and when both parties are satisfied that you are who you say you are, you will demonstrate two knots for them, they will tell you which knots to form so make sure you have your knot rope with you. One boy will demonstrate a sheet bend and the other will make up a reef knot or a fisherman's knot.

'Now split up into teams of two but don't all go to the same places together. The first group that gets back here will be awarded a merit badge. So, before you go, let's see you tie the three knots we have just mentioned.

'Oh, and one other thing, when you tie the knots make sure you tell the guest visitor the purpose of the knot you have just demonstrated for them.'

The little group of twelve boys and two girls, all part of the First SS Orion Scout Group, gathered around Chunky, who went over the knots for those who could not remember. Akela gave the description of the people to be found; 'one male, one female about forty years of age. The lady will wear a red scarf; the man is wearing a safari jacket and shorts. They will be together and waiting for you to approach them. They will not talk to you until you have identified yourself.'

Five minutes later: 'Make sure you all return here by twelve o'clock,' Chunky said. 'Are you ready, get set, go! Don't forget the first pair back wins the prize.'

The children dashed off in all directions; Andrew and Steven paired up together, both of them wearing the neckerchief which identified them as scouts of the First SS Orion Troop. First they went up on the sun deck. They had decided to go to the top and work their way down the decks. The spray was really lashing over as the ship ploughed through the waves, but the spray was light caught on the wind and gently covering them, cooling them down. Men were playing deck quoits and tennis on the top deck and people were laying around in swimming trunks and swimsuits. It was easy to quickly check this deck; no one was wearing a safari jacket.

They slipped down to the deck below, walking fast and peering at the passengers sitting or lying on the wooden lounger seats. The promenade deck was always popular; many of the fitness fanatics chose to run or walk at a pace for hours on end around these boards. The two boys clambered down the set of steps leading to the deck below. They passed a small group of scouts who had just completed that deck and they had found no one. They exchanged pleasantries and assured each other they had not discovered the mystery guests.

Almost as soon as they had passed the other scouts, Andrew noticed a couple partially hidden behind newspapers. Not wanting to alert the other scout group, he pushed Steve towards the railing and pointed out to sea.

'I think I've found them Steve. It's the two people behind the newspapers behind us.'

'You sure, Andy?'

'Yes, look at his jacket.'

The two boys made their way back and politely addressed the couple sitting with the newspapers.

'Excuse me sir, are you the scout leaders we have been asked to find?' asked Andrew.

'That's right, my boy, you are the first to find us. You had better give me your names.'

The two young boys obliged.

'And now I'd like you to demonstrate a sheet bend.'

Stephen passed his piece of rope with a loop skilfully woven at the end. Andrew tied the knot and displayed it with skill and panache to the scoutmaster.

'Well done, young 'un, that's perfect. Now I understand you've to get back and claim your prize. As he said this, the other boys they had passed were returning to the steps and saw Andrew and Stephen demonstrating to the couple and quickly came forward to establish their knot-making skills, realising that because they had not been observant in the first place; they had walked past the couple quietly sitting down.

The boys raced along the passageway down the main staircase and found Akela and Chunky, explaining to them what happened and that the scoutmaster had taken their names and asked them to demonstrate a sheet band.

Later that day, the two boys were presented with a leather woggle with the badge of the SS Orion. Both Steve and Andrew were very proud to be presented with this, although Andrew's Dad did not come to see him receive it, not realising how important it was to his son.

Later that evening after dinner, the Bakers all went to the cinema together before the children went to bed and the Mum and Dad went up to the bar for a nightcap. Andrew placed his necktie and woggle on the chest of drawers and stared at it from his bunk; simple as it was, this was the first time he had been given something for merit he had achieved.

Tuesday 27th January 1959 – Crossing the Equator

Susan had been ill most of yesterday suffering from seasickness caused by the large, heavy swell of the Indian Ocean. This morning the waves had evened out considerably, and as usual Dad and Andrew were amongst the first at breakfast. The menu was especially printed telling us of the impending celebration that afternoon. But as this was only breakfast it was more of a reference than something more details – things like:

Neptune's Breakfast

Seaweed Sandwiches

Mermaid Boiled Eggs with Toast

Davy Jones' Big Fry

and as usual, there was always orange juice, milk, coffee and/or a pot of tea.

Around the table the conversation consisted of the ceremonies surrounding the crossing of the Equator and at eleven o'clock on the sun deck, the officer had asked for a gathering to tell everyone of the procedure and just what would take place and where. Much interest was gathered and the hilarity started when four of King Neptune's Maidens all sailors turned up in scanty costumes and dyed mop heads turned into wigs.

Andrew and his friends gathered and listened to learn about the traditional crossing of the Equator activities. An hour later, lunch was served as a seafood buffet on the pool deck. The water was lowered in the pool to assist anyone to wanted to take part, but was not a swimmer. The boys pushed forward to place their names on the list for the greasy pole pillow fight and the traditional dip, Equator-style, into the pool.

While the lunchtime diners were finishing their meal, the crew made ready the pole over the pool; this was secured to stop it moving and a small handrail was erected to assist in mounting the pole. Already the spectators were gathering and taking their seats for the afternoon's spectacle. It didn't take long for the pool deck seats to fill, and all the other places adjacent, to witness the Equatorial Shenanigans.

First to arrive amongst a fanfare from the band was King Neptune and his Mermaids. Once ensconced on his throne and surrounded by the mermaids with their assistants, he adjusted his long flowing wig and a cloak of seaweed and cockleshells. On obtaining the instruction of precisely when they were crossing the equator he declared the ceremony open.

The Pirate pageant started the festivities and the pirates paraded in front of the crowd, many had handmade costumes with wooden cutlasses; some of the men dressed as female pirates with balloons under their jumpers and many of the females came in tight shorts and wet T-shirts. The parade was deemed a success and King Neptune had the winning lady and gent thrown into the pool by his helpers to reward their efforts.

The greasy pole battles commenced and one after the other they were tumbled into the pool, many of the contestants didn't even manage to crawl along the pole to the combatant position, before they unceremoniously swivelled and splashed into the pool. After the winner was declared he was given a kiss from King Neptune's helper and then thrown into the pool to the riotous applause and laughter of the spectators.

The Master of Ceremonies then called everyone in the order they had placed their names in the book to be ceremoniously dunked. King Neptune came down from his throne and stood by the pool; a large bucket of ice cream and a paintbrush about twelve inches wide were set down beside a large wooden chair. The line formed and one by one the victims of the Equator Festival sat in the chair. King Neptune plastered them with the ice cream, said a few choice words to each one; his helpers then stood them up and pushed them backwards into the pool. Two men vigilantly assisted them towards the ladder and made sure their safety was in order. Each time somebody hit the water a loud cheer went up and the ship's photographer was on hand to record the happy event.

The afternoon passed by festively and everyone had a good time. Andrew, Susan and their friends all took part and later at dinner, Andrew told his Mum and Dad what happened and they replied, 'yes, we know, we saw it all from the deck above, and yes, we saw you being thrown into the pool.'

That evening after dinner, the ship had a big fancy dress party and the revellers partied into the night.

Thursday 29th January – The Cocos and Keeling Isles

After breakfast Andrew and Susan raced up to 'C' Deck pushing open the heavy doors which led onto the deck and made a beeline for the railings. They peered out to the azure blue sea. Dolphins raced alongside the ship, jumping and diving, surfing on the wake as the bow ploughed and churned the calm waters.

The children breathed in the now familiar smells of the polished brass and the scrubbed decks. They peered into the water and spotted an abundance of flying fish leaping and skimming over the dancing waves. They ran first to the port side and then to the starboard; peering into the distance scanning the horizon.

That morning at breakfast the table talk had been about the arrival of Orion at the group of islands known as the Cocos Isles. A leaflet was left on the table telling everyone who cared to read it, a little of the history of the island.

The Territory of the Cocos (Keeling) Islands is also known as the Cocos and Keeling Islands and part of Australia; located in the Indian Ocean, southwest of Christmas Island and approximately midway between Australia and Ceylon. The territory consists of two atolls and twenty-seven coral islands, of which two—West Island and Home Island, are inhabited with a local population of approximately six hundred people speaking a language derived from Malay.

Susan and Andrew decided to play a game of deck quoits while passing the time waiting for their respective friends to arrive, it wasn't long before Andrew's mates turned up.

'Table tennis, John?' asked Andrew.

'Yep, why not,' replied John.

Richard and Susan came; Janice joined them as they were walking along the deck towards the tables.

'Got to keep our eyes open for the Island. We'll be there in about two hours, so they'll be coming into sight soon,' remarked Susan.

Janice asked, 'Which islands are you talking about?'

Susan decided to tell everyone what they had learned from the breakfast brochure.

The boys played their first game of table tennis; no one else was as good as John and Andrew and refused to play with them, but happily played amongst themselves on one of the other tables. The time passed quickly and it wasn't long before the ships tannoy announced that the Islands would be coming into view in the next hour and the ship would be stopping offshore for three hours to unload supplies and mail.

In the distance a cloud was forming on the horizon. From past experience the boys knew that this could be just what they had been waiting for. All around them the flying fish were skimming over the azure blue water. By now Andrew was out of his shirt enjoying the rays of sunshine beating down.

Susan said, 'I am going to find Mum and Dad and tell them the islands are coming into view.' She scampered off, her mate Janice followed. The two girls had been inseparable since meeting on the ship. The boys played another game of table tennis, occasionally stopping to go and indulge in yet another tub of ice cream.

Soon afterwards the foghorns were belching steam and emitting a noise to waken the dead. By now the Cocos Islands were in full view and the ship was steaming directly towards them. Passengers were arriving on all decks and leaning out over the railings, many of them holding drinks with little coloured umbrellas in them. Men stood with pints of ale, but didn't stay too long. In the main they got fed up and went back to the bar. The ship still had quite a way to go. They could get at least another pint in before it became really interesting!

Twenty minutes later, the ship was moving very slowly and it had slipped in between the two islands. The Captain was up on the bridge deck and he beckoned to one of his officers who spoke into the walkie-talkie. Suddenly there was the not unfamiliar sound of the anchor chain being released, and it crashed uncontrollably into the sea and vanished into the clear blue waters. The lowering of the anchor was the signal for all the people on the shoreline to head for their little canoes.

Soon dozens of little boats appeared, some paddling, some with small sails but all heading out towards this giant ocean liner anchored just off their coast. A lighter and a couple of small tenders made their way out; these carried fresh fruit – the storeroom doors to the pursers and galley areas opened. The gangway was lowered and various dignitaries made their way to be greeted by officers of the Orion.

The natives, in their colourful costumes, bobbed like a flock of ducks on the surface of the water all around the ship. Both boys and men dived into the sea for coins or any objects that were thrown. Andrew and Jack saw a waiter throw a teapot into the sea. The natives scrambled for this prize and one of them held it high about the water on retrieval before placing it in his canoe. A treasure to behold.

For several hours the islanders bounced in the tide, awaiting any handouts which may come their way. Occasionally garlands of flowers were seen around the necks of both men and women who had managed to secure them from the fisherman in the canoes.

The Orion gave a mighty blast and belched steam from the whistle on the funnel. The ship's engines shuddered into life. Boys, girls, men and women; all who had retreated to their daily activities, jumped back into life, many of them heading for the walkways and ship's railings. By this time, the canoes were already paddling towards the shore and heading for safety.

The anchor chain was rumbling link by link around the capstan on the fore deck. The crew were positioned on the decks ready to secure and operate any necessary winches. Officers appeared on the bridge deck with walkie-talkies. The Orion, now free of its metal tether, engaged its gear system and the mighty propellers agitated the azure blue sea into a frenzy. Hundreds of seagulls swirled all around the ship. Sharks' fins could be seen cutting through the surface as the last of the garbage could be seen being discharged from the metal double doors, which were dramatically clanged too as the ship made ready for sea.

Three mighty blasts sounded from the foghorns. The flags that had been flying were lowered; the Blue Peter was changed and new flags were run up the mast. Slowly but very surely, the Orion started to turn and head for the channel between the two main Islands; West Island and Home Island.

People gathered at the village of Bantam on the Home Island all still waving as the Orion turned into the passage and headed once again for the open sea.

The Swimming Lesson

Andrew and Stephen sat by the swimming pool; the sun was strong and beat down on the them. 'Time to get wet Steve,' said Andrew.

'Yep, it's too hot just sitting here.'

They made their way to the ladder and inched their way into the pool, neither of them could swim and they were quite envious of the boys and girls who just jumped into the water.

Andrew was developing a technique of pushing himself off the steps and crashing and splashing his way through the water to a fixed point further along the railings. He did this time after time, trying to get a little further each time. It wasn't very successful, but he was getting more confident in the water. The two boys did what they could in the water, both of them were out of their depth and as the ship gained a little more speed, the water in the pool splashed from end to end, depending on the pitch and toss of the ship.

Dozens of people surrounded the pool, some bathing, many just spread eagled and getting a tan, several of the boy's mates and friends gathered around, like a lagoon it really was a focal point; this was the social area for many of the younger passengers.

The afternoon drifted on, afternoon tea came and went; a team of boys and girls headed into the whist drive which was taking place in the lounge. While entering the lounge, Andrew caught sight of his Mum and Dad. They were sitting at the card table with two friends. Susan had found them just a few minutes earlier and the little group sat enjoying the session of whist drive.

The trouble was, the boys found it difficult to sit for too long, they needed to be occupied and so they toddled off to find a talent competition just about to start at one of the other venues on 'C' Deck. Because this was the late afternoon, the act were mostly young people; teenagers playing guitars or singing hopefuls. Andrew and Stephen sat down amongst the other guests with a couple of ice creams and watched and listened to the entertainment. The conjuror was the best; somehow he really did manage to pull a rabbit from a hat to the gasps and astonishment of the young crowd.

'I thought you weren't allowed to have pets on board the ship,' said Andrew.

'You're not,' his mate replied. 'I wonder if the Captain knows he's got it on board.'

'Don't forget, he flew a load of pigeons around the lounge as well.'

As the day progressed, the two lads decided to go back to the pool area, they sat around for a few moments. Most of the passengers had gone off to get ready for the evening meal. Unbeknown to Andrew, his father had followed the boys on deck to tell him not to be too long as it was nearly dinnertime.

On seeing his son, still not making much progress, he lost his temper with Andrew and yelled at him, 'If you don't swim properly now, you are not coming into this pool again. Do you understand?' He pushed the boy away from the railings and Andrew, who was quite scared of his father, splashed and floundered in the water.

'Now swim boy, swim! Arm over arm; that's it! You can do it!'

Andrew crashed and splashed in the water, salt water getting up his nose and in his eyes. After a lot of splashing about, he realised he had got to the other side.

'Now then, I told you, you could do it. Now turn round and to it again.' His father didn't seem so scary this time and Andrew crashed back down the side of the pool, totally out of control but a little more confident of his ability.

Next time he looked up, his father had gone, leaving the boy to his own devices. The two boys scrambled up the ladder. Andrew was delighted at his achievement but shaking from the fear his father had instilled in him. He would have liked to go into the pool again, but decided his Dad may still be angry with him. Little did he know, his father was secretly delighted, he knew now that his son would improve with practise.

That night, after evening meal the ship had arranged a Tropical Island dance and fancy dress. Everyone came in grass skirts or wearing 'shipwrecked' costumes. Some carried cardboard spears. There were men dressed up in hula skirts with a pair of coconuts tied around their chests like a lady's bra. The band played on into the early hours, lots of different cocktails were available from the bar and many young couples were getting to know each other better.

The ship ploughed on, crashing through the waves and creating the most intensely coloured blue and green fluorescence along the side of the ship. Several young couples cuddled along the railings looking out to sea, deep in their own world, but all of us with the same goal. Everyone was heading to Australia, the land of opportunity.

A Visit to the Bridge

The following day, was much the same as the previous, but with one large exception. Today we had all been invited to join the ship's Captain on the bridge. At eleven o'clock, the Bakers were formally introduced to the Captain of the ship. Captain Edgcombe, who in turn introduced the First Officer, who he explained would answer any questions we had and give us an insight into how the ship was run.

The Bakers and one or two other families mercilessly bombarded the officer with questions, which were probably very mundane to him. Andrew piped up, 'How often do you see whales at sea?'

The officer smiled and indulged the young boy. 'Quite frequently actually. We had some in sight this morning. You see because they are quite large, occasionally an alarm will sound indicating the close proximity to the vessel.'

'Do you ever run any over?' asked Andrew.

The officer smiled again, 'No lad, the whales move out of the way of the ship well before the Orion comes anywhere near them. Occasionally you can record them on the Ferrograph, but the vibration from the vessel makes sure they are always at a safe distance. No, the only reason you see them is because they are curious, they probably like to see other large objects in the ocean and at different periods of the year they too follow migratory journeys.'

The officer allowed the families to look through the powerful static binoculars mounted in two different positions on the port and starboard sides of the viewing platform.

Andrew looked into the ferograph to see what was happening below the ship. Various shoals of fish were pointed out to him and the depths they were swimming at. The officer flicked a switch and suddenly the undulations of the seabed were pointed out, these looked like little mountains on a flat base.

It wasn't too long before the crew asked us to vacate the bridge as there was another group waiting to visit. One of the junior offers told us there would be at least six other visits before lunch that morning. This was a really popular thing to do on the ship.

The Bakers made their way down to the passenger decks. Andrew and Susan dashed off to find their friends. Celia and Bob headed to the coffee lounge for elevenses and to listen to the outcome of the tote which they had invested six-pence in.

Andrew soon found his friends by the pool and quickly settled into an excited diatribe into what he had seen and done on the bridge of the ship. The boys jumped and splashed in the swimming pool but this time he swam very badly backwards and forward in the swirling water as it crashed backwards and forwards with the motion of the ship.

Lunch came and went; the boys played Ping-Pong and deck quoits. They challenged the girls to a game of deck tennis, and then they all jogged round the deck before ending up jumping into the swimming pool again to cool off. Daytime merged into the evening; the ship was putting on a variety show, which was enjoyed by one and all.

Chapter 5

Sunday February 1st 1959   Arriving in Australia

The family rose early and went to morning Mass, then carried on to the dining room. Few people were there because during the night a squall had blown up. The ship had pitched and tossed but it didn't last too long and the morning produced a red sky, so bright it looked as it if had been painted on the very edge of the horizon with an artist's brush.

Mum and Susan decided to give breakfast a miss and headed back to the cabin.

Dad and Andrew polished off a plate full of bacon, sausage and eggs and went on the deck for a swift walk round. En route they met several friends and passed the usual morning pleasantries, but the comment which cropped up several times was, 'Looking forward to tomorrow Bob?

This was the last day aboard the ship for anyone who was departing at Perth so many people were really excited about the situation they found themselves in.

'It'll soon be our turn son,' Bob turned and addressed his young protégé. 'Are you looking forward to it? You know that Perth is the first stop for the ship in Australia? We will have to sail on for a few more days to Adelaide.'

'Of course Dad, it'll be great to get to Perth tomorrow, then we'll know what Australia is like.'

Dad smiled at him and tousled his hair. 'I'm going to see if your Mum is okay.'

Andrew looked over the railings to see how many porpoises were riding the wake of the ship. This was a normal activity now and true to form about six to eight giant fish were surfing the foam, darting up and down, washing through the waves. It wasn't long before one of Andrew's friends came by.

'Fancy a game of Ping-Pong?'

'Yes, okay, let's go and get a table before it gets busy.'

The boys scampered off towards the sports deck. En route they saw Chunky, the Scout Master and said a polite 'Good morning' giving the scout a salute as they passed. Moments later they were attacking the Ping-Pong balls like old adversaries. For a couple of hours they batted the ball backwards and forward across the table, the boys were getting to be good players with all the practise they had on the journey. Two other friends had joined them and competition between them was fierce. The two lads ceased their table tennis for a while so that they could go around the ship with their autograph books and collect a few

Then the announcement for ice-cream came across the tannoy and all activity stopped. The boys made a bee-line for the iced delight of the morning.

With a couple of pink ice-cream tubs in their hands the little group headed down to the pool deck and whiled away an hour or so jumping in the water and swimming a few lengths. As each day went by, Andrew's swimming had become more accomplished and considerably more improved. The officers and crew organised a drawing programme which the boys took part in before heading off to their lunch time meal.

The ship cruised on, rapidly closing the distance between their present position and the first Australian port, Fremantle.

That evening the gentlemen dressed in their dinner jackets and the ladies resplendent in their best evening dresses, headed upstairs for the Landfall Dinner in the 'A' Deck restaurant. Celia, Bob, Andrew and Susan sat together with their friends Bill and Sandra. Every now and then the couples would get up and have a waltz or a quick-step. Sandra reached out for Andrew's hand 'Come on young man, if it's the last think I do before we reach Australia I am going to teach you to waltz in time to the music.'

Moments later she had swept him into her arms and they were moving to one-two-three in a little square on the floor. Andrew didn't mind too much about this, he just didn't want his mates to see him in case they laughed.

The night passed by quite quickly. Mum was dancing with Bill and later on he gave Susan a whizz round the floor. The band played on late into the night. Many couples looked into each other's eyes. It was an evening of nostalgia; some couples would be saying goodbye on arrival in Fremantle in the morning.

Fremantle

After breakfast the children made their way up to the deck and in the distance, on the horizon, the shores of Australia could be seen. The excitement buzzed all over the ship. Many people were hanging over the railing, some with binoculars, some without but everybody was pointing and shouting to friends. It was as if the ship had been infected with happiness fever.

Andrew saw his Mum and Dad coming through the double doors. 'Dad! Dad! Look we've got to Australia! I can see it!' he pulled his Dad to the railings.

'Well, blow me down,' said Dad. He called to his wife, 'Look Celia, you can see the shore in the distance.'

The little family clung to each other, peering into the distance, willing it to be closer. Together they went to the deck where the ship's notices were displayed.

'We will be in Fremantle by twelve o'clock,' Dad announced. 'At one o'clock we will be on a coach, so make sure you children are ready. Now listen to me,' he said, 'I know you will want to see the ship berthing, but as soon as it has and the moment the first gangway goes down you come back to the cabin and we'll depart together. Is that clear now?' Dad had spoken.

Excitedly the children dashed off to find their friends. Many families were already mustering in the departure areas, luggage was being moved from cabins and into lobby area, stewards and porters were moving deck luggage and baby carriers. Andrew caught up with a couple of his mates both of whom were going to Sydney. By now the ship was closing on the port; tugs were connecting ropes and the pilot had already come aboard.

The Orion was getting ready to dock; the precise manoeuvres had already started and the ship was slowly turning to be pulled to her berth. The quayside in the distance was crowded with people, already waving and cheering, even though the ship was still a good way from the quayside.

An hour later, the ship was tied up, the tugs had gone, and officials were talking to the people due to depart the Orion. The gangways were all in place and the Purser was busy issuing labels and giving forms to the departing groups of passengers.

Soon the instruction came to make your way steadily to the shed marked with a giant 'A'. Excited passengers made their way down the gangway, some greeted by the awaiting well-wishers, who threw their arms around each other and kissed. Others excitedly made their way to the immigration desk in Shed 'A' to be allocated a place to stay for a while.

Buses could be seen from the ship's deck, lining up awaiting their passengers. Dad had his flock together and pretty soon we too were making our way down the gangway, through the throngs of well-wishers, passengers and officials, everything looked bright and fresh. The sea air permeated around and the sun beat down. There was hardly a breath of air. Mum was already complaining that it was too hot.

An official-looking man in a peaked hat came up to us and requested, 'Make your way to the buses please.' He checked the tags we were all wearing so he knew we were on the tour around Perth and Fremantle. We all climbed aboard the modern buses and settled ourselves into the plush seats.

Mum turned to Dad, 'Thank God these are up to scratch. I was half expecting four horses and a carriage!' She mopped her forehead.

Andrew said, 'You're sweating Mum.'

She pulled him up immediately, 'Horses sweat, you will recall I told you this before. Ladies glow, I do hope you won't forget your manners now.'

She looked at him disparagingly. He withered back in his seat. Andrew knew when not to make a smart reply. Just then, the driver arrived and swung himself into his seat.

'Good day, everybody,' he shouted. 'That means 'Hello, and you'll hear that every day from now on, so how's about you all shout it back? 'Okay! Good day everybody!' the driver shouted again.

Very half-heartedly the passengers said 'Good day' back to him, but it was only the children that put any enthusiasm into the greeting. All the English people seemed a little reserved. The driver started the bus engine and immediately the air conditioning started to cool the interior of the vehicle. Dad smiled at Mum, he knew she was uncomfortable. 'That's better, Bob,' she smiled back at him.

The bus pulled away from the dockyard area and immediately it was evident that a lot of thought had gone into the development all around. Plants were on both sides of the road; beautiful Oleander and palm trees adorned the wide esplanade, the bus was driving along. Soon we turned onto a modern free way which was wider than we had ever seen before. Modern buildings were all around, parkland areas seemed to be on both sides of the road, and the grass verges were wide and green with palm trees offering a little shade from the blistering sun. Wattle, palm and eucalyptus were growing in abundance and every hundred yards or so, water was pumping through giant spraying machines which created watery rainbows for the children to leap in and out of, in their effort to keep cool.

The bus driver switched on his intercom to the bus and in a loud Australian accent announced 'I would like to welcome you Poms to Fremantle. I know this is all new to you, so the first thing I want you to understand is that Australian people have a habit of giving nicknames. Hence we call all the English, Poms, all the Irish, Micks and all people with ginger hair, Blueys. If you're not feeling well, then your Crook. Now all the Brits call us Aussies so it's not all one-sided. Please understand that none of these slang names are meant to offend, in fact it's the opposite. It's a term of endearment because it shows you're been accepted for who or what you are. Now, not to go on about it but the girls on the bus will be called, Sheilas which is just a generality and any male who we don't know the name of will be called Bruce. And just so you know my name is Wayne because my dad came from just down the road and that's a very Australian name.

'As we drive down these local roads taking us away from the dock area, I am going to tell you a little about the history of the town and how it evolved. Fremantle is actually a city in Western Australia. It has a population of around 23,000 people. It is located at the mouth of the Swan River which is incidentally where I am going to take you today. In 1819 it was settled on by colonialists after a naval officer, Captain Charles Howe sailed in and pronounced possession of Western Australia and established a camp at the mouth of the Swan River.'

The bus sped on; the driver constantly had the attention of his charges as he called out titbits of information. The roads were so much wider than in

England and large trees were apparent everywhere. Several big buildings dotted the paved areas surrounded by green lawned areas.

'You will notice several large Victorian buildings and I will point out a number of well-preserved nineteenth century Heritage sites as we pass them. And here's one coming up now; if you look to the left in a moment you will see the beautiful National Hotel, the architect designed a tower at the highest point to enable a view of the city. This was at one time the highest point around. Not far away a similar style building with its cream cornices and other outlining features is the Fremantle Markets, where fruit and all sorts of fresh purchases are sold and traded every day. Thousands of people flock here for their weekly or even daily produce, everything is fresh and as you see. What a beautiful building.'

The bus, dodging the various traffic jams, weaved its way through the trucks and barrows. Policemen attempted to make the bustling traffic jams flow. Changing gear and uttering expletives at the same time, the road had narrowed for a short distance, but soon the big vehicle was making headway again. All the passengers had settled in the pleasantly cool atmosphere and the bus driver had a really laid-back but knowledgeable attitude, which entertained the visitors he transported proudly around the city.

'Not sure if I mentioned it, Cobbers, but it took the local citizens one hundred years to make Fremantle a city. You remember I told you it was first settled in 1819? Well, in 1929 it was declared a city and had a big celebration. I bet a few tinnies were opened that night!'

Like a Chinese whisper, it passed around the bus that a 'tinnie' was a beer in a tin.

It didn't take long for the bus to roll into the city suburbs, large houses; many of them constructed colonial style with corrugated tin roofs and large surrounding verandas. All of them set in substantial well-developed gardens and trees engulfed the properties. Each house was the subject of admiration from the occupants of the bus. Most of the migrants had come from the terraced areas of the suburbs and cities of Britain. Many of the gardens were in bloom and it was noticeable that the trees, as well as the shrubs were also in flower with colour in abundance.

The driver pointed out that we were on part of the Manjaree Heritage Trail. The local indigenous people 'the Whadjuk' lived in the area prior to the European settlements in the Swan River areas and it had been their custom to set fire to the surrounding bush in order to promote new growth around the perimeter area. He then went on to describe how this would be done as a controlled exercise when the wind was in the required direction.

The luxury coach pulled off the road into a small clearing with a restaurant and a tourist shop. He told his passengers that we would be stopping for an hour to give everyone a chance to stretch their legs, get a beer, take in the view and go to the privy. The visitors filed out of the bus and immediately wished they hadn't.

'Wow, isn't it hot, Dad,' Andrew turned to his father. Mum was almost visibly wilting under the midday sun. Susan was already making a beeline for the shade.

As a family, the Bakers filed into the tourist shop which fortunately had an air conditioning system on, although it wasn't as cool as the bus had been. Everyone was glad to be out of the sun. For ten to fifteen minutes all the passengers looked at maps and pens, pennants and ashtrays, books about wild flowers and trees and all the other tourist paraphernalia that make up a shop of this nature. The one thing that was different, that no one had ever seen before, was a complete range of artefacts made from mulga wood.

Wayne who had been browsing in the shop decided to interject and tell a small group gathered around the objects.

'Couldn't help noticing your interest folks. This wood is really prolific around several areas in Australia, especially around Western Australia and Queensland. It's part of the acacia plant family and grows like a large shrub in the desert regions. The Aborigines use it for food and make cakes from the seeds, they also get a honey substance from the shoots, as well as to tools to scrape the soil. Some tribes make woomeras because it's a hardwood, but most importantly the wood is very colourful with its light and dark veins which contour its structure. It has proved to be a natural wood which has come to symbolise Australian artefacts.'

With this Wayne proudly pointed to the many items on display and said, 'Now I'm going for a beer to wet my whistle.'

Mum and Dad purchased a bottle opener with a mulga wood handle and a date holder displaying the Swan River on a mulga stand. Andrew purchased a Western Australia pennant, then they all trooped into the restaurant for a drink and an ice-cream.

With one and all refreshed and ready to go again, they quickly queued like a crocodile and got back on the bus.

The man next to Dad said, in a Scottish accent, 'Damned hot out there, I'm glad to be back on the bus.'

Only the bus driver smiled 'I'll soon have you cool again. Right now we're going to head for the Round House which is not too far away. This is the oldest building in Western Australia.'

The bus jerked into action and was soon ploughing up the road; the air conditioning pushed out the cool air for which everyone was eternally grateful. It didn't take long before the coach pulled into the parking area of this historic building.

'Now the choice is yours, Cobbers. You can get off the bus and walk up the steps to get a fine view of the Swan River or you can stay on the bus and keep cool. The peak we are on is the highest around here and is known as Arthur Head from which you can see a fine panorama of the original settlement area of the Swan River.'

Dad, Susan and Andrew got off the coach and climbed the steps to the oldest public building. Mum declared that she would stay on the cool bus. They then walked around to a grassed area looking at all the views surrounded by eucalyptus trees. Just the look on Dad's face told us he was in his element even though it was hot. At least he had arrived at the Australia he was looking for. Wayne in the meantime stayed on the bus and gave the remaining passengers a potted history.

'The Noongar people inhabited the area that is now known as Fremantle, originally this was known as Walyalup, an aboriginal word.' Wayne cleared his throat; he was now impressing his captive audience. 'The area was considered as a site for the possible British settlement in 1827, when Captain James Sterling, in HMS Success explored the Swan River. He then sent a favourable report to the British government, who had for some time been suspicious of the French colonial intentions towards the Western portion of Australia. Now I don't have to tell you folks, that the Brits and the French have never exactly seen eye to eye.'

He took a deep breath and continued, 'Now, as a result of Stirling's report, Captain Charles Howe Fremantle of the ship HMS Challenger, a 603 ton 28 gun frigate was instructed to sail to the West Coast of Australia to establish a settlement there. On May the second, 1829, Fremantle hoisted the Union Flag in a bay near what is now known as Arthur's Head and if you look out of the bus window at your partners and mates, that's where they are right now.

'Now in accordance with his instructions, he took formal possession of the West Coast of New Holland 'in the name of George IV of the United

Kingdom. The settlement of Perth began on the 12th August 1829. Captain Fremantle left the colony on the 25th August after providing much assistance to Sterling in setting up the colony. It was only then that Sterling decided to name the port settlement Fremantle.'

Wayne took a swig from his bottle of water, opened the bus door to a furnace like blast of hot air and let his charges back onto the bus. Once on board and settled in their seats, he made a comment that some of you folks are already starting to look like lobsters and that was the reason all Aussies wear hats.

'Well while you've all been outside sweltering, we've had a bonzer time in the cool bus learning the history of Western Australia and about the Port Settlement of Perth and Fremantle. I'm now going to drive you past a number of heritage buildings on your way back through the suburbs while you take a swig of water and enjoy the air conditioning on the bus. With that Wayne started the engine and moved off from Arthur Head. The driver skilfully manoeuvred the bus down the hill through the gum tree covered lanes and soon we were all travelling along the leafy wide suburb with its beautiful houses.

Quickly arriving at the more densely populated areas and onto the perimeter of the city Wayne pulled the bus into a lay-by took another drink of water, leaned over and switched the microphone on.

'Fremantle is renowned for its architectural heritage from the times of convict built colonial-era buildings, a jetty, port and prisons. Built of limestone with ornate façades in a succession of styles, it gave rise to an Edwardian precinct for shipping companies and merchants following the development of the harbour.

'The Round House is the oldest building in Western Australia and was constructed as a gaol, but when the first shipment of convicts transported from Britain arrived in 1850 it became obvious that the Round House was inadequate and so a new gaol was built'

After pausing for breath, Wayne drove to the building he had been talking about. It wasn't long before we were turning into the port area.

'Well that was a terrific tour, Dad, I really enjoyed that.' Andrew smiled at his Dad. 'This Australia place may be okay after all.' He winked at Mum and Dad.

'Cheeky young pup!' Mum tousled his hair, 'c'mon now off the bus. Say thank you to Wayne as you get off and stay together as we go up the gangplank.'

Back on board the Bakers made a beeline for their cabins to get a quick shower before dinner. It was noticeable that night that there were many vacant spaces around the dining hall, and a few new faces filled some of the spots. Conversation that evening buzzed with the activities of the day.

Mum and Dad agreed that Wayne had been most informative. 'I hope we get him tomorrow for the short tip along the Heritage Trail.'

At the bar that evening all the men were sampling and passing opinion on the Australian Beer. Some were for it, some against, but a lot was swallowed, that's for sure.

The following morning all the Bakers were up bright and early, a shower and a quick cup of tea was enjoyed before the family made their way along to the dining room for breakfast. The menu contained lots of fruit, such as passion fruit and papaya which was not so well known in Britain, and the favourite Australian breakfast, Steak with two eggs was running alongside the traditional dishes. The Fremantle trip was very popular with many migrants wanting to get a glimpse of Australia and the people who didn't go on the first trip had waited to hear the comments of the people who had been.

The buses lined up as previously and people were ushered on filling each bus in rotation. Andrew caught a glimpse of Wayne waiting by the door of his bus.

'Quick Dad, let's get on Wayne's bus.'

'You can't do that lad, you have to go where you are told,' said Dad.

'Not me Dad, I'm going on Wayne's bus. He was good yesterday,' and with that he bolted two buses down the quay and waved at Wayne.

'Hiya cobber,' he called.

The Aussie seeing the little lad smiled and waved back. Other members on the queue followed suit and Mum, Dad and Susan chased after Andrew.

'Don't shout at him Bob, Australia likes people with initiative.' Wayne stuck up for the little lad as they climbed aboard his bus.

By this time the orderly emigrants waiting in line had fragmented and many of the other people were getting on the buses they had previously been on, having recognised the drivers they had previously encountered. It wasn't long before the air conditioned buses were pulling away from the waterfront leaving the Orion to collect the vittles for its onward journey.

'Welcome aboard, Cobbers. Good Day to all the Bruce's and Sheila's who were with me yesterday. Today it is my privilege to take you along to see some of the Heritage sites of Fremantle and to tell you of a little bit of the history of Fremantle. Those of you who travelled with us yesterday will travel past some of the sites we visited yesterday, on the road out of the harbour district is the one we have to take to get us into the town. En route I will tell you of the history of the country and the buildings as we pass them. As you know this is a short trip so we won't be stopping at too many sites, but we will stop for a bathroom call and to get a drink should you require it.

'By the way, the Australian slang for a toilet is a 'dunny' so if you need one urgently, just sing out and let me know otherwise we will stop in an hour and a half.'

During the next hour, Wayne passed many buildings, pointing them out as he approached them. 'The National Hotel; you will note, this has changed quite a bit as it had a major fire in 1907. The Fremantle Markets; you can buy just about anything in these many of them are run by stallholders from all over Europe. All the migrants tend to sell the products that are popular in their homeland and on many days you will find the Australian Aborigine playing their Didgeridoos busking for whatever money they can make.

'The Fremantle Prison, a very impressive building if you're driving past it, we could tell you a hundred stories about that place, but just ensure you never make the inside of it, or you'll have another one to tell.'

Wayne drove on, he was trying to fit in as much as he could. We drove along a long road with many warehouses. Suddenly he slowed the bus right down 'I'm going to show you the biggest dingo in town.'

We approached a warehouse with a painting of the Australian wild dog the height of the whole building.

'This is the listed flour mill and is very well known on the Heritage route. It's called the Dingo Flour Mill.'

We carried on down the road and turned into a wide area with several road junctions. Wayne pulled the bus over and pointed to some toilets and a small delicatessen where everyone could get some refreshments.

'Don't get lost now, Cobbers and take your cameras – have a look at that beautiful building over there.' Wayne pointed to the Fremantle Town Hall. 'You've got twenty-five minutes before we're off again,' he said.

Time went by quickly and Wayne counted all his charges back on the bus. 'Okay Cobbers, don't you agree that was one of the most beautiful buildings the Town Hall?' Wayne was back in full swing after his little refreshment.

'Have any of you old boys, heard of Aussie Rules? It's the game of football we play in this state. It has an oval ball a bit like a union ball, but slightly thinner.' Wayne went onto tell us a few facts about the sport as he pulled the bus out of the square and down the street.

'Organised Australian Rules football to give it the correct title was first played in Fremantle, in the early 1880s, with the Fremantle Football Club. The Club went through a lot of changes in those early years but it's now settled down. The East Fremantle Sharks are by far the most successful club in Western Australia. The Dockers and the West Coast Eagles are two other clubs that are great rivals. I could talk a lot about football, but I know it's not what the Sheilas want to hear about.'

The bus progressed along a long built up drive with purple jacaranda and golden wattle adorning both sides of the road. The coast area loomed up quickly and the bus cruised along a road known apparently as Cappuccino Strip. This is on the South Terrace and known for its alfresco style dining. Fish and seafood restaurants and coffee houses vied for the trade in the busy waterfront area. A number of old buildings on the harbour have been renovated, including a Little Creatures Brewery which occupies a former boat shed and an old Crocodile farm.'

Andrew piped up, 'Do they really have crocodiles there?'

'Yes definitely, crocodiles are very prevalent in the Northern Territory and are hunted daily for their skins,' replied Wayne.

The driver paused, and then pressed on with his dialogue. 'This is the area where the Annual Sardine Festival is held each year, which attracts thousands of fish food lovers. There is also a chilli festival and the Fremantle Boat Show.' He pauses for a moment and the bus cruised on.

Next to the Boat Harbour is Bathers Beach which is a flat beach and very popular with swimmers. As the bus drove along this beautiful beach, several people asked Wayne if we could stop and have a paddle. The sand was almost white and appeared to be very firm. The waves were just lapping at the edges and beckoned to one and all to come in. A few people were running down the beach and diving in. At this moment most of the people who were on the bus appreciated that this was the life-style they were all looking for.

Unfortunately Wayne declined the request, 'Sorry Cobbers, but we've got to get you back now otherwise the ship will leave without you.' And with that he found a sensible car park in which to spin the bus around and steadily proceeded back to the harbour where the S.S. Orion was berthed, patiently waiting.

Once again, one and all said their goodbyes and thank yous to Wayne who had proved to be both hospitable and knowledgeable about the city he loved.

Almost to the tick of the clock, the Orion slipped her moorings, smoke belching from her funnel and a cacophony of blasts from the ship's horn. Very slowly the giant ship inched her way from the quayside breaking the tangle of coloured streamers tethering relatives and friends from the loved ones on the ship. The band played nostalgic tunes as the ship slid away, guided by the ever present harbour tugs gently manoeuvring alongside the hull in case a nudge was necessary. Another blast from the ship's horn and the mighty propellers engaged the tumultuous churning azure blue waves. Peacefully and without any fuss or palaver, the ship gathered speed and cautiously pulled away.

Many people stood watching for a half hour of so but the excitement of the day was pipped by the sound of the *Roast Beef of Old England* over the loud speakers, the migrants on the first dinner call made their way to the dining hall.

The table was a buzz with the Fremantle trip and what one and all thought of Western Australia while the passengers dined and made excited but polite conversation about the day's activities, the ship efficiently ploughed its way through the sea settling into a steady rhythm and motion.

The dining room was now filled with guests, some new, some regulars; the delicious smells permeated their way from the galley. Waiters in white starched uniforms carrying stainless steel tureens and giant fully loaded trays scurried back and forth.

Australian accents could be heard, brashly dominating some of the tables of the newly embarked guests and in general for a few hours, life on board progressed back into the routine the Bakers had come to be acquainted with.

Mum and Dad, Andrew and Susan made their way to the promenade deck. Andrew and Susan climbed the rail, the perimeter protection and peered over. By now the ship was at full speed and crashing its way through the pitching waves, land was just a green and yellow line on the horizon.

The ship was far out to sea and making its way on its new course for South Australia, for the Bakers, and many others, this was the final destination.

The Ball

That evening was to be a big Ball to celebrate the Australian landfall. By eight o'clock everyone was in evening dress and ball gowns. Many friends sat in groups and enjoyed drinks from the bar. Men compared the Australian beer and ladies drank cocktails with cherries and little Australian flags stuck in blocks of pineapple. The music played and people danced the foxtrot and the quickstep, ladies twirled their skirts and flirted with the men in evening dress.

Muriel, Mum's friend, got up and beckoned to Andrew. 'Come on, little man, let's have a waltz!'

Andrew protested 'I can't dance; I've never danced in my life!'

But Muriel was already placing his arms behind her waist, 'You've danced with me before, so none of your protesting!'

Slowly she guided him, one-two-three, one-two-three she glided in a little square formation until, Andrew, though very jerkily in his movement, slowly came to grips with what he was doing and quickly fell into the rhythm.

For the next five hours the band played and the lady with a low dress and receding neckline sang the night away. The band sounded like Glen Miller with a prominent trombone saxophone. Mum and Dad danced only because Mum made Dad get up; Mum was accomplished but Dad disliked dancing.

'Bob you really do have two left feet!' Mum pushed him around the floor until they both decided to call it a draw.

Meanwhile the ship ploughed on, couples walked hand in hand along the deck. The night air was warm, but the ship created a breeze. Many couples leaned over the railings watching the fluorescence as the ship broke the waves.

The dancing and merry making went on for a long time but Mum and Dad decided, around ten o'clock to have an early evening. Slowly they made their way along the deck, taking in the night air and smelling the oh so familiar ozone of the sea, combined with the oil and scrubbed deck smell, which had already started as the night shift crew started to swab the decks.

Wednesday 4th February 1959 The Southern Ocean

The morning broke with sunlight streaming through the porthole; it was Wednesday fourth February 1959. After showering, the family collectively made their way down to the dining hall, enjoyed their breakfast, chatted with their fellow diners and enjoyed conversation with Mervyn the new table guest, who had joined at Freemantle. Mervyn was a schoolteacher and he was to take up a new appointment in New South Wales.

Susan whispered to Andrew, 'I think he's really dishy!'

'Cor, that's just like a girl to say stuff like that! I bet he can't play football,' replied Andrew.

After breakfast the two children made their way upstairs and found their friends. The little group went for a game of deck tennis and then played quoits in between leaning over the rails and counting the dolphins leaping in and out of the water as the ship ploughed on, slowly tossing through the Southern Ocean.

Dad did the tote, gambling his six-pence and when the announcement came and the ship's mileage shown on the easel in the lounge, Dad had lost. Mum chirped up, 'I told you not to gamble Bob, you know you always lose!' Andrew and Susan grinned at Dad being told off.

'Shall we go for a swim Sue?'

'Yes, okay. Will you go down to the cabin for the cosies?' said Andrew. 'I want to see if our mates are around,' he continued.

'Okay,' said Sue and quickly dashed off. 'I'll meet you by the pool.' She muttered tossing her head sideways as she ran off.

The two children spent the next hour soaking up the sun and jumping in and out of the pool. By now Andrew had mastered the art of swimming, although his style was still very cumbersome and ungainly. Lunch came and went. The children spent time on the deck playing quoits, going to a scout meeting and generally enjoying themselves.

In the evening the whole family visited the cinema on board and watched a cowboy film after which they headed for the lounge and a couple of drinks with friends before bedtime.

Thursday 5th February 1959 The Australian Bight

That night as the family slept, the ship ran into some foul weather. By three o'clock the Orion was really starting to rock and roll. By breakfast Mum was being seasick and it turned out that hundreds of other passengers were in a similar plight. Mum was wailing as Susan and Andrew entered their parents' cabin. 'Let me die, Bob; just let me die!' she had turned a pale green colour and was attempting to vomit into a bucket.

The stewards were running up and down the passageway with mops and buckets, bouncing off the sides of the passageway as they went, hardly managing to keep on their feet. On deck, passengers were clinging to the rails as they tried to make their way around the deck, most were keeping away from the side of the vessel as copious amounts of water sloshed over the wooden railings. Seagulls soared overhead seemingly adding to the mayhem which had unfolded over the last few hours.

Andrew and Susan made their way to the pool deck although Susan was still suffering. En route they met up with two of their mates, but by the time they got there the swimming area it was roped off and a large sign read 'NO SWIMMING TODAY'. The water in the pool had been lowered, but it still sloshed backwards and forwards crashing into the sides and making a large splash which carried on the wind and splashed on the wooden floor, making it more slippery than it already was.

Slowly the children made their way along the deck to the observation deck, where they could watch the waves crashing as the mighty ship pitched and tossed in her attempt to penetrate the stormy seas. Great clouds of water formed a geyser of showers as it broke the ever-climbing waves and showered back with the wind onto the see-through sheet, which was protecting the children and other onlookers. People watching felt they were on a roller-coaster as the mighty ship climbed out of the wave and plunged headlong into the unforgiving mountain of water, before burying its stern like a giant whale, only to judder and vibrate with the stern of the vessel pushing it onwards to repeat the manoeuvre time after time again.

As eleven o'clock the tote was called and the mileage achieved was announced. Many people were surprised that the ship was still making way in the heavy weather and the tote was won by a little old lady who had simply taken a random guess at the distance. The Captain took the opportunity to announce to his protégés that the ship was passing through a section of the ocean known as the Australian Bight, notorious for its temperamental weather conditions and that the current situation was not uncommon. He also told us that we would be out of the storm in about another four hours and that the Bight was 720 miles long. The news was welcomed all over the ship and a large round of approval could be heard up and down the vessel.

The children decided that if they couldn't swim or play on the deck, then they would go to the cinema and that's exactly what they did. By the time dinner was being called the ship was achieving a little more speed and had settled into a gentle swell. It was still rocking and rolling but not in the ferocious manner of the previous twelve hours or so. Needless to say, the dining hall was considerably fuller; however, mother had decided she still was going to abstain.

The bar filled up that evening and the usual dance band played late into the night and as we went back to our cabins to get our last night's sleep aboard the Orion, passengers were already placing their suitcases outside their doors for the porters to move early in the morning ready for disembarking. Last thing that night, Bob Baker did the same.

Susan and Andrew went to their cabin but found it difficult to sleep. Tomorrow they would arrive at Port Adelaide.

6th February 1959 – The Final Destination

That morning bright and early, with the sun streaming through the porthole window, the children woke to find the ship had already docked at Outer Harbour. The Bakers made their way down to the dining hall for breakfast. Three other passengers on the table were also disembarking. Dad tipped the steward and thanked him for his service over the last five weeks and we all said goodbye around the table and promised to keep in touch.

Susan and Andrew agreed with their parents to meet them back at the cabin again at ten o'clock because the disembarking time was eleven o'clock sharp and Dad had to see the Purser before then.

Andrew took his library book back. He had been reading the *Castle of Adventure* by Enid Blyton. He then went up to the promenade deck to find his friends and say goodbye. Moments later the children met up again, the sun was getting hotter and already it was a glorious day. The ship was really alive and people hustled and bustled up and down every corridor and passage. Luggage was gathered at all the muster stations and open spaces, which families had designated as meeting places.

Andrew and Susan made their way down to the cabin as promised. Dad was handing over an envelope with cash in it to the steward and quickly marched his assembled family down to the lift to take them to the Purser's office.

Mr Baker picked up some paperwork from the pursers office, and signed a few documents, all other bills had been paid the night before. He changed a few pounds into Australian currency which coincidently were also pounds, shillings and pence; these had kangaroos and emus illustrated on the face of the notes. The family excitedly made their way to the gangway to wait in an orderly queue until it was their turn to walk down the swaying gangway and take their first step onto South Australian soil.

In an orderly fashion the Bakers walked into a giant customs shed, collected the luggage on the concrete deck under a six-foot high sign displaying the letter 'B'. After collecting the hand luggage, the family formed another queue in order to pass the customs men standing by trestle tables. The porters moved the heavy luggage to the train station just a few hundred yards away.

The customs were asking everyone if they had purchased goods in Port Said or Suez. Many people were showing the poofs and leather camels which the customs men were interested in. We saw 'How much' the Scotsman have his camel taken off him and many other people had similar objects confiscated. We learned later that items like this were often stuffed with used surgical dressings and that was why the authorities did not want them to enter Australia.

Mum had packed the camel she bought in the day chest and this was not accessible as it had been taken to the hostel by a truck, along with other too big to carry items. It turned out that this one was packed with sand, which as the other material used for filling these leather items. For us the customs check was uneventful and soon we were outside standing together as a group and moaning about the heat, along with hundreds of other new migrants.

The Outer Harbour where the migrants disembarked consisted of a rough stone pier with compacted material on the surface area. In several areas huge concrete cubes appeared to be strewn in an unorthodox manner these littered the area in general. There was an air of hasty construction which was untidy and unrefined.

The new migrants were unceremoniously being ushered to a place that had been flattened and bulldozed to form an area about the size of a small sports field. All around was a desolate compacted desert, with rough stony ground, plant life and what appeared to be an old railway line. A gentle but very hot breeze was blowing. Salt bush rolled into balls four to six feet in diameter. these were dashing about the plain, encouraged by the breeze causing clouds of dust. In the distance little circular plumes of sand and debris, like skeletal fingers of sand, were trying to reach for the sky, constantly moving, whipping across the surface area, then vanishing into miniature clouds. The sun beat down relentlessly getting hotter as the time passed by.

The migrants were growing in number and appeared to be scattered around the area in little groups. Ants dashed backwards and forwards on the hard-baked soil, some large and black; others were red and small.

By now the majority of the disembarking passengers had passed through the customs. The clearance men in khaki shorts and bush hats disappeared.

Porters had pulled luggage laden trolleys with miscellaneous boxes and cases from the ship's hold into an area ready to load onto the trains destined to arrive sometime in the future.

'It won't be long now,' one of the porters told the waiting crowd for the tenth time.

The ship moored up at the harbour wall was sending wisps of smoke into the cloudless sky. Now that we were all standing on Australian soil, it was hard to imagine we had sailed 13,000 miles in the cream painted moored-up vessel, which had been our home for nearly five weeks. At that moment we all looked fondly at the old ship, each of us with our own memories, thoughts and re-collections. All of us recording and evaluating the reason for being here at this moment.

Mum was wearing her best navy and white dress with a floral pattern, together with her wide-brimmed hat to keep the sun of her pale complexion. As children we had all tried and succeeded in getting a suntan; Mum had set out to do the opposite and continued to look like the white rose she aspired to be.

In the distance, a puff of smoke could be seen. This aspired to be in competition with the dust clouds and the whirlies which continued to form, only to vanish again amongst the sun baked desert and rampaging salt bush.

Slowly the smoke plume formed beneath a recognizable shape. The train grew in stature and appearance, ploughing through the rolling debris and gaining visibly with every moment.

The bushmen porters scrambled over the large irregular stones close to the track. 'Keep back now! keep back!. Keep away from the track until the engine has stopped.'

The men waved their arms in an effort to assert some crowd control.

People were already surging forward with baggage in their hands even though they did not know precisely where the train was going to stop. Apart from the large water tower, there was no platform—just a few red flags stuck in the rocks.

Moments later the giant locomotive with its massive cow catcher affixed to the front of the engine, roared its way belching steam and clanking noisily towards the red flags, and with a screech of brakes traumatically finally affected a stop. Smoke belched from its funnel; steam spouted in anger from its valves. The massive wheels of the cast iron and steel contraption enveloped in a white, damp misty cloud. For a few minutes every junction, bearing and valve appeared to agitatedly spit out vapour or smoke. The forward carriages had open ended verandahs, just like in the wild west films. Behind them a few wood and metal carriages, more like the ones we were used to in Britain, but with sliding doors. Most of the doors were wide open and appeared dangerously precarious. Many of the waiting migrants likened them to cattle trucks amongst other derogatory comments

Andrew and Susan thought this was great fun. This train was just like the trains they had seen in the cinema. Most of the new arrivals simply wanted to get on into Adelaide and didn't really mind how they got there. As the people thronged forward they mounted the stairs, which had folded down to the rail track level, luggage was passed up to the rapidly filling carriage, folks took their seats, happy to be on the last leg of a long journey.

Mum turned to Dad as she clung on to her best hat, and with tears forming in her eye, she said quietly but with true emotion, 'Dear God, Bob, what have you brought me to?'

The End

Printed in Great Britain
by Amazon